Learning Maya™ 5|

Rendering

Alias|**wavefront**®

Learning Maya 5 | Rendering

Credits:

Christoph Berndt, Petre Gheorghian, Jill Harrington, Alan Harris, Cathy McGinnis

Special Thanks:

Paolo Berto, Michael Bossuyt, Steve Christov, Brian Cho, Shawn Dunn, Bill Dwelly, Erica Fyvie, Lee Graft, Deion Green, Bob Gundu, Dave Haapalehto, Rachael Jackson, Tom Kluyskens, Andreas Kraemer, Danielle Lamothe, Robert MacGregor, Alan Opler, John Patton, Lorna Saunders, Carla Sharkey, Michael Stamler, Larysa Struk, Marcus Tateishi

ISBN 1-894893-43-3

Printed in Canada.

10 9 8 7 6 5 4 3 2 1

Learning Maya 5 | Rendering

Learning Maya 5 | Rendering

INTRODUCTION

The *Learning Maya™ 5 | Rendering* book explores the final stage in the 3D Computer Graphics production process by examining the techniques and tools that will allow you to become proficient and effective using the Maya® renderer.

This book is project based. Each chapter contains several examples, usually with supporting data files where appropriate. In lessons where involved concepts are introduced, simple test beds are explored with and without example scene file data.

In many cases, the purpose of these lessons is to teach concepts and provide examples that demonstrate how something works while still providing techniques that the reader can embellish for themselves in their own projects. The book is organized for a very hands on progressive approach where the reader is strongly encouraged to work through the provided example data files using Maya.

The following sections provide a very brief overview of some of the key topics discussed in this book.

Materials

This section describes materials and their interaction with lights. The Hypershade workflow is explored in depth and several Utility nodes are introduced to demonstrate the power of Maya's shading networks and integrated renderer.

Concepts covered:

- Understanding Shading Networks and Hypershade
- Materials and their interaction with light
- Anisotropic shading
- Layered Shaders

- Shading Maps
- Surface Shaders

Textures

This section introduces various methods of combining textures for sophisticated effects. Special attention is placed on efficiency and animation requirements.

Concepts covered:

- Working with Textures in a complex Shading Network
- Various techniques for combining and modifying textures
- Texturing issues for animation
- File texture Filtering and the use of BOT files
- Displacement mapping
- mental ray for Maya's .map files
- mental ray for Maya's Bake Sets

Lighting

Lighting is an important step in the planning and layout of a scene. This section will describe the most important criteria to keep in mind as well as the workflow approaches that can be implemented.

Concepts covered:

- Lighting Workflow using IPR and Hypershade
- Direction and distribution of lights
- Multiple methods of controlling light attenuation (decay)
- Light Linking
- mental ray for Maya's Area Light

Cameras

This section will focus on advanced camera attributes and matching live images.

Concepts covered:

- Camera basics
- Working with Film Gates and Film Backs

- Using Image Planes
- Non-square pixels
- Aspect Ratios
- Matching live action workflow
- Clipping Planes

Shadows

This section will describe in depth the theory and applications related to shadows. An emphasis will be placed on Depth Map Shadows but Raytraced Shadows will also be covered.

Concepts covered:

- How Depth Map Shadows work
- Optimizing with Disk Based Dmaps
- Volumetric Lighting Effects
- Raytraced Shadows
- mental ray for Maya's Shadow Maps
- Motion Blurred Shadow Maps

Raytracing

Raytracing is a powerful rendering feature in Maya that can produce realistic reflections and refractions.

Concepts covered:

- How Raytracing works in Maya
- Reflection/Refraction/Shadow limits
- Memory and performance options

Controlling Renders

Typically, the highest quality results must be achieved in the shortest render time. This section will present all of the important tools for controlling the final rendered results.

Concepts covered:

- Anti-aliasing
- Motion Blur

- Tessellation and How to Control it
- Memory Requirements and Optimizations
- Multi-pixel Filtering
- Render Diagnostics
- mental ray for Maya's Sampling Quality
- mental ray for Maya's Approximation Editor

Special Effects and Compositing

Adding special effects can greatly enhance a scene's quality and produce some interesting results.

Concepts covered:

- Controlling Light Glow and Shader Glow
- How to use Depth of Field
- What to expect with Motion Blur
- When to Render for Compositing
- Matte Opacity

Hardware Rendering

The new Hardware Renderer delivers superior image quality.

Concepts covered:

- How to use the Hardware Renderer
- How to adjust and optimize when using the Hardware Renderer

Vector Rendering

It is now possible to output the most common vector formats. This expands the value of Maya for those working in the print and web publishing industry.

Concepts covered:

- Using the Vector Renderer
- Working with Fills
- Working with Render Layers

Global Illumination and Caustics

Global Illumination is a technique used to describe Indirect illumination and Caustics is a sub-set of Global Illumination. mental ray for Maya is used to simulate these effects.

Concepts covered:

- How to use Caustics
- How to fine-tune Caustics
- How to use Global Illumination
- How to fine-tune Global Illumination

Final Gather and HDRI

Final Gather can be used in conjunction with Global Illumination to obtain a finer level of diffuse detail. The Final Gather process can make use of a High Dynamic Range Image as the basis for illuminating information in a scene. This is known as Image Based Lighting.

Concepts covered:

- Using Final Gather
- Combining Final Gather and Global Illumination
- Using HDRI images

mental ray® for Maya shaders

This chapter will cover several examples of how to use mental ray for Maya shaders to create complex effects that may not be easily reproduced using another renderer.

Concepts covered:

- How to use Contour Shaders
- How to use mental ray for Maya's Material Shaders
- How to use mental ray for Maya's Photon Shaders
- How to use mental ray for Maya's Shadow Shaders
- How to use mental ray for Maya's Volume Shaders

CHAPTER 1

Materials

A **material** is a set of instructions that describes how the surface of an object will look when rendered. It is not just a collection of attributes you can texture map, but also a mathematical description of how light will behave when it strikes the surface. Maya provides many attributes to fine-tune the "look" of a material whether it will be a cartoon effect or photorealism.

In this chapter, you will learn:

- Materials and Shading Networks
- Layering Shaders and Textures with a Layered Shader
- Ramp Shader
- Shading Maps
- Surface Shaders

IPR

IPR stands for *Interactive Photorealistic Rendering* and is currently only available for the Maya renderer. IPR is a type of software rendering that allows you to adjust shading and lighting attributes and see the updates in real time. When you do an IPR render, it writes out a file (deep raster file) that contains all the sample information for each pixel in the image. This file is a temporary file and is written to the *iprimages* directory. It will have a name like *_tmp_ipr.iff*. This file is similar to the file that gets written out when you do a normal render in the Render View in that it gets overwritten every time you do a new IPR render. As long as that project is the current project, the file will get overwritten when an IPR render is started in that user session. However, IPR does not prefix the camera name on the file like a normal render does. This means if you change cameras and do an IPR render the deep raster file will overwrite the same file. A regular render will add the prefix of the camera to the file and generate a new file. If you want to save the file permanently so that it does not get overwritten you can do a **File → Save IPR file** in the Render View window. This is useful if you are working on a large scene and the IPR file took several minutes to generate. If this is the case, you can save out the IPR file and work on other things and still return to it at a later time. If you have saved out an IPR file you can **fcheck** it to view the image component of the file.

Note: IPR files can be quite large and will consume large amounts of disk space.

The IPR file is created using a *z-buffer* approach that means one sample per object per pixel. This means that the size of the file is somewhat capped by the resolution of the image in that if every pixel has an object behind it, it is a big file. It doesn't matter how complex the geometry is, i.e. a large ground plane that covers every pixel will be the same size as a complex scene that covers every pixel. Also, the file size will increase with things like transparent objects. The IPR file needs to keep one sample per object for each pixel so if there are many transparent objects covering a pixel, the number of samples goes up. Fog will also cause the same problem. When the user marquees a region to start tuning, all of the samples for those pixels are loaded into RAM. The amount of RAM is the number displayed in the top right corner of the Render View. Having something like fog or transparencies will make this number large even for a small marquee region because of all the samples for each pixel. The amount of memory is not just proportional to the number of samples, it also is proportional to the amount of time it takes to do each update in the marquee region.

You can also create IPR files from a shell using the render command with the flag *-ipr*. This allows you to create multiple IPR images at one time which you can load in at a later time for tuning. If you have a large scene that took twenty minutes to generate an IPR image, you can set up an animation and generate the IPR files overnight. You should create a simple camera animation that focused on sections of your scene that you want to tune.

IPR Rendering

- Open the file called *aeronChair.mb* and press the IPR render button in Render View.

  You will see that Maya renders the scene and then a message appears at the bottom of the Render View window that says:

  ```
  select a region to begin tuning
  ```

- Use the **LMB** to draw a region around the portion of the image you want to tune.

  Once you do this, you can begin tuning your lights and materials.

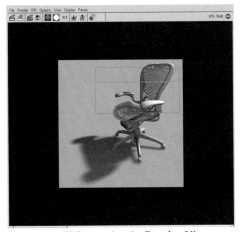

IPR running in Render View

- You can move lights, add new lights, modify light attributes, and delete lights with IPR updating. You can also create, assign, and edit new materials within an IPR session.

- Stop IPR with the red Stop Sign shaped button in the Render View window.

Tip:	IPR files can require large amounts of disk space, so depending on your available disk space, you may find it helpful to hide any unnecessary objects to keep the file size as small as possible.

Note:	IPR is currently not supported in mental ray for Maya.

UNDERSTANDING SHADING NETWORKS

Shading Networks

A **Shading Network** can be defined as *a graph of connected nodes which can be used to shade objects.* These networks generally contain what Maya classifies as materials and textures, but they do not have to contain just these nodes.

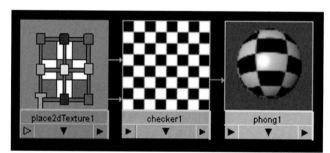

Phong Shading Network with Checker color texture

The idea behind the Maya architecture is to have many simple nodes that can be connected together in a virtually infinite number of combinations rather than fewer and very complex nodes. For example, you will not find all of the conceivable light attributes on a single node; instead you will have attributes for the **Light** on one node, attributes for the **Light Fog** on another node and attributes for the **Light Glow** on another node. While this may seem inconvenient at first, it will become apparent that this is actually a powerful method for augmenting a material.

Shading Groups

A **Shading Group** is a set of objects to be shaded with the Shading Network. Below is a diagram of a Shading Group called *Phong1SG* (the SG stands for Shading Group). You can see a cone and a sphere connected to the Shading Group; these objects comprise the *set* which will be shaded by the shading network. In this case, the shading network is a *Phong* material with a *checker* connected to it:

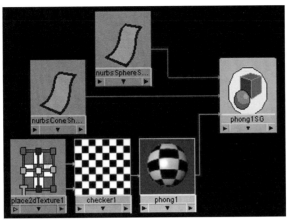

Shading Group with attached Shading Network

Note: At render time, Maya determines which objects will be rendered by going to all of the Shading Groups and collecting all of the objects contained in each group. If an object is not a member of any Shading Group, it is not rendered.

Connecting Shading Networks to Shading Groups

The shading network is connected to an attribute on the Shading Group called a *Port*. In a typical workflow, this connection will be made automatically. Below is a view of the Attribute Editor showing the three ports on a Shading Group:

Surface Material

This port is used most frequently as it is used to shade NURBS and Polygonal surfaces.

Volume Material

This port is used to shade volumes such as fogs and some particle types.

Displacement Material

This port is used for displacement mapping surfaces so it is used in conjunction with the Surface Material port.

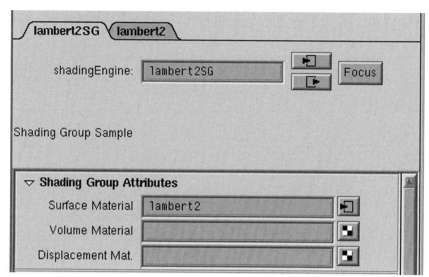

Shading Group Attribute Editor

All Shading Groups have the same three ports for generality so that any Shading Group can shade any type of object. Each port has a shading engine associated with it that will evaluate the network attached to it.

Maya Shader Library

The Shader Library is a collection of over sixty shading networks comprised of various example material types. These networks can be used as is or as a basis to create your own materials or shaders. You can preview the library directly in the **Hypershade** via the *Shader Library Tab* located in the bottom panel. To use one of the shaders from the library, simply **MMB** drag it into the Hypershade or **RMB** → **Import Maya** file. Once you have dragged or imported the file, it will appear in the *Materials Tab* and can be assigned or manipulated like any other material. You cannot assign Shader Library materials directly from the Shader Library tab.

MATERIALS

Materials are similar to what were called shaders in Alias Studio™/ PowerAnimator™ and Wavefront's Explore. They are called *materials* in Maya to avoid any functional associations that the word *shader* might imply. A material is essentially a shading model that calculates the surface characteristics and determines how a surface will be shaded. The use of the word shader and material are interchangeable and correct for this

description. The common industry term for this description is shader and
you will find this term used throughout this book.

Materials and their interaction with light

The single most important thing for you to do when creating an effective
material is to concentrate on how the object's highlight appears. This one
factor can dramatically improve the look of the material even before any
textures are applied. Look around you and take note of the various ways
light falls across surfaces. Notice how shiny objects have a bright small
highlight and how a dull surface has barely any highlight at all.

Let's take a closer look at how light reflects off surfaces. The following
diagram illustrates how some portion of incident light is scattered as it
reflects and some portion of the light can be reflected at a more consistent
angle. The light reflected at a consistent angle results in an intense bright
region called a **Specular Highlight**. The scattered light is referred to as
Diffuse light.

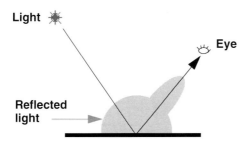

Reflected light

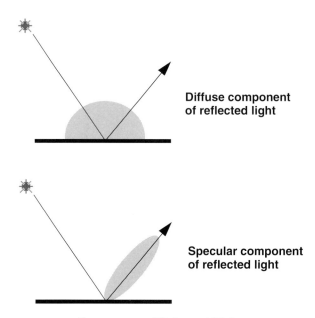

Components of Refracted Light

In reality, the *specular component* vs. the *diffuse component* of the total reflected light will vary depending on the characteristics of the surface.

If you consider the amount of reflected light in terms of percentages, the maximum value when the diffuse and specular components are added together would be 100%. This would mean that all of the incident light is being reflected off the surface. A value less that 100% would mean that some of the incident light was absorbed. A value greater than 100% would not make much sense since it would suggest that more light was being reflected than was actually coming from the light source. In Maya, the diffuse component and the specular component are controlled separately which gives you the flexibility to simulate virtually any real world surface. It also means, however, that there is nothing to stop you from entering numbers you want for one component without considering the other. In order to achieve realistic looking surfaces though, it is a good idea to ensure that diffuse + specular color values do not exceed 1.0.

Lambert Material

The **Lambert** material works well for matte surfaces. It simulates surfaces where most light rays will be absorbed by uneven, tiny surface imperfections. When light rays strike such a surface, they bounce around in the nooks and crannies instead of being reflected back from the surface. Any rays that actually are reflected will be scattered at close to random angles so you won't see a specular highlight. There is very little correlation between the *angle of incidence* and the *angle of the reflected* rays.

The extent to which the scattered light is absorbed or reflected is controlled by the **Diffuse** attribute. This attribute exists on all of the basic materials.

Since light reflected from a surface is what gives you the sense of its color, low diffuse values close to **0.0** mean very little light is scattered so the surface will look dark. A high diffuse value approaching **1.0** means that a lot of light is scattered so the surface will look very saturated.

An example of a Lambert surface with a **Low Diffuse** value is something like coal. In this case, most light is absorbed by the surface imperfections.

Examples of Lambert surfaces with a **High Diffuse** value are things like the surface of the moon or colored chalk. In this case, the surface imperfections cause the light to be scattered and some amount of it is actually reflected, giving these surfaces a strong sense of color.

Tip: The Lambert shading model is used to compute the diffuse component of surface illumination. All other more complex shading models derive their diffuse component from Lambert.

The following image shows two Lambert materials with different diffuse values; otherwise all of their attributes are identical.

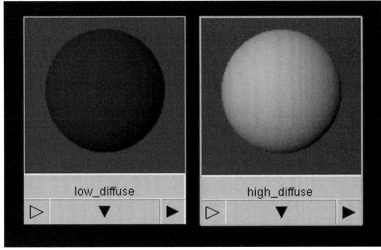

Different diffuse values

Phong, PhongE, and Blinn

Very smooth surfaces such as glass, mirrors, and chrome will have a very low diffuse value approaching zero. This is because they reflect very little scattered light. The light doesn't get scattered because there are few surface imperfections which would cause it to bounce at random angles. Instead, most of the light rays are reflected off the surface at a similar angle resulting in a *specular highlight*. Because the Lambert material does not simulate the specular component of surface illumination, for these types of surfaces you can choose from several other materials: **Phong**, **PhongE**, and **Blinn**.

Both Phong and Blinn shading models approximate the surface physics of incident light reflecting off a smooth surface. They are named after computer scientists Bui Tuong Phong and James Blinn.

The **Specular Shading** attributes on these three material types control how coherent the light rays are as they are reflected off the surface. If the light rays are reflected at close to the same angle, a tight highlight results. If the rays are more scattered, a bigger and softer highlight will result. If the rays were to become scattered enough, you would end up with the look of the Lambert shading model.

At the other extreme, these shading models can simulate a mirror's almost perfectly smooth surface where very little light is absorbed and the reflected rays are very coherent.

Unlike the diffuse attribute which is common to all of these materials, the attributes which control the specular highlight appearance have different names on each material.

Phong: Cosine Power affects the size of highlights on the surface. This attribute can be thought of as shininess. Low numbers create big highlights while high numbers produce small highlights typically seen on very shiny surfaces.

PhongE: Roughness and **Highlight Size** work together to affect the size and look of the highlight.

Blinn: Eccentricity affects the size of highlights on the surface. Low values such as **0.1** produce a small highlight (very shiny surface). The default value is **0.3**.

Blinn vs. Phong vs. PhongE?

While all three of these materials produce specular highlights, they each provide very different visual results. This visual impact is likely to be the determining factor in terms of which one to use, although it is worth noting that there is a slight increase in rendering time associated with using more complex materials such as Blinn.

The order of rendering performance from fastest to slowest:

- PhongE
- Phong
- Blinn

  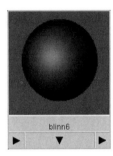

Comparison of materials Phong, PhongE, and Blinn

Phong is less complex than *Blinn* in several respects. *Phong* does not take into account changes in specularity due to the angle you are viewing the surface at.

Blinn is a more sophisticated and true to life shading model where surfaces appear shinier at more severe angles. This can be controlled by the **Specular Roll Off** attribute on the Blinn material.

The Specular Roll Off also allows surfaces to reflect more of their surroundings when viewed at glancing angles. The following images show the effect of this attribute on Reflectivity.

Tip: Use a Specular Roll Off value of **0.3** to simulate a wet surface, such as wet paint.

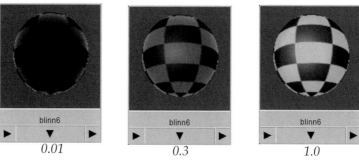

Effect of Specular Roll Off on Reflectivity (Reflected Color mapped with checker)

You will also see that the Specular Roll Off affects the transition between the specular color and the diffuse color.

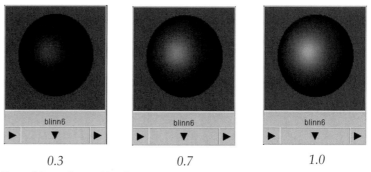

Effect of Specular Roll Off on transition from Specular Color to Diffuse Color

---

Tip: The soft highlights on Blinn surfaces are less likely to exhibit roping or flickering for thin highlights than the harder highlights on Phong surfaces. Use the Blinn surface material for surfaces with bump or displacement maps to reduce highlight roping or flickering.

Specialized surface materials

So far you have looked at the most frequently used materials. There are several other materials in Maya. These materials are:

- Anisotropic
- Layered Shader
- Shading Map
- Surface Shader

Anisotropic

The purpose of the anisotropic shader is to simulate surfaces which have micro-facet grooves and the specular highlight tends to be perpendicular to the direction of the grooves. If an anisotropic surface is spun against the grooves, the shape and location of the highlight will change depending on how the groove direction changes. Examples of uses for this material are CDs, satin holiday ornaments, the bottom of frying pans, nylon twill purses, and tote bags, etc.

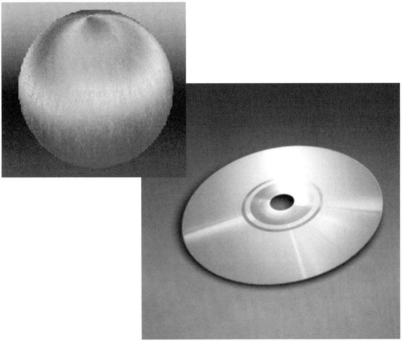

Examples of Anisotropic material - scene files:
satinOrnament.mb, anisoCD_Finished.mb

Exercise: CD part I - Anisotropic Shader

In this exercise, you will create and apply an anisotropic material to a falling CD to reproduce the rainbow style highlights characteristic of a CD's undersurface. Later in this chapter you will complete the CD using a Layered Shader. A movie file called *ansioCD* is available to show the final results.

1 Open anisoCD1.mb

This file contains a CD (NURBS) that was animated as a rigid body colliding with a ground object. The simulation has been baked to allow scrubbing in the Time Slider. The CD geometry is made up of different pieces so different materials can be applied to the various sections. All pieces are parented under one rigid body node.

2 Work with the camera Persp1

There are two cameras in the scene. Persp1 is the animated camera that is set up for this exercise. Make sure when you render that you are rendering this camera.

3 Create and assign an anisotropic material

- Use the **Create** menu in the Hypershade to create an anisotropic material.

- **Assign** it to *mainCDbody* and *mediumRing*.

4 Tune the anisotropic material

- Use the values shown below as a guideline:

    Set **Diffuse** to **0.05**;

    Set **Angle** to **180**;

    Set **Spread X** to **37**;

    Set **Spread Y** to **0.1**;

    Set **Roughness** to **0.4**;

    Set **Fresnel Index** to **8.4**.

Note: The diffuse value should be low because this material is meant to simulate the smooth plastic coating on the underside of a CD. Nearly all reflected light from a very smooth surface will be represented by the specular component. The micro grooves in this coating will produce anisotropic highlights controlled by the following attributes.

Spread X controls how much the grooves spread out in the X-direction. It ranges from **0.1** to **100**. (The X-direction is the surface's U-direction, rotated counter-clockwise by the Angle attribute). When this value is increased, the surface appears smoother in that direction (the specular highlight in that direction shrinks). When the value is decreased, the highlight spreads out more in that direction, making the surface appear less smooth.

Spread Y controls how much the grooves spread out in the Y-direction. It ranges from 0.1 to 100. (The Y-direction is perpendicular to the X-direction - see the Spread X attribute above.) When this value is increased, the surface appears smoother in that direction (the specular highlight in that direction shrinks). When the value is decreased, the highlight spreads out more in that direction, making the surface appear less smooth.

Roughness controls the overall roughness of the surface. It ranges from 0.01 to 1.0, with larger values giving a rougher appearance. As this value is increased, the specular highlights are more spread out. This value will also affect the Reflectivity of the material, if Anisotropic Reflectivity is turned on.

Angle defines the X- and Y-directions on the surface relative to the surface's intrinsic U- and V-directions. X is the U-direction, rotated counter-clockwise by the Angle attribute. These X- and Y-directions are used by the shader to place the microgrooves that control the anisotropic properties of the shader. This value ranges from 0 to 360 degrees.

Fresnel Refractive Index affects the look of the anisotropic highlight. (It does not affect the way light from other objects bends when passing through the material, if the material is transparent and you are raytracing). As you increase the Fresnel Refractive Index, the highlight becomes brighter.

For transparent objects, you may want to set the Fresnel Index to match the object's Refractive Index. This will give the most physically accurate result for the highlight.

If **Anisotropic Reflectivity** is turned on, the Reflectivity of the material is calculated directly from its roughness.

If this attribute is turned off, the value in Reflectivity is used instead.

5 IPR Render

- At frame **57**, a variety of highlights will be clearly visible in the render.

- **IPR → IPR Render → persp1.**

- Define a tuning region that encompasses the entire CD.

   Note the quality and shape of the specular highlights. They are long and spread out across the surface, not round.

6 Map specular color with rainbow ramp

The colored highlights that occur on CDs generally run from the inside of the CD to the outer edge and are typically a variety of colors from the visible light spectrum. On real CDs, these "rainbow" colors appear due to the diffraction of light (diffraction is the term for the light splitting into its individual wavelengths as it passes through a medium such as a prism). A colored ramp texture will be used to fake the appearance of diffraction.

- **Map** a **Ramp** onto the **Specular Color** attribute.
- Set **Type** to **V Ramp** and **Interpolation** to **Smooth.**
- There is a pre-made ramp called *rainbowSpecRamp* that already exists in the file that you can use as reference.
- Set the **Repeat UV** attribute on the ramp's texture placement node to **1** and **10** respectively.

7 Adjust the lighting

When working with the anisotropic material, the direction, distribution, and intensity of the lighting is vital to the success of the look you are going for. Normally, multiple lights are required at various angles to the surface to see the anisotropic highlights well.

- Increase the intensity of *spotLightShape2* to see the impact it has on the brightness of the highlights. Moving this light also drastically affects the results, as shown below.
- Try adjusting the lights to get a feel for the significance of their intensity and position relative to the surface.

  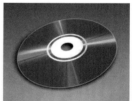

8 Save the file

- When you are finished, **Save** the file as you will complete the CD in the Layered Shader exercise.

Layered Shader

This node can be used in two different ways. It can be used to **layer materials** or it can be used to **layer textures**. However, there is a newer node specifically designed for layering textures that will be covered in the next chapter on textures.

When using the Layered Shader node, ask yourself if you need to see different material types on different areas of the same surface or if you need to see different materials at the same time such as clear coat over car paint. If not, then you should use a **Layered Texture** rather than a **Layered Shader**. It is best to avoid using Layered Shaders unnecessarily because they are very expensive to render.

Layered Shader general workflow

Layering materials takes longer to render than layering textures. However, you may need to use it for specific results.

1 Create Materials to use as Layers

Before you can layer anything, you will need a couple of simple materials.

- Create a **Phong** and a **Lambert** material.
- Make the Phong material **Blue** and the Lambert material **Red**.
- **Map** a *checker* to the **Transparency** of the Phong material. Change the **U,V repeat** to **8, 8** on the *place2Dtexture* node for the checker texture.

2 Create a Layered Shader Node

- In the Hypershade, create a **Layered Shader** node.

3 Connect the Materials to the Layered Shader node

- Open the Attribute Editor for the *Layered Shader* node.
- With the **MMB, drag** the red Lambert into the box in the Layered Shader attributes.
- With the **MMB, drag** the blue Phong into the box in the Layered Shader attributes.

  You will notice that each time you drag a material into the rectangle, a new icon appears. These icons represent the layers.

- Click on the small **X** under the green layer icon to remove it.

  The green icon is simply the default layer that you can get rid of once you have added your own layers.

4 Shuffle the Layers

You now have a Layered Shader with two materials in it. However, the swatch for the Layered Shader will appear to be completely red. This is because the red Lambert material (without any transparency) is on top of the blue Phong. You need to change the order of the layers in order to see the Phong on top of the Lambert.

- In the Attribute Editor for the Layered Shader, use the **MMB** to drag the Lambert icon to the right of the Phong icon.

  You should now see both the layers in the swatch.

Tip:	The order of the layers from left to right in the Attribute Editor represents the layer order from uppermost to lowest.

5 IPR Render the Scene

- **Create** a **Sphere** and some lights.

- **Assign** the **Layered Shader** to the *sphere* and do an IPR render.

  You will notice that the specular highlight falls across both the Phong and the Lambert regions of the surface (because even though the Phong is transparent in those regions, its specular highlight is visible). This essentially defeats the purpose of using the layered materials.

  To get the look you were going for (different parts of the surface show different materials), you will need to change the layers again.

6 Manipulate the Layers

With IPR still running:

- **Break** the connection between the checker and the Phong in the Hypershade.

- **Create** a connection between the checker and the Lambert.

- In the Attribute Editor for the Layered Shader, swap the layers using the **MMB** as you did earlier.

  Notice how in the IPR render, the specular highlight no longer shows on both the red and the blue regions.

Tip:	In more complex layered materials, you may need to apply a specular map to control the specular highlights on different layers.

The shading network would look something like this:

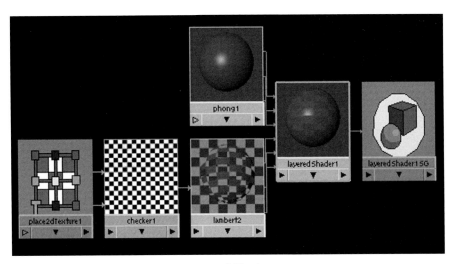

Layered Shader

Exercise: CD part II - Layered Shader

In this exercise, you will complete the CD that you started earlier in this chapter. You will use a Layered Shader to add the foil base visible under the clear grooved plastic on the underside of a CD.

1 Open the file

- Use the file you saved from part I earlier or open *anisoCD2.mb.*
- Make sure you are viewing/rendering through the *persp1* camera.
- **IPR Render** frame **57** for test rendering throughout this example.

2 Create a Layered Shader

- **Create** a **Layered Shader** material in Hypershade.
- Assign the Layered Shader to *mainCDbody* and *mediumRing.*
- Open the Attribute Editor for the Layered Shader.
- **MMB** drag *anisotropic1* from Visor or Hypershade into the red rectangle in the Attribute Editor for the Layered Shader.
- Click on the small **X** under the green default layer icon to remove it.

3 Create a Blinn for the foil coating

A Blinn material will be used to create a silver/gold foil base coating on the CD. This layer will go under the anisotropic clear plastic coating.

- **Create** a **Blinn** material in Hypershade.
- Open the Attribute Editor for the Layered Shader and **MMB** drag the Blinn into the red rectangle.

  At this point, you will not be able to see the Blinn layer because the anisotropic material has no transparency.

4 Adjust the transparency on the anisotropic material

- Increase the transparency on the anisotropic material to a suitable level for clear plastic. This will reveal the Blinn layer below.

5 Tune the Blinn material

- Adjust the Blinn attributes until you are happy with the results.

  There are guidelines for polished metal surfaces in the section on **Specific Material Examples** at the back of this chapter.

  (Hint: Very low diffuse, high Specular Roll Off, low Eccentricity)

6 Add a reflection map

Although the Diffuse, Eccentricity, and Specular Roll Off will be the primary attributes you tune on the Blinn shader, adding a reflection map will enhance the visual impact of the foil.

- **Map** the **Reflected Color** attribute on the Blinn with an **Env Chrome** from the Environment Textures section of the Create Render Node window.

  This makes the CD appear as though it is reflecting a pseudo-environment.

- Adjust the Reflectivity attribute to increase or decrease the brightness of the reflection map.

- Adjust the colors on the Env Chrome texture if you do not want a blue look. It is also possible to turn off the floor of the texture.

7 Make final adjustments

If you have been test rendering at the same frame, you should check some other frames throughout the animation to make sure the values you are using provide expected results.

The camera angle and the lighting positions/settings are an important part of the overall effect in this exercise. Experiment with different lighting to see how it affects the overall image.

The Layered Shader lets you combine the features of the various shading models together to produce one final result. This extra flexibility does come at the expense of increased render times but gives you results that may be otherwise difficult to achieve.

The file *anisoCD_Finished.mb* is a completed version of this example.

Tip: The file *anisoCDBlendCol.mb* demonstrates an alternate method of achieving a similar appearance in the shading but with the use of a blendColors utility node rather than a Layered Shader.

Ocean Shader

The **Ocean Shader** is used to create open water effects and can be used in conjunction with Fluids.

Ramp Shader

The **Ramp Shader** allows extra control over the way color changes with light angle, brightness or the viewing angle (facing ratio). You can give your objects a flat, toon-like look by using the Ramp Shader.

This shader shares any attributes with other material attributes. All the color-related attributes are controlled by ramps. There are also graphs for defining Specular Roll Off and Reflectivity, providing performance improvements by avoiding complex shading networks and making toon shading easier to achieve.

Exercise: Ramp Shader

In this exercise, you will use the Ramp Shader to give some bouncing balls a flat, toon-like look.

1 Open the file
- Open *bounce.mb*. This file consists of a number of spheres using dynamics to bounce on a primitive plane. There is also a very large Area Light which is why the illumination is so bright.

2 Create a Ramp Shader
- **Create** a **Ramp Shader** material in Hypershade.
- Assign the Ramp Shader to all the spheres.
- Open the Attribute Editor for the Ramp Shader.
- You'll notice that many of the common material attributes are controlled by ramps.

3 Edit the Ramp attributes to create a toon shader

- Under the **Color** section, create another ramp handle in the ramp field by LMB clicking in the field. Set the **Selected Position** of this ramp handle to **.157**.
- Select the first ramp handle and under **Selected Color**, change the RGB values to **0,0,1**. Select **Interpolation** and change this to **None**.
- Select the second ramp handle and under its **Selected Color**, change the RGB values to **.381, .631, 1.0**. Select **Interpolation** and change this to **None**.
- Change **Color Input** to **Brightness**.

4 Edit the Incandescence attribute to create a toon outline

- Under the **Incandescence** section, create another ramp handle. Set the **Selected Position** of this ramp handle to **.236** and change the **Interpolation** to **None**.
- Select the first ramp handle and under **Selected Color**, change the HSV values to **-1,-1,-1**.
- Render into the Render View window and you will notice flat bands of color surrounded by a black outline.

5 Add specular shading

- Under the **Specular Shading** section, change **Specularity** to **1.0** and **Eccentricity** to **.058**. This will change the size and the brightness of the highlight.

Shading Map

A **Shading Map** is a node which allows you to **remap** the output from a material to create custom shading results. Recall that a material is a mathematical formula or set of instructions on how to shade the surface. For this reason materials are also known as shading models. The purpose of the Shading Map is to allow you to control the final shaded results to go beyond what is possible with the standard materials in Maya.

A shading map allows complete control over the transition from the highlight to the shaded area of a surface. For example, to achieve a cartoon look you can do simple banded shading.

Car designers sometimes use shading maps in renderings. This allows for more variation in the look of the paint to avoid surfaces which look flat and monochromatic.

Even more complex materials that have a translucent scattering layer can sometimes have a non-Lambert falloff in *diffuse* intensity. This can be roughly simulated using the shading map to help get more natural looking skin, for example.

This can be a very powerful feature in that one can remap the output of any shading model using a shading map. The remapped outputs of different shading models can then be recombined to create a new shading model.

Layered Shader with a shading map

Car paint can be represented in any number of ways. The purpose of this exercise is to show the use of a shading map for the control and placement of highlights on a car body.

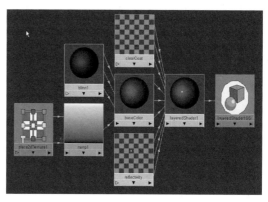

Layered Shader network using a shading map for control of highlights

Paint Base Layer

1 Create a Layered Shader

- Open the file named shadingMap.mb. In Hypershade, create a **Layered Shader node**.

2 Create a Blinn material

- In Hypershade, create a **Blinn** material.

3 Create a shading map

- In Hypershade, create a **Shading Map** node.

4 Connect the Shading Network

- Open the Attribute Editor for the Layered Shader node.
- Use the **MMB** to drag the shading map material from Hypershade to the **Layered Shader Attributes** section of the Layered Shader node.

  In the **Shading Map Attributes** section, you will notice two attributes called **Shading Map Color** and **Color**.

- Use the **MMB** to drag the Blinn material from Hypershade to the **Color** attribute of the **Shading Map** section of the shading map node.
- Map the **Shading Map Color** with a **Ramp** texture.

5 Edit the Ramp attributes

- Set the top color in the *ramp* to white.
- Set the bottom color in the *ramp* to black.

- Move the middle ramp handle to the 0.9 position and change the color to a pale blue - RGB values of 181, 217, 213.

- Create another ramp handle and place it at the 0.1 position, change its color to a dark blue - RGB values of 58, 65, 83.

The ramp will look as follows:

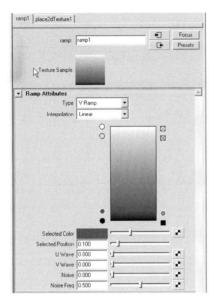

6 Clean up the Hypershade window

- In Hypershade, click on the Layered Shader node and graph the **Input connections.**

Clear Coat Layer

Just as on a real car, a clear polished shader needs to be layered onto a matte base to create two separate highlight regions.

1 Create the clear coat layer

- In Hypershade, create a **Blinn** material.

- Make the shader completely transparent.

- Ensure that the **Refractive Index** is set to 1.0. (AIR preset).

- Make the **Specular Roll Off** -10 and keep the **Eccentricity** low (between 0.1 and 0.05).

  A point highlight is created.

- Reduce the **Reflectivity** to zero.

The clear coat Attribute Editor will look like this:

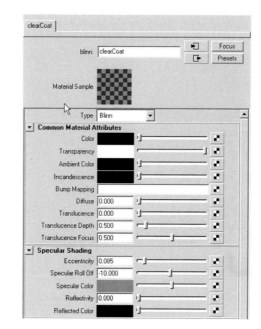

2 Add the clear coat to the Layered Shader node

- **MMB** the clear coat Blinn node onto the Layered Shader node

- Using the **MMB**, reassemble the order of the nodes so the clear coat layer is in front of the base layer.

Reflection Layer

Although reflections can be added to the clear coat layer, custom reflection effects will be isolated with their own layer.

1 Create the reflection layer

- Create another Blinn shader.

  This shader will be the main reflection shader. In cases where you are raytracing, this shader will pick up the surrounding elements.

- Increase the **Specular Roll Off** to a very high level (between **0.89** and **0.95**) and decrease the **Eccentricity**

  This will ensure that the reflection will only be seen on angles oblique to the camera's eye.

- Open the color swatch and change the specular color value to **4**.

To see the reflection when the Specular Roll Off is so high, the **Specular Color** has to be superwhite.

- Once the specular color is superwhite, the reflection needs to be lowered to not have washed out reflections.

Tip: Typically the **Reflectivity** value should be **1/specular color** (a specular color value of 4.0 should have a Reflectivity of **0.25**).

- Set the color to be black.
- Increase the **Transparency** to **1.0** and reduce the **Refract Index** to **1.0** (AIR preset).
- **MMB** the clear coat Blinn node onto the Layered Shader node.
- Using the **MMB**, reassemble the order of the nodes and position the reflection layer in front of the other layers.

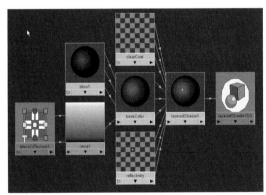

Layered Shader network using a shading map for control of highlights

2 Assign the Layered Shader to the car geometry

- Select the Car body and RMB assign the Layered Shader to it.

3 Set your Render Globals for Raytracing

- In the **Raytracing Quality** section of the Render Globals window, turn on **Raytracing** and set **Reflections** to a value of **4**.

4 Render your scene

Surface Shader

A special node called **Surface Shader** is a light weight *pass-through* node that simply allows you to translate the names of any node's outputs to the names required for it to be a valid *Surface Material.*

What this means is that a node must have at least one of the following specially named output attributes to be a valid node and directly connect to a **Surface Material Port** of a Shading Group:

- *outColor*
- *outTransparency*
- *outGlowColor*

If the node connected to the **Surface Material Port** of a Shading Group does not have at least one of the above attributes, none of the objects assigned to that Shading Group will render.

Note: It does not matter which attribute of a node is connected to the **Surface Material** port of a Shading Group; only the **outColor, outTransparency** and **outGlowColor** attributes of the connected node will be used.

The Surface Shader node is simply a means to translate an arbitrary network of Maya or user-written nodes with arbitrarily named output attributes into what the renderer will recognize as a shading network.

Use Background Shader

This material becomes important in workflows involving compositing in the production pipeline. This will be covered in detail in the chapter on compositing.

SUMMARY

Materials are the foundation for shading your surfaces. A material is a set of instructions that describes how the surface of an object will look when rendered. It is not just a collection of texture maps but also a description of how light will fall across the surface. Maya provides a number of tools to help you define the materials in your scene.

In this chapter, the following topics were covered:

- Understanding Shading Networks

- Materials
- Common Material Attributes
- Layering Shaders and Textures with a Layered Shader
- Shading Maps
- Surface Shaders

Textures

One of the most important aspects of a scene is the look of the *textures* mapped to the various objects and surfaces. These textures give the objects relevance to their surroundings, enhancing the visual quality and believability of the scene. It is important to keep in mind that this is a slower process than most would think; a certain amount of *tweaking* is involved in designing and applying textures.

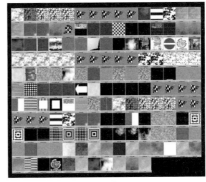

Texture Icons

In this chapter, you will learn the following:

- How to use textures to build a Shading Network

- Texturing Issues for Animation

- File texture Filtering and the use of BOT files

- Displacement Mapping

- mental ray for Maya's Displacement Mapping

LAYERED TEXTURE

Exercise: Layering scratches and logos

In this exercise, a Layered Texture node is used to give a helmet some scratches and logos. The Layered Texture node is designed to composite multiple textures, using various blend modes, directly inside Maya.

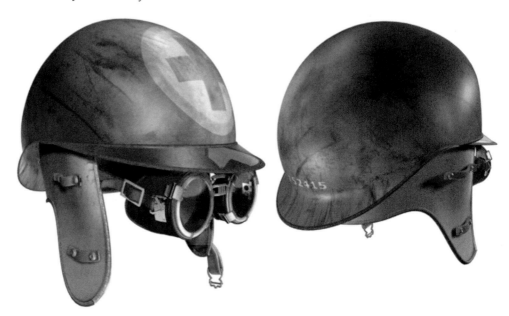

Layered Texture Helmet

1 Open the file

- Open the file called *layeredTextureHelmet.mb*.

  The final shaders are included in the file as examples. The goggles, helmet, and leather liner are all on separate **Render Layers**.

Tip: If the layer bar is turned off in the UI, you can turn it on using **Display** → **UI Elements** → **Channel Box/Layer Editor**.

---

2 Interaction and render optimizations

The *goggles* and *liner* can be set to non-renderable to optimize the rendering of the helmet during the exercise.

- Under Layer go to Layer Attributes, and click the "Renderable" box of the Render Layer tabs to toggle the goggles and liner to non-renderable.

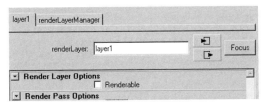

Renderable turned off on goggles layer

Setting a Render Layer to be non-renderable prevents the geometry in the layer from rendering but it does not hide the geometry in the modeling view. In this scene, the goggles and liner geometry are quite heavy and slow to interact with. To optimize the interaction speed in the modeling view, there are several things you can do.

- You can hide the *goggles*, *visor*, and *liner* until the final render. This may be the most convenient way to work.

If you would prefer to leave the geometry visible but want to improve the interaction performance, you can try the following:

- Rather than hardware shading all objects, **Smooth Shade Selected Items** can be turned on in the **Shading** menu.

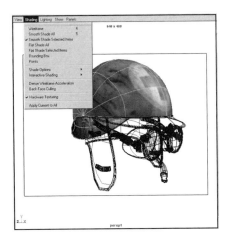

- You can toggle the **Show** menu's **Isolate Select** → **View Selected** to filter all non-selected geometry from the modeling view.

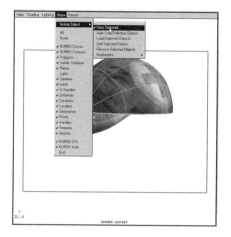

3 Create a new Blinn material

- **Create** a **Blinn** material and assign it to the *helmet.*

- **Name** the Blinn material **newHelmet.**

  Blinn is suitable because of its metallic appearance.

4 Create a Layered Texture Node

- **Create** a **Layered Texture** in Hypershade from **Create → Layered Texture**.

- **Drag** the Layered Texture onto the *newHelmet* Blinn and connect to **Color**.

- In the Attribute Editor for the Layered Texture, click inside the red outlined rectangle twice to create **2** new layers. This results in **3** layers in total.

  The **top** layer is furthest to the **left** and the **bottom** layer is on the far **right**. It is possible to rearrange the order of the layers at any time by **MMB** dragging and dropping them within the red outlined rectangle in the Layered Texture Attribute Editor.

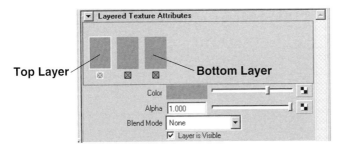

Top Layer — Bottom Layer

5 Map the bottom layer

- Click on the **bottom** layer icon to make it the active layer.
- Set the **Blend Mode** to **None**.
- **Map** the **Color** attribute with a File texture called *khaki.tif*.

  The bottom layer will not be visible yet because the middle and top layers are not set up. To temporarily make a layer invisible, click on the layer icon and then turn off the **Layer is Visible** flag.

- Make both the **top** and **middle** layers invisible for now.

Bottom layer only

6 Map the middle layer

- Go back to the Attribute Editor for the Layered Texture node.
- Click on the **middle** layer icon to make it active.
- Turn the **Layer is Visible** flag back on for this layer.
- Set the **Blend Mode** to **Multiply**.
- Map the **Color** attribute with a File texture called *scratch1.tif*.

This mode multiplies *scratch1.tif* and *khaki.tif* (on the layer below). In areas where *scratch1.tif* is white, *khaki.tif* is unchanged because white is 1,1,1 in RGB. Where *scratch1.tif* is black, *khaki.tif* becomes black because it is multiplied by 0,0,0.

Scratched layer multiplied with bottom layer

7   Map the top layer

- Go back to the Attribute Editor for the Layered Texture node.
- Click on the **top** layer icon to make it active.
- Turn the **Layer is Visible** flag back on for this layer.
- Set the **Blend Mode** to **Add**.
- Map the **Color** attribute for this top layer with a File texture called *logoRedcross.iff*.
- Map the **Alpha** attribute for this top layer with the *alpha* output from the *logoRedcross.iff* File texture.
- In the Attribute Editor for the *newHelmet* material, set the **Hardware Texturing** quality to **Highest**.

  This will make it easier to visualize the results of the Layered Texture effect in the modeling view.

- Adjust the texture placement attributes to position the red cross at the front of the *helmet*.

  This can be done with the **Interactive Placement** tool or by entering numbers in the *place2dTexture* node's Attribute Editor.

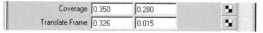

Suggested 2D texture placement for logoRedcross.iff

- Set the **Default Color** attribute to **black** on the *logoRedcross.iff* File texture. This step is important because adjusting the **Coverage** on the texture placement (in the last step) has exposed the **Default Color** surrounding the logo. Because the **Blend Mode** is **Add**, setting the **Default Color** value to black (**0,0,0**) leaves the layers below unchanged.

Logo layer added

8 Adjust the brightness of the logo

The alpha channel is acting as a mask between the red cross logo and the layers below. To reduce the amount of color information from the logo that is being added to the layers below, the alpha channel can be multiplied down with the Alpha Gain attribute.

- Lower the **Alpha Gain** value on the *logoRedcross.iff* File texture until the red cross appears duller and the scratches are visible.

Alpha Gain lowered on **logoRedcross.iff**

9 Add a detail to the back of the helmet

It is possible to map the **Default Color** attribute of the logo texture to add another texture detail without creating another layer in the Layered Texture.

- Open the Attribute Editor for the *logoRedcross.iff* File texture.

- **Map** the **Default Color** with a File texture called *serialNumber.tif*.

- Adjust the texture placement attributes for the serial number to place it at the back of the *helmet*.

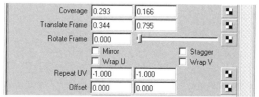

Suggested 2D texture placement for serialNumber.tif

- Lower the **Color Gain** on the *serialNumber.iff* File texture to make it blend in with the rest of the helmet.

Serial Number added to back of helmet through Default Color

Exercise: Creating a Rusty SpaceJet

In this exercise, you will build a material for the body of the spaceJet. You will create a shading network using various connected nodes to achieve a rusted beat-up metal look.

1 Open the file

- Open the file called *spaceJet.mb*.

2 Create the Layered Texture

You will start by building a Layered Texture and working up the base layer to resemble rusted metal.

- **Create** a **Layered Shader** node and rename it *hullLayeredTexture*.

- Set the **Compositing Flag** to **Layered Texture** in the Attribute Editor and **Create 3 Layers**.

- **Click** to select the layer icon closest to the right hand side.

  This will be your base rusty metal layer.

3 Create the Base Layer

To create the base metal layer, you will be using a **stucco** texture that has one of the channel fields mapped with a **solid fractal** and the other with a **crater** texture.

- **Create** a stucco texture and **map** it to the color channel of the base layer in the **Layered Texture** created above.

  Since this is the bottom layer, you do not need any transparency so set the **Transparency** value to **0.0**.

  However, in order to see the texture effects on the base layer, you'll need to set the top 2 layers' **Transparency** value to **1.0**.

- **Rename** the stucco *baseMetal*.

- Set the **Shaker** attribute to **6.0**.

  Shaker controls the smoothness of the transition between the **Channel1** and **Channel2** attributes. The lower the value, the smoother the transition.

- **Map** a **Solid Fractal** to **Channel1** on *baseMetal*.

  Under the **Color Balance** of the solid fractal tab, adjust the **Color Gain** to a moss green color.

  Adjust the **Color Offset** to a fairly dark brown color to simulate a dirty appearance.

  Adjust the **Ratio**, **Ripples**, and **Depth** to create a detailed fractal pattern. The following are some suggested values:

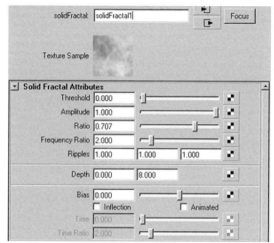

Suggested Solid Fractal Attribute values

- **Map** a **crater** texture to **Channel2** on *baseMetal*.

    Set the **Shaker** to **1.1**.

    For Channel1, choose a **pale steel blue** color.

    For Channel2, choose a very **pale warm grey**.

    For Channel3, choose a **medium rust** color.

    These colors will help to simulate the look of steel with rusty patches.

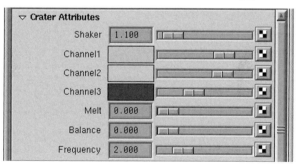

Suggested crater colors

- **Map** a **solid fractal** to the **Color Gain** on the crater texture created above.

    This helps break up the texture a bit and adds more realism to the look.

- Adjust the solid fractal's attributes to the following suggested values:

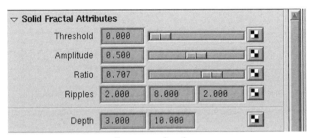

Suggested values

At this point, the shading network for the *baseMetal* layer should look something like this:

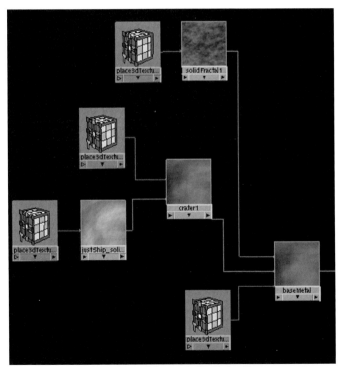

baseMetal section of the mainHull shading network

You have now created the **base** layer in your Layered Texture. You need to see how it renders and start tweaking it and adjusting the placement. In order to see these results, you need to connect the Layered Texture to a material and assign the material to the hull of the *spaceJet*.

4 Connect the Layered Texture to the Material

- **Create** a **Blinn** material and name it *mainHull.*

- Set the **Diffuse** attribute to **0.61**.

- Drag with the **MMB** the *hullLayeredTexture* onto *mainHull.* Connect to **Color**.

5 Assign mainHull to spaceJet

- With the perspective view in hardware textured mode (**6** key on your keyboard), drag the *mainHull* material onto the main hull section of the *spaceJet.* This geometry is called *main.*

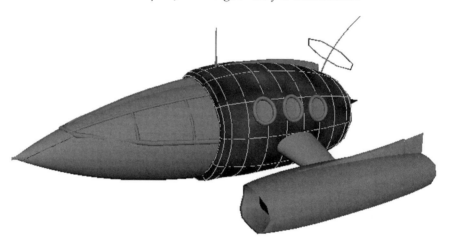

6 Render the spaceJet

- In a Render window, select **Render → Snapshot → Persp**.

- Do a render region of the *mainHull* area to view the texture.

Note: IPR may not update reliably to show the changes in 3D texture placement, so use render region instead.

---

7 Adjust the 3D Placements

At this point you will need to adjust the texture placement. Because the rusted metal is comprised of 3D solid textures, they each have a *place3dTexture* node. This is the node you will manipulate in order to control the placement.

- Use Hypershade to select one of the *place3dTexture* nodes. A green 3D cube will highlight in the modeling view.

| Tip: | It may be useful to share one texture placement for all three of the solid textures that make up *baseMetal* so that it is easier to adjust them all at once. |

- Adjust the scale and re-render the render region until you are happy with the look of the texture. Setting the **Scale X** to a value of **2** makes the *spaceJet* look like it is weathered in a lengthwise direction.

- The *baseMetal* node also has a *place3dTexture* node that you may wish to adjust. Suggestions:

    Set **Scale X** to **2**;

    Set **Scale Y** to **2.01**.

8 Add the Decal Layer

At this point you will go back and work on the middle layer of your Layered Texture to add a decal to the side of the *spaceJet*.

- Open the Attribute Editor for *hullLayeredTexture*.

- **Click** on the **Middle Layer** to make it active.

- Set the **Transparency** channel back to being fully **Opaque** so you can see your work.

- Click on the **Map** button for the **Color Channel**. In the Create Render Node window, click on the **Textures** tab. Choose **As Projection** from the 2D Textures options. Now click on **File**.

- In the Attribute Editor for the File texture, click on the small folder icon to the right of the **Image Name** attribute. Choose the image called *decal.tif*.

    By doing this, you are applying the decal as a PLANAR projection. This means that the image is being projected through worldspace very much like a slide projector. The green placement in the modeling view shows which way the texture is oriented so all you need to do is position it.

9 Position the Decal layer

- Open the Attribute Editor for the *place3dTexture* node and click on the **Select** button at the bottom.

    This is the best way to make sure you have selected the correct placement manipulator once you have several of them in a scene.

- **Translate, Rotate,** and **Scale** the 3D placement until it is roughly in position.

- Do a **Render Region** to see the results.

  You will notice that the decal is being repeated. In order to control this, you need to turn **OFF** an attribute called **Wrap**.

- Open the Attribute Editor for the **Projection** node. In the **Effects** section, turn Wrap **OFF.**

- Redo the **Render Region**. The decal should now only show up inside the 3D placement manipulator.

  The projected texture will show up only on parts of the surface that are inside the 3D placement manipulator when Wrap is **OFF**. If the decal is showing up on the opposite side of the *spaceJet*, make sure that the 3D placement is scaled so that it does not engulf the opposite side of the *spaceJet*.

- **Repeat** the above procedure for the **Transparency** channel on this layer. This time use an image called *decalTransp.tif* as the projected image.

- **Reuse** the *place3dTexture* node that you already positioned for the color map. To reuse the placement, connect *worldInverseMatix* to *placementMatrix*.

- Remember to turn **OFF** Wrap on the new *projection* node.

- Redo the **Render Region**.

  You will notice that while you now have a decal on the side of the *spaceJet*, the overall look of the base layer has changed. This is because of an attribute called **Default Color**.

  When you turned Wrap off, the texture map no longer covered the entire surface that it was mapped to. So, Maya applies the Default Color to any regions outside of the textured region. The Default Color in this case, is being added to the color information from the base layer which is throwing off the look. For this reason, it is important that you set the default color correctly so that it does not interfere with the other layers in the Layered Texture.

Tip: It is possible to texture map the Default Color attribute to create a Layered Texture look.

---

10 Adjust the Default Color of the Decal

- Open the Attribute Editor for the projection node that is connected to color. In the **Color Balance** section, set the **Default Color** to **Black**.

  By setting the Default Color to black, you are essentially adding **0,0,0** to the regions outside of the decal. This results in no change to the look of the base layer.

- Open the Attribute Editor for the projection node that is connected to Transparency. In the **Color Balance** section, set the **Default Color** to **White**.

  In this case, you want the regions outside the decal texture to be fully transparent. Since white is fully transparent, you need to set the default color to **White**.

- Redo a **Render Region** to see the effect.

  You have now finished the middle layer of *hullLayeredTexture*.

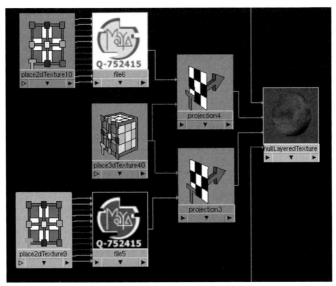

Decal layer section of the mainHull shading network

11 Add a Dirt Layer

At this point, you will build a dirt layer to add to *spaceJet* Material.

- Open the Attribute Editor for the *hullLayeredTexture* and make the top layer active.

- Make the color **Black**.

- Click on the **Transparency** map button and choose **Leather** from the Create Render Node window.

Tip: The Leather texture is very good for simulating all sorts of bumpy, knobby, or scaly surfaces. Try experimenting with it for organic effects.

- Open the Attribute Editor for the leather texture and set the following values:

  Cell Size to **0.31**;

  Density to **0.86**;

  Spottyness to **1.0**;

  Randomness to **2.0**;

  Threshold to **0.94**.

To improve the dirt effect of the leather texture, you will now use something called **Color Remap** to extend the level of control you have.

What the color remap does is take the original colors that were in the original texture and replace them with a user defined ramp. That way, you can change the colors and/or map other textures into the ramp. This gives a great deal of control over the final look.

- Open the Attribute Editor for the leather texture and go to **Effects → Color Remap → Insert**.

A **ramp** appears. Notice how the color of the leather has been changed by the ramp.

The way it works is that the lightest values are replaced by the color from the top of the ramp and the darkest values are replaced by the color from the bottom of the ramp. The middle tones are replaced by the ramp colors in between.

- Open the Attribute Editor for the *RemapRamp* and set the following:

  Type to **V Ramp**;

  Interpolation to **Bump**.

- Select the top color entry of the ramp and set it to:

  H to **0**;

  S to **0**;

  V to **0.514**.

- Select the bottom color entry of the *RemapRamp* and set it to **Black**.

- Click on the handle on the middle color entry of the ramp. Set the **Selected Position** attribute to **0.395**. Map the **Selected Color** attribute with a **stucco**.

  Mapping the middle color entry of the ramp with a stucco helps to break up the pattern.

Tip: You can move the ramp color entries up and down manually using the handles on the left side of the ramp.

- Open the Attribute Editor for the stucco.

  Set the **Shaker** to **5**.

  Set **Channel1** color to **White**.

  Set **Channel2** color to **Medium Grey**.

The last thing you need to do is reverse the colors of the remap output to complete the dirt layer. You will do this by inserting a **reverse** node between the *outColor* of the *RemapRamp* and the **Transparency** input of the top layer of *hullLayeredTexture*.

- In Hypershade, create a **reverse** node from the general utilities menu. **Drag** the *RemapRamp* onto the reverse node. Connect *outColor* to **Input**.

- Break the connection between *RemapRamp* and *hullLayeredTexture*.

- Open the Attribute Editor for *hullLayeredTexture*. Click on the Top Layer to make sure it is active. Drag the *reverse* node from Hypershade to the **Transparency** channel in the open Attribute Editor.

  You have now broken the existing connection between the *RemapRamp* and the *hullLayeredTexture* and inserted a *reverse* node.

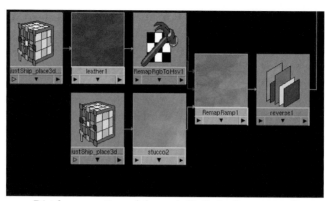

Dirt layer section of the mainHull shading network

You can see that the surface of the *spaceJet* now has a nice spotty dirt layer on it that resembles grease and splattered space bugs.

12 Add a Specular Map

Now that you have completed all the work for your color channel, you can move on to some of the other attributes on your *mainHull* material. Because you have created such a beat-up rusted metal, you need to have highlights that make sense. Essentially, you don't want the rusted areas to look as shiny as the smoother areas. Specular maps are very useful in helping fool the eye into seeing this effect.

To do this, you will reuse the **crater** texture you mapped onto the *baseMetal* layer.

- In Hypershade, show the Input nodes for *mainHull*.
- Find the crater texture that is connected to *baseMetal*.
- **Connect** *crater.outColor* to *mainHull.specularColor*.

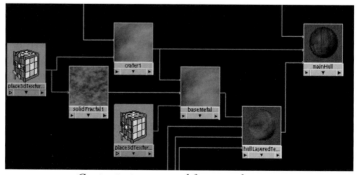

Crater texture reused for specular map

13 Add the Bump Maps

You will now add some bump maps to complete the look of your *spaceJet* hull. The first bump will be a 3D solid texture to give a greater sense of roughness to the rusted metal. The second bump map will be a File texture that gives a panelled look to the hull.

- Open the Attribute Editor for *mainHull* and **map** a **Solid Fractal** to the **Bump** channel.

- Some suggestions for the solid fractal attributes are:

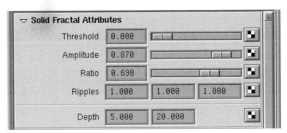

Suggested settings

You want this bump map to enhance the effect of the color and specular maps so in this case you can again reuse a 3D placement. You will reuse the placement connected to the **crater** texture.

- **Delete** the *place3Dtexture* node that is connected to the *solid fractal* you are using as the bump map.

- **Drag** the *place3Dtexture* node connected to the crater texture you have connected to **Specular color** and *baseMetal,* and connect it to the Solid Fractal that you are using as a bump map. This should automatically connect the *worldInverseMatrix* to the *placementMatrix* for you.

At this point you are finished with the first bump map. To complete the entire *mainHull* material, you will add a second bump map for the detailed panelled look.

- In Hypershade, **Create** a File texture node.

- **Map** the image name attribute with a file called *engineBump.tif.*

Note: Be sure that when you create the File texture, you are NOT creating it as a projection. It should be set to **Normal**.

- **Create** a *bump2d* node in Hypershade.

You need to connect the File texture to the 2D node. Normally, if you map a File texture to the bump channel of a material, Maya will connect the *outAlpha* from the File texture to the Bump Value of the bump node.

However, if you **fcheck** the image file (*engineBump*), you can see by pressing the **A** key, that there is no alpha channel. In this case you need to use the color information instead. The problem is that you cannot connect the **Out Color** attribute to the *BumpValue* directly since the data types do not match. In order to accomplish this, you will use a **Luminance** node.

- **Create** a **Luminance** node in Hypershade.
- **Drag** the **File** texture onto the Luminance node. Connect **Out Color** to **Value**.
- **Drag** the Luminance node onto the *bump2D* node. Connect **Out Value** to **Bump Value**.

You now have a bump map network but it is not connected to the rest of your *mainHull* material. Since you have already mapped a texture to the bump channel on *mainHull*, to apply this second bump you will chain the bump maps together.

- **Drag** the *bump2d* node onto the *bump3d* node that is already connected to *mainHull*.
- Connect **Out Normal** to **Normal Camera**.

Note: In order to find the input called *Normal Camera*, you will need to go to **Right Side Filters** at the top of the Connection Editor and turn on **Show Hidden**.

Now the *mainHull* material will show the results of both bump maps. The complete bump map section of the *mainHull* network should look like this:

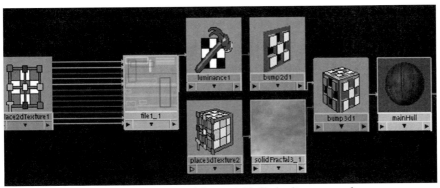

Bump map section of the mainHull shading network

Now that you have completed the bump mapping process, the *mainHull* material is complete.

Using ramp color entries to combine textures

Ramp textures are useful tools for developing textures. It allows you to combine other textures into the ramp and the ramp controls how they interact. If you look at a ramp, it has position markers that define a specific U or V value along the texture. If you select one of these position markers in the Attribute Editor, there will be a color associated with it. You can then map that position marker's color and depending on the **Interpolation** settings, the texture will be blended with the other colors of the ramp.

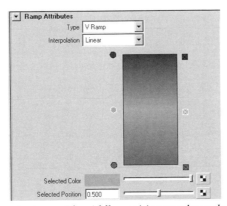

Ramp texture with middle position marker selected

The above diagram is a default ramp with the middle position marker selected which is shown in the **Selected Color** attribute.

- **Create** a **Checker Texture** and **map** it onto the selected color of the middle position marker. You should end up with a ramp that has a checker map in the middle which fades nicely to the colors defined by the top and bottom position markers. The ramp itself will not show the changes but the swatch representing the texture will. **Add** textures to the other position markers.

Ramp textures

The ability to map the position markers of a ramp gives you greater flexibility and control in building textures. By manipulating the **Type** and **Interpolation** of the ramp and texture mapping more position markers, you are able to build interesting textures for your scenes. The following object has a bump map that was created using only **ramp** and **grid** textures.

Bump map from ramp textures

TEXTURING ISSUES FOR ANIMATION

Animation of an object must be considered when applying textures. For example, you have used many 3D textures on the *spaceJet*. Because 3D textures are defined in worldspace, the *spaceJet* will appear to slide through them once it is translated or deformed. There are several things that can be done to prevent this from happening (a movie is provided called *spacejet* to show the results of the following solutions):

- Parent the *place3dTexture* nodes to the animated transform node
- Create Texture Reference Objects
- Convert to File textures

Parenting the place3dTexture node

In the case of a **non-deforming** object, parenting the *place3dtexture* nodes to the animated transform node will allow you to move the object and the textures together. As long as the object does not deform, the textures will translate, rotate, and scale with the textured object.

Parenting 3D texture nodes under animated transform nodes

- Select the animated object.
- Open Hypershade and use the icon to graph materials on selected objects.
- Select all of the *place3Dtexture* nodes used on this animated object and group them.
- From either the Outliner or Hypergraph windows, you can drag and drop this group into the hierarchy of the animated object.

Texture Reference objects

In the case of a **deforming** object, you will encounter crawling or swimming 3D textures or projected textures so you need to consider using either a texture reference object or converting the 3D and projected textures to 2D File textures.

A **Texture Reference Object** is a copy of the original object. This copy does not deform and is used as a *reference* for texture placement on the original object. The idea is that the original object can be deformed and the 3D or projected texture placement information will be based on the non-deforming reference copy.

Some **advantages** of using this method are:

- You have the ability to animate the solid texture attributes.

- There is no fixed resolution.

- It does not require storing texture maps on disk.

- It is quick to setup.

Some **disadvantages** are:

- File size can increase due to extra copies of geometry.

- Very noisy 3D textures can sometimes look like they are crawling or shimmering when animated.

- 3D textures take longer to render than surface mapped File textures (however, very hi-res File texture can also be slow).

Create a Texture Reference Object for the spaceJet

The scene file *spaceJetWarp.mb* demonstrates the necessity for special handling of the 3D textures due to deformations applied to the spaceJet. In the following steps, you will create a texture reference object to prevent swimming textures.

1 Open the scene file spaceJetWarp.mb and create a reference texture

- **Select** the *spaceJet* (make sure you select the whole hierarchy - the root node is called *spaceJet*).

- Select **Texturing** → **Create Texture Reference Object** to create a Texture Reference Object.

- Because the texture placement nodes were already set up with respect to the original surfaces, the Texture Reference Object will be at the same position as the original surfaces so that the textures look as intended.

Note: If you create a Texture Reference Object prior to positioning the textures, you would simply position all the 3D and projected textures relative to the Texture Reference Object rather than the original geometry. In this case, it would not matter whether the reference copy sits in the same location as the original.

- **Translate** the new templated Texture Reference Object so that it is right on top of the original.

  This will ensure that the textures look the same as they did before creating the texture reference object.

- **Save** this file under a new name.

- Batch render a small sequence or test render different frames in the animation to see that the textures are now looking as if they are sticking to the surfaces.

Note: Do not parent *place3Dtexture* nodes to animated transforms when you are planning to work with Texture Reference Objects. If you were originally animating the objects with parented textures, be careful when later creating a texture reference object that you do not leave any parented textures. If you forget, the texture placements will move but the reference object will not. This will cause the textures to slide over the surface in the animation.

Converting to File textures

Another option when dealing with animated and/or deforming geometry involves converting 3D or 2D procedural textures into File texture parametric maps. Once the conversion is done, the File textures are automatically mapped onto the surfaces.

Some **advantages** of using this technique are:

- It is possible to touch-up or otherwise manipulate a File texture in an Image Editor.

- It is generally much faster to render a File texture than networks of complex procedural textures. However, very high resolution File textures will also take a long time to render and use lots of memory.

- In the event of crawling or shimmering texture problems, it is often easier to fix once the textures are converted to File textures (see File Texture Filtering).

Some **disadvantages** are:

- You can no longer animate texture attributes.

- The resolution is fixed.

- It can require large amounts of disk space to store image files.

- Very high resolution image files can require large amounts of memory during rendering.

- Converting to File textures for many surfaces will produce a separate material for each surface. This can lead to a large number of materials in Visor and Hypershade.

How to Convert to File textures

- **Select** the texture, material, or shading group that you wish to convert.

- **Shift-select** the surface you want to create a File texture for.

- In Hypershade, use **Edit → Convert to File Texture.**

  You will notice that there is an option box for this feature. The options will allow you to specify the resolution, whether or not anti-aliasing will be applied, and whether or not to bake the lighting into the resulting texture.

Converting to File textures on the spaceJet

The scene file *spaceJetWarp.mb* demonstrates the issues surrounding 3D texturing an animated and deforming surface. In this exercise, you will convert the projected and 3D procedural textures to 2D File textures using the **Convert to File texture** feature.

1 Open the scene file spaceJetWarp.mb

This is the same scene file that you used to test the *texture reference object*. In this exercise, you will convert the 3D procedural and projected textures to 2D File textures as an alternative approach to resolving the texture swimming problem.

2 Convert the material associated with the main part of the ship

To try this workflow, you will first convert the material that is assigned to the spaceJet's *main* body.

- **Select** the *main* object in the Outliner or the perspective view.

- Click on the **Graph Materials on Selected Objects** button in Hypershade.

  This will display the shading network assigned to this surface.

- **Shift-select** the *mainHull* Blinn material node in Hypershade.

  Both the surface and the material node are selected.

- Select **Edit → Convert to File Texture** from the Hypershade menu.

  From the option box, leave *anti-aliasing* off and set the **X** and **Y** **resolution** to **1024**. This will create a higher resolution File texture.

- **Press** the **Convert Texture** button.

  This may take a few minutes depending on system performance.

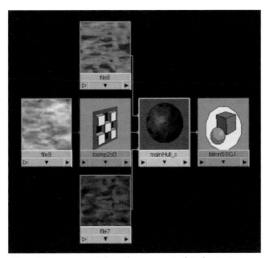
Resulting material with converted File textures

The conversion results in a baking of the 3D textures into File textures. A new material is created and assigned to the surface. The original material remains intact and can be re-assigned if needed. In this case, the original material is still shading the other surfaces on the spaceJet.

- **Rename** the new material *mainHull_new*.

3 Re-connect the bump texture

The resulting new material is a good representation of the original with one exception:

> The chained bump node's information (the panel grooves) is missing in the resulting File texture connected to the bump channel on the *mainHull_new* material.

> To correct this you will duplicate the original File texture and *bump2d* node used to create the panel grooves and add it to the new (*mainHull_new*) shading network.

- **Select** the *spaceJet_bump2d* node in the original (*mainHull*) shading network.

- **RMB** select **Edit → Duplicate → Shading Network.**

> This will duplicate the *bump2d* node as well as its Input nodes, including the File texture and its placement node.

- **MMB** drag and drop the duplicated *bump2d* node onto the *bump2d* node which is already connected to the *mainHull_new* material.

- In the Connection Editor, connect the **Out Normal** attribute of the duplicated *bump2d* node to the **Normal Camera** attribute of the *bump2d* node already connected to mainHull_new.

4 Adjust the final bump effect

You have now recreated the chained bump map of the original material. However, you may notice that the visual results look different than the original look of the bump map.

- Adjust the **Bump Depth** attribute on the *bump2d* nodes until the bump effect looks like the original.

5 Convert the remaining surfaces on the spaceJet (optional)

The workflow for converting the rest of the surfaces associated with the mainHull material is as follows:

- Using **RMB** on the *mainHull* material in Hypershade, select **Select Objects With Material.**

  All of the surfaces still associated with this material will be selected.

- **Shift-select** the *mainHull* material.

- Open the options for **Edit → Convert Material to File Texture**, set the **Resolution** back to a lower value because the remaining surfaces are smaller than the main hull section, then click on **Convert Texture**.

  Maya will create and assign a new material with the resulting File textures for each surface. This may take a while.

Details About Convert to File texture Feature

The name of the underlying function is called **Convert Solid Texture**. It has two components: a UI written completely in MEL and a command. When you specify the shading node and surface, depending on the shading node's type (i.e. texture, shader, shading group) and depending on how many surfaces were specified, the convert solid command will be run on each surface for each channel in the shading network.

For example, if a Blinn is chosen and there are connections to color and transparency, the MEL script will run **Convert Solid Texture** twice; once on the node connected to color and once using the node connected to transparency. The MEL script will then duplicate this shading network, connect the computed File textures, and re-assign the surface to the new shading group.

- **Convert solid** is like doing a mini-render so be aware of all surfaces that have **Double Sided** by default. This will affect convert solid because a discontinuity will be observed anywhere the normal was flipped. The shading operates using camera normals, so the normal flip will occur around the silhouette of the surface as seen from the active camera. This is turned off by default when converting.

- When the **Baked Lighting** option is used, shadows are not included in the computed result by default. It is possible to turn on an option to include the shadow information. (For more, see the online documentation).

- **Bake Transparency** specifies whether to compute transparency when baking lights. This will sample both the color and transparency of the network.

- The options under **UV Range** specify the amount of the surface to sample in UV space. For example, if you select one or more faces on a poly object, instead of sampling the whole surface only the selected faces are sampled.

- Bump mapping has the effect of tweaking the normal depending on a texture. You may want to convert a bump map but be aware that the normals cannot be represented as a pixel map.

- When anti-aliasing is turned **ON** in the options window for **Convert Material to Texture**, double the resolution and average four pixels to get the resulting pixel color.

- The active camera is important if sampling needs information from *NormalCamera*. Most rendering nodes (for example, crater or marble) are not sensitive to the camera used but there are others (for example, camera projection and baked lighting) which will be very dependent on the camera used. In these situations you should be aware that the camera in the active view will be used.

- **Convert Solid Texture** will construct the output by connecting the sampled node's name with the surface's name. If this file already exists, the version number will be appended to the file. The file will be written to the *sourceImages* folder of the current project.

Known problems and limitations:

- Depending on how the isoparms are positioned on a NURBS surface, the samples could all be taken in a very small area of the surface.

- If a polygon is used, the surface must have unique normalized UVs. If a polygon has non-unique UVs, or convert solid determines that UVs are missing, there are no error messages generated and the convert solid will be wrong.

- Chord length texturing mapping (Fix Texture Warp) is ignored.

- Only NURBS and polygon surfaces may be converted.

FILE TEXTURE FILTERING

When rendering File textures, Maya by default applies filtering. The filtering contributes to the overall quality and speed of the final rendered image.

Filtering is controlled by several attributes found in the Attribute Editor for a File texture as well as many other textures found in Maya. You will look at the primary filter type called MipMapping as it applies to File textures.

MipMapping

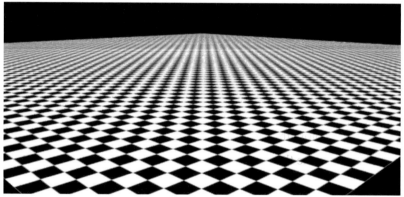

Checker floor

Why filter File textures? In a perspective view of a plane (receding to a vanishing point), a single pixel in the final image may correspond to thousands of pixels in the source checker pattern. Determining the final color for a single pixel would require an immense computation. To reduce the amount of work required to compute the final pixel color, a technique called *MipMapping* was developed to produce quicker filtering.

MipMap filtering in Maya means that Maya stores multiple resolutions of the same texture. For example, if you have a 512x512 image, Maya stores the 512x512, then 256x256, then 128x128, then 64x64, then 32x32, etc.

Note: Storing such multiple resolutions means that it is most optimal for the MipMap to deal with square resolutions that are a multiple of 2 (meaning 2^x); i.e. 1024x1024, 512x512, 256x256, etc. This is particularly true for bump maps, though close to square resolutions still produce very respectable results. Extreme non-square ratio textures may cause problems.

The renderer chooses the appropriate level of File texture image to use based on how much screen coverage there is and how obliquely the object is being viewed. The further away or more oblique, the more the renderer tends to use a lower-res/blurry version of the texture. (Actually, in general the renderer is getting texture values by interpolating between two levels of the MipMap).

This helps the renderer by reducing the amount of work it needs to do to resolve the final color of a pixel, but how does it affect the image quality?

In terms of quality, the filtering acts like a form of anti-aliasing for textures. By using lower resolution versions of a texture, the resulting pixel colors are more of an average of the surrounding colors on that texture map. This lends to a somewhat blurry look to the receding parts of the textured surface in the rendered image.

However, the upside is that this "averaging" prevents detectable shifts in color for a single pixel from frame to frame. If the resulting distant pixel colors were very precise at all times, you would see very noticeable texture crawl or shimmering during animation because the same pixel could have very different colors from frame to frame depending on the viewing angle.

The trick is to strike the right balance between the sharpness of the texture in the final render vs. the amount of crawling in the texture during animation.

Tip: When particular File textured surfaces are crawling, shimmering, flickering, etc. (over an animation), it is best NOT to play with the anti-aliasing shading samples first. The first choice would be to play with the File texture's filter attribute values.

The **Filter Size** is internally computed by Maya based on the above mentioned criteria (how much screen coverage there is and how obliquely the object is being viewed). The **Filter** and **Filter Offset** under the **Effects** section are attributes that can be used to alter the results that Maya calculates.

Tip: It is not recommend that the **Filter** be set to **0**. Setting **Filter** to **0** or a very small value will tell the renderer to ignore the internal filter size computation. This will force the renderer to use the highest level of the MipMap.

Higher Order Filter Types

In some situations, adjusting the filter attribute values will not help. In this situation, the more optimal solution would be to employ a higher order filter, such as the **Quadratic** filter. The quadratic filter does more computations in projecting screen pixels to texture space, thus resulting in much cleaner results. This is the Maya default Filter type.

Pre-Filtering File Textures

The **Pre-Filter** and **Pre-Filter Radius** attributes found under the File Attributes editor, are used to correct File textures that are aliased or contain noise in unwanted areas. When Pre-filtering is on, the image file uses a **Gaussian** type filter to get rid of noise and aliasing, contributing to a better quality image. The Pre-Filter Radius will determine the size of the filtering radius. The default value of **2.0** works for most images, but you can increase the radius to provide even smoother results. This can be particularly useful when bump or displacement mapping.

Block Ordered Textures and Caching

In the Attribute Editor for File textures, there is an attribute called **Use Cache**. This attribute can be used as an optimization if you are finding that your renders are running into swap space. Using swap is very slow so you want to avoid this.

By turning **Use Cache** on, you use a lot more disk space but less memory. This is because the renderer does not need to keep whole textures in RAM during the render. Instead, it uses **tiles** of the texture called **BOT** files as it needs them. BOT stands for **Block Order Textures**.

BOT are enabled by turning **Use Cache ON** for each File texture. If this flag is **ON** and the File textures are not already BOT format files, then Maya will automatically create BOT textures from the image files and store them in the TMPDIR at render time.

The File textures can be pre-converted to BOT by using the *makebot* MEL command:

```
makebot -i "in_image" -o "out_bot_file";
```

In this case, the resulting BOT files can be stored in a directory you specify. For example:

```
makebot -i "in_image" -o "/usr/tmp/out_bot_file";
```

Once the BOT files are created, you need to change the path and name in the File texture's Attribute Editor to point to the BOT files. If the textures are already in BOT format, this saves time at the start of the render. It also allows you to know how much disk space is being taken up by the BOT files on disk before you start rendering.

Technical Details

A BOT texture on disk is a compressed MipMap structure with 8x8 texel pages. (A **texel** is a texture element derived in much the same way as pixel is a picture element). The *textureCache* is a 256 texel page cache in memory; that is, it can hold 256 of the 8x8 texel pages. There is only one *textureCache* for the entire rendering session and the cache is shared between all File textures.

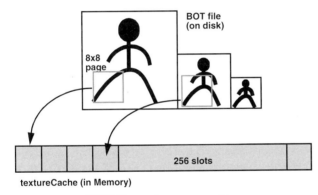

BOT files and texture caching

The *textureCache* is demand loaded. When part of a texture is required, if it is not already in the cache, it is loaded from disk. If the *textureCache* is full, the least recently accessed pages are removed and replaced with the pages being loaded.

BOT textures have the advantage of reducing the amount of memory required to keep textures in memory. If the image file has already been converted to a BOT texture file, the Maya renderer can use it much more quickly than when it has to convert the file to BOT texture on its own.

BOT textures do have some limitations as well. If multiple renderers/ processors are using the same BOT file, there can be an I/O bandwidth problem which will cause all the renderers to slow down (having a copy of the BOT texture for each processor is about the only work-around). If the image files are not BOT texture files to begin with, then TMPDIR can get full quickly with all of the temporary BOT files.

If different shading networks reference the same File texture image, a single copy of the image is kept in memory and shared by all the shaders.

BOT Files and Pre-Render Optimization

There is a command that creates smaller and more efficient Maya binary files reserved for rendering. By deleting information not relevant to the renderer, these "leaner" files can help reduce overall memory used and decrease render times. To do this, run your files through *Optimize Scene Size* with all the flags checked on. BOT files are created and relinked (texture assignment). Information used to edit the scene is deleted.

Tip: For Maya files with file referencing, it is best to export all first otherwise some optimizations may be missed.

The usage for this pre-render setup is straightforward. Use *maya -optimizeRender -help*, for a list of flags and descriptions for this command.

DISPLACEMENT MAPPING

Sometimes, rather than modeling the details of a surface, it is more convenient to use a **displacement map**. Displacement mapping uses a texture to alter the shape of geometry. This is different than a bump map which simply alters the surface normals to create the illusion of surface relief.

Displacement Map   **Bump Map**

Displacement mapping in Maya

The displacement map is connected to the Shading Group node instead of the Material node. This is because it is applied to the geometry rather than the shading. To see the connections in Hypershade, select the Material node and click on the *Output Connections* button. Then select the Shading Group node and click on the *Input Connections*. This will show the Displacement map, the Material node, and all of the geometry that belongs to the Shading Group. The following snapshot of the Hypershade shows an example of the nodes and how they are connected:

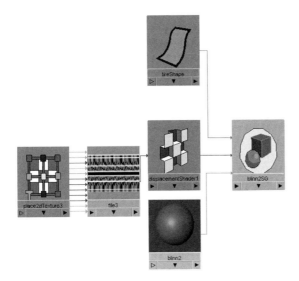

The Displacement node is connected to the Shading Group directly

There are two types of Displacement mapping available in Maya. When working with the **original** method, the **Bump** channel on the material is mapped automatically. This is required for correct surface normals; without this bump map the surface will not shade properly. To use another bump map in addition to the one the displacement map requires, just follow the same chaining technique used earlier to apply two bump maps to the *rusty hull* material for the *spaceJet*. Drag and drop the second bump node onto the displacement's bump node. Connect the **Out Normal** to **Normal Camera**.

A newer type of displacement is called **Feature Based Displacement Mapping**. Its purpose is to add interesting details to surfaces. In order to capture small details with the original displacement method, the tessellation had to be increased for the entire surface. This would often lead to crashes from running out of memory. The feature based displacement mapping solves the problem by attaining high quality displacement tessellation with minimum triangle counts. To achieve this, the tessellation is built so that the triangle density is greatest where the details are. This technique decouples the effect of tessellation parameters and displacement mapping parameters.

Exercise: Feature Based Displacement

This exercise will make use of **Feature Displacement** to create the treads on a tire. Open the file called *TireDisplacement.mb*. There are two display layers; one contains the tire geometry and the other contains the chrome rim. The rim layer can be made invisible to optimize test renders. The final material and displacement map is provided in the file as an example.

1 Adjust the Tessellation for the non-displaced tire

- Adjust the tessellation on the tire just high enough to capture the shape of the surface. There is no need to increase the tessellation parameters beyond this point for displacement mapping.

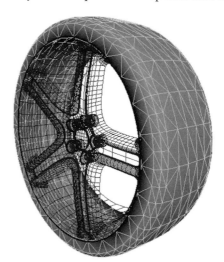

2 Visualize the Displacement Texture

Because displacement maps cannot be previewed in hardware texturing, the following technique can be very useful.

- **Map** the texture *tread.tif* to the **Color** channel on the material called *newTire*.

This is the intended displacement texture but mapping it to the color channel (temporarily) will help to position it and also help when setting the displacement attributes.

tread.tif File texture

- Turn **ON** Hardware Texturing by pressing the **6** key.

- In the Attribute Editor for the *newTire* material, under the **Hardware Texturing** section set the **Texture Quality** to **Highest**.

  This increases the resolution of the display of the texture, making it easier to see the placement.

- Adjust the placement of the tire tread texture using the *place2dTexture* node.

Tip: It may be helpful to use the **Interactive Placement** in conjunction with **IPR**. Remember to use the **Middle Mouse Button** to move the handles on the interactive placement manipulator.

Default placement   **Adjusted placement**

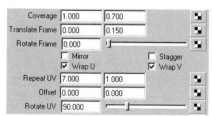

Coverage	1.000	0.700	■
Translate Frame	0.000	0.150	■
Rotate Frame	0.000		■
	☐ Mirror	☐ Stagger	
	☑ Wrap U	☑ Wrap V	
Repeat UV	7.000	1.000	■
Offset	0.000	0.000	■
Rotate UV	90.000		■

Suggested values for the texture placement

- Set the **Default Color** on the *tread.tif* File texture to **black**.

  Because the **Coverage** has been adjusted to less than **1.0**, the **Default Color** is visible on the sides of the tire. Setting the Default Color to black (rgb 0,0,0), intentionally prevents the sides of the tire from being displaced when this texture is applied as a displacement map.

- Set **Display Render Tessellation** to **ON** in the tire's Attribute Editor to see the tessellation triangles.

Display Render Tessellation turned on

3 Connect the Displacement map

- Drag the *tread.tif* File texture onto the *newTire* material. Connect to **Displacement map**.

  This automatically connects the tread texture to the Shading Group node.

4 Tuning the displacement attributes

The displacement attributes are found in the Attribute Editor for the geometry, not the texture map.

- Make sure the **Feature Displacement** flag is turned **ON**.

If the original tessellation triangle is large and the texture details are fine, then the **Initial Sample Rate** has to be large (from **30** to **50** or even higher). If the triangle is small and the texture details are not that fine, then Initial Sample Rate does not have to be very high (usually the default of **6** is good enough).

Observe how sharp the texture details are and if there are many clean lines or curved details. The sharper the features and the cleaner the lines, the higher the **Extra Sample Rate** needs to be.

- For each tessellation triangle, observe how much texture detail is in the triangle.
- Set the **Initial Sample Rate** based on your observations.
- For now, set the **Extra Sample Rate** to **0**.
- Disconnect the **File** texture from the **Color** channel.
- Test render the tire to see the results of the displacement map.

  It is not possible to use IPR to help tune the displacement attributes because the displacement map is applied to the geometry, not the shading. Changes in the shape of the geometry are not supported by IPR.

- If not enough details are captured, try increasing the **Initial Sample Rate**. Use the lowest acceptable value.
- If the features are too jagged, try increasing the **Extra Sample Rate**.

  This attribute refines the displacement results. It is a good idea to try it at 0 and see if the quality is good enough. This will help to keep the triangle count as low as possible. Increase it only if the quality is not good enough.

In the case of the tire, the triangles are medium sized where the tread lies on the surface and the texture details are fairly small (fine) relative to the size of the triangles. In order to capture enough information about the texture details in each triangle, a medium-high **Initial Sample Rate** is required.

To refine the results, the **Extra Sample Rate** should be increased from **0** very slightly until the edges of the texture details look acceptable.

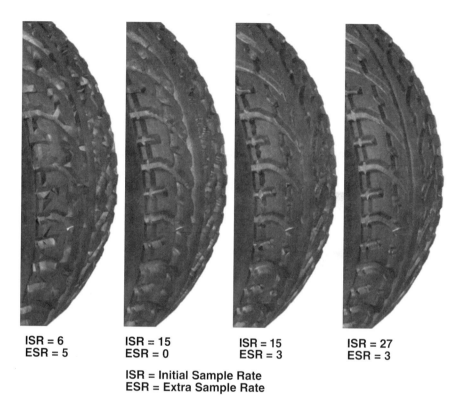

ISR = 6   ISR = 15   ISR = 15   ISR = 27
ESR = 5   ESR = 0   ESR = 3   ESR = 3

ISR = Initial Sample Rate
ESR = Extra Sample Rate

5 Using the Displacement to Polygon tool

Under the **Modify** menu on the main menu bar, there is a **Convert** menu that contains a tool called **Displacement to Polygon**. This tool is very useful because it bakes out the displaced surface as a polygon mesh, providing a great way to visualize the results instead of test rendering. The resulting polygonal object is created in the same location as the original and can be used instead of the original surface (in which case, the displacement map serves as a modeling tool). While the original surface is preserved, there is no *history* relationship between the original surface and the polygonal object. If changes are made to the original surface or any of its tessellation or displacement attributes, the **Displacement to Polygon** tool must be used again to see the changes.

Note: The tire used in this exercise is NOT a good case to test the **Displacement to Polygon** tool. In general, when the texture details cover the entire surface, **Feature Displacement** will result in a very high number of polygons. This creates a very heavy file relative to a NURBS surface. In these cases it is not advisable to use the **Displacement to Polygon** tool.

The following images show an example of the **Displacement to Polygon** tool results:

The texture is mapped to the color channel for placement visualization only. After the **Displacement to Polygon** tool is invoked, the displacement map is visible in the resulting polygon mesh. The polygon object is created in the same location as the original NURBS surface (the two surfaces are visible in the above image).

- To try this, open the file called *AWlogoTireDispl.mb*.

  This is the tire shown above with the Alias | Wavefront™ logo used as a displacement map.

- Test the **Displacement to Polygon** tool.

- Try different setting for the **Feature Displacement** attributes and redo the **Displacement to Polygon**.

  This will help you to gauge the impact of the Feature Displacement attributes.

- Try changing the tessellation settings and redo the **Displacement to Polygon**.

  This will help you to gauge the impact of the tessellation settings and how they interact with the Feature Displacement settings.

Transparency Mapping using outAlpha

If you map a File texture to the Color channel of a material and look at it in hardware shading or hardware rendering, you will notice that the Alpha channel is used as the transparency automatically (if the File texture has an Alpha channel that is). However, the same is not the case in software rendering. In order to do this in software rendering, it is necessary to pass the *outTransparency* from the File texture before connecting it to the Transparency channel.

outTransparency

A material's transparency is the opposite of a File texture's Alpha channel which is generally based on opacity:

alpha opacity, (0 = black = transparent; 1 = white = opaque)

material transparency, (0 = black = opaque; 1 = white = transparent)

In previous Maya releases, there was no easy way for the alpha value of a File texture or Layered Texture to act as a material's transparency. The *outAlpha* of the File texture or the Layered Texture would have to be sent through a reverse node prior to connection to the material's Transparency attributes.

To compensate for this, Maya has an *outTransparency* attribute, accessible from the node's pop-up menu. In the Hypershade or Connection Editor, connect the outTransparency attribute of the File or Layered Texture to the Transparency attribute of a material. This will allow you to see an embedded alpha in hardware shaded mode.

The default drag-and-drop creation of File or Layered Texture nodes does not automatically connect the outTransparency of the texture to the transparency attribute of the material. This is because it can cause confusion when alpha in not available in the texture. So that the outTransparency is always connected when creating File or Layered Texture nodes, you can set the following environment variable:

```
setenv MAYA_USE_OUTTRANSPARENCY_CONNECT
```

Each channel (R,G,B) of the outTransparency attribute is the reverse of the node's outAlpha attribute. This makes it easier to define the opacity of a material using the Alpha value.

By default, a Layered Texture's Luminance value is used as its Alpha. To use the actual Alpha or the outTransparency, turn off **Alpha is Luminance** in the Layered Texture's Attribute Editor.

MENTAL RAY FOR MAYA TEXTURING

Texture Reference Object in mental ray for Maya

Texture reference objects are supported in mental ray for Maya and are setup exactly the same way as in Maya.

Baking in mental ray for Maya

The procedure for baking information (convert to File texture) with mental ray for Maya is done by using **Bake-sets**. Bake-sets allow users to bake a variety of objects with different baking options such as illumination, shadow, shading, and textures using this method. You can also save different baking parameters, making it easier to re-bake when needed.

You can also bake objects that have not been assigned to a bake-set. If this is the case, then the objects are automatically assigned to the initial bake-set, and the baking proceeds.

To do a simple batch bake in mental ray for Maya:

- Select one or more objects for which you want to bake.
- Select **Lighting/Shading → Batch Bake (mental ray)**.
- Set the desired options, then click **Convert**.

Note: Pre Maya 5, the mental ray for Maya baking options were found in the **Hypershade → Edit → Convert to File Texture**. Now they are found in the rendering menu set under **Lighting/Shading**.

To create a bake-set in mental ray for Maya:

- Select one or more objects for which you want to create a bake-set.
- Select **Lighting/Shading → Assign New Bake Set → Texture Bake**.
- Adjust the bake-sets attributes in the bake-set Attribute Editor. If you want to edit the bake-set later, RMB click on the object and select **Baking → Baking Attributes**.

Displacement mapping in mental ray for Maya

Set up displacements the same as you would for Maya. mental ray for Maya provides the opportunity to optimize a displacement by using the Displacement Approximation Editor. By default, mental ray for Maya will use Maya's tesselation settings for surface approximations. If you want to override this, you can use mental ray for Maya's Approximation Editor under **Window → Rendering Editors → mental ray → Approximation Editor**.

Approximation refers to the number of triangles used to approximate or define the surface of an object. The key when tessellating displacements is to use many triangles in areas that have high curvature and fewer in flat areas, as they require less definition. In mental ray for Maya, tessellation can be controlled by a base approximation and then for purposes of displacement, a displacement approximation. The process is quite efficient, so that areas without displacement will use less triangles, thereby reducing render times.

The general workflow for using displacement approximation is first to apply the base approximation, which will affect the entire object. Keeping the base approximation as low as possible and then increasing the values of the displacement approximation will give the best results. This is because displacement approximation can only add to the number of triangles or at the very least, equal the number of triangles. It cannot create fewer triangles that are required for the base approximation. A good benchmark to keep in mind is that scenes generally need a number of triangles that is in the same range as the number of pixels in the rendered image.

The various subsections within the Approximation Editor will help to further refine the displacement tessellation. For a more detailed look at the Approximation Editor, see the *Controlling Renders* chapter.

- **Parametric** approximation creates a regular grid of triangles that are good for creating soft displacements that don't have any hard edges.

- **Distance** approximation will measure the distance between displacements at the vertex level. It will increase the number of triangles in areas of high curvature, so that they are more detailed and can be approximated much more accurately. Again, it will create fewer triangles in flatter areas, concentrating on creating more triangles in areas of high curvature.

- **Angle** approximation looks at the angle that neighboring triangles form on the surface. This parameter is particularly useful for displacements when there are areas of sharp peaks as well as flat. It is crucial to set an upper tessellation limit when using angle approximation to avoid excessively large numbers of triangles being created at the sharp edges. When setting displacement approximation parameters, any of these three can be used, as well as in combination with one another.

SUMMARY

Creating great textures is an important factor in producing a convincing image. Textures help determine the style you are reaching for from extreme realism to cartoon. If you have a strong grasp of the tools used to create textures, it opens up the door to your artistic abilities.

In this chapter, the following topics were covered:

- How to use Textures to build a Shading Network
- Texturing Issues for Animation
- File Texture Filtering and the use of BOT files
- Dealing with Displacement Mapping
- mental ray for Maya's Displacement Mapping

CHAPTER 2
Summary

Lighting

Lighting a Maya scene is much like lighting a scene for photography, film, or theatre and, as an element of design, light must be considered a basic influence at the beginning of the creative process and not something to be added later. This is especially true in computer graphics where lighting is based on mathematical algorithms and creating real world lighting effects can require a solid understanding of the software application.

Light Fog Effect

In this chapter, you will learn the following:

- Lighting basics
- Decay Rates and Intensity Curves
- Color Curves, Color Mapping, Barn Doors
- Light Linking
- mental ray for Maya Lights

CHAPTER 3

LIGHTING CONCEPTS

The basic premise of good lighting is that, when done right, light gives objects or characters "meaning" in their surroundings. It also provides an appropriate and intentional atmosphere that will be logically interpreted by the viewer.

The design potential of light is inherent in its physical characteristics. By controlling its **intensity, color,** and **direction**, light becomes a key factor in creating a scene. Lighter and darker areas help to compose the frame and guide the eye toward certain objects and actions.

Choosing Light Types

Once you have determined the direction and distribution of lights in a scene, you will also need to consider the type of light source.

Maya provides a selection of different light types that all have attributes that can be edited and animated to simulate real world lighting. These lights can produce a range of qualities from soft and diffuse to harsh and intense because they each have different characteristics. While it is likely that your combination of lights and techniques will vary with each production, the design principles of combining sharp and soft edged light, different angles, intensities, and shadows remain the same.

Directional Lights

Directional Light

You will notice that the **Directional Light** icon depicts several parallel rays. This is because its purpose is to simulate a distant light source such as the sun where the light rays are coherent and parallel.

This type of light will typically produce a harsher, more intense quality of light with harder edges and no subtle changes in surface shading because of its parallel rays with no decay. Directional Lights are not very expensive to render because the angle is constant for all rays and decay is not computed.

Note: The position of the Directional Light will become important later in the section on shadows from Directional Lights.

Point Lights

Point Light

The **Point Light** icon depicts light rays emanating from a single point outwards in all directions. Its purpose is to simulate an omni-directional local light source such as a light bulb or candle. This type of light does have decay and will typically produce a more subtle, yet richer shading on surfaces.

Ambient Lights

Ambient Light

An **Ambient Light** is normally used as a non-Directional Light to simulate the diffused scattered or reflected light you see in real life.

However, you can adjust the **Ambient Shade** attribute which will allow you to specify how much of the light comes from the source. If set to 0.0, it acts like an RGB multiplier, allowing you to control the overall contrast levels in the scene. However, it is very difficult to determine the edges of objects at this setting with no other light source. The **default** is set to **0.45** to give a slight hint of shading on surfaces. If **Ambient Shade** is set to **1.0**, it is fully directional, i.e. the location of the light matters 100%.

Rendering Ambient Lights are quick to render because they have no decay and create no specular highlights. Often they are used as a secondary light source, supporting a stronger light source such as a spot or directional. Be aware that only using an Ambient Light for illumination has limitations. For example, bump maps will not show up.

Tip: Without radiosity, you could try to come up with a general level of Ambient Light intensity, based on the total number of lights, their separation in space, their average color, and the average color of the objects in the scene. For example, if you have an object sitting on a ground plane you could set the light color to match the ground plane so it will look as if the light was reflecting up onto the object from the ground.

Spot Lights

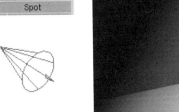

Spot Light

A **Spot Light** has a cone of influence in a specific direction. This is controlled by the **Cone Angle** attribute which is measured in degrees from edge to edge. The Spot Light also has **Decay**, **Dropoff**, and **Penumbra** which will be covered later in the chapter.

Area Lights

Area Light

Point, **Directional**, and **Spot Lights** are all abstract lighting models in the sense that they are zero size lights that exist at a single point.

Because all lights in the natural world occupy some amount of space, Area Lights can help to produce a more realistic lighting distribution; an Area Light's lighting computation reflects the size and orientation of the light.

There are three effects that are difficult to achieve using light sources other than Area Lights:

- Straight, long, specular highlights (like those found in a car advertisement)

- Soft lighting distribution

- Realistic shadows that vary from hard to soft

Specular highlight size and orientation

Simply position and scale the light using IPR to see the specular highlight interactively (make sure you have a specular shader, i.e. non-Lambertian).

Soft lighting distribution

The size, orientation, and position of the Area Light's 3D *icon* in the modeling view controls the lighting distribution.

- If you have a large Area Light, more light is emitted. The light can be non-proportionally scaled to modulate the distribution.

  A real world analogy would be a window with a shade that pulls down; as you lower the shade, the size of the window opening gets smaller and the amount of light is reduced.

- The farther away the object is from the light, the less light is cast onto the object. Quadratic decay is factored in by default.

Realistic shadows

The size and shape of an Area Light can help to achieve realistic raytraced shadows that dissipate as the receiving surface "sees" more of the Area Light. This normally requires a relatively high number of shadow rays and can be expensive to render.

Depth Map Shadows can also be used with Area Lights. However, at this time, the results will be computed in the same way as a Point Light.

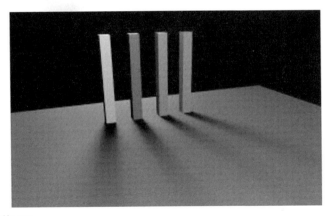

Optical effects

Any light that is visible to the camera lens has the potential to produce an optical effect (Light Glow). Optical effects for an Area Light reflect the shape of the Area Light. This is particularly evident in a "halo" effect.

Area Light Limitations

- Depth Map Shadows do not reflect the size and orientation of the Area Light.

- The specular highlight produced by an Area Light on an anisotropic shader is poorly defined.

- The specular highlight produced by an Area Light on plug-in shaders will not reflect the size and orientation of the Area Light. Enhancements had to be made to the architecture to support a proper specular direction. These enhancements are not exposed to the API as of yet.

Volume Lights

volumeLightShape1

Volume Light

The **Volume light** illuminates objects within a given volume. Volumes can be *spherical, cylindrical, box*, or *cone* shaped. The advantage of using this type of light is that you have a visual representation as to the extent of the light. In addition to the common attributes found in all lights, volume lights have attributes that allow greater control over the color of the volume. The **Color Range** section allows the user to select one color or blend between colors within the volume. You can control the direction of a light within the volume by using the **Volume Light Direction** attributes.

Default Lights

If there are no lights in a scene, Maya will create a Directional Light when the scene is rendered. This light is parented to the rendered camera and illuminates the scene regardless of where the camera is facing. After the render is complete, Maya removes the default light from the scene.

Light Intensity

Intensity can be defined as the actual or comparative brightness of light. Like most other render attributes, it can be modified either by using the slider or by mapping a texture to the channel.

Tip: It is possible to enter negative values for intensity - this will subtract light in the scene and can produce dark spots instead of hotspots on specular shading models.

The **Emit Diffuse** and **Emit Specular** flags are on by default and will control the diffuse or specular shading results for the light. Ambient Lights do not have these attributes.

Decay Rates

Decay refers to how light diminishes with distance. In Maya, it is possible to alter the rate of decay for Point and Spot Lights by adjusting the **Decay Rate** in the light's Attribute Editor. The initial default is **No Decay**. The other settings are **Linear**, **Quadratic**, and **Cubic**.

Note: For computer animated characters or other elements which must match live action shots, it is very important to consider the decay rate. For example, if your character is moving towards or away from a light source, the intensity of the light cast onto the character must appear to increase or decrease as it would in real life or it will not be believable when it is later added to the live shot. This is especially true if the character will be placed next to a live actor who is also moving towards or away from the light source. For this reason you may choose to work with **Quadratic** decay for realism.

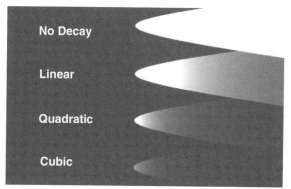

Light Decay

No Decay - Light reaches everything.

Linear - Light intensity decreases in direct proportion to distance ($I=1/d$).

Quadratic - This is how light decays in real life ($I=1/d*d$)

Cubic - Light decays faster than real life ($I=1/d*d*d$)

The decay factor occurs only after a distance larger than **1** unit. Otherwise, the decay factor can result in over-exposure in lighting with distances less than **1** unit.

Note: Area Lights have **Quadratic** decay built-in. While it is not possible to turn this off, it is possible to change the Decay rate to further manipulate the decay results.

Precision lighting

While Decay rates offer a mathematically accurate way to have light fall-off over distance, they do not allow for any control in precision lighting.

Being able to do precision lighting is crucial to working on special effects, i.e. being able to interactively clamp lighting at an exact spot, or to easily specify the light intensity at an exact distance, etc. Currently, Spot Lights have all the tools to perform precision lighting.

Tip: When beginning to work with decay on Spot Lights, it is best to use either the decay approach, or the precision lighting approach, as mixing both may yield unexpected results.

Decay Regions

The first useful tool is **Decay Regions**. The primary purpose of this tool is to allow regions to be lit or non-lit within the same cone of light. The Decay Regions can be used in conjunction with the Decay rates to control effects such as table lamps or car headlights (using light fog) where the visible light beam emanates from a broad region rather than a single point in space.

- **Create** a Spot Light with light fog.
- In the Attribute Editor, go to **Light Effects** → **Decay Regions.**
- Turn **ON** the **Use Decay Regions** flag.
- Turn **ON** the manipulators by selecting **Display** → **Camera/Light Manipulator** → **Decay Regions.**

  You can interactively move the manipulator's rings in the modeling view to define the regions of illumination.

Tip: An alternate way to adjust the regions is to open the **Region** subsections of the **Decay Regions** section in the Attribute Editor and enter values in the **Distance** fields. This tool can also be very useful as an interactive measuring tool to determine distances from the light.

Intensity Curves

At times it is important to be able to control the exact intensity of a light at a given distance from the light source. Intensity curves allow precise control over this behavior.

- In the Spot Light's Attribute Editor, click on **Light Effects** → **Intensity Curve** → **Create.**

  A curve is created and connected to the light's intensity channel.

- With the light still selected, open **Window** → **Animation Editors** → **Graph Editor...**
- Press **a** to frame all in the view or use **View** → **Frame All**.

  There will be a number of key frames on the curve.

Notice that the vertical and horizontal axis represent **intensity** and **distance** for this curve.

You can edit this curve as you would edit any other animation curve in Maya by moving keyframes, adding or deleting keyframes, changing tangents, etc.

Tip: To try this with a Point Light, create a Spot Light and set up the intensity curve. Then convert the Spot Light to a Point Light in the Attribute Editor.

Color curves

Similar to intensity curves, **Color curves** allow you to individually control the red, green, and blue values of the light over distance.

- To create color curves, open the Spot Light's Attribute Editor, click on **Light Effects → Color Curve → Create.**

Tip: Don't delete any of the color curves because this can give unexpected results. Instead, if you want to take out all of the green component, for example, delete the middle keys and set the remaining two keys to an intensity value of 0.

Color mapping lights

Another way to specify light color is to map a texture onto the color channel. This essentially allows the light to act like a movie projector which can project the texture onto the objects in the scene.

Tip: Mapping the color channel of a Spot Light with a water texture can create realistic looking Caustic patterns especially when the texture is animated.

In the file *movieScreen.mb*, there is a drive-in movie screen which needs to have an image sequence projected on it.

1 Use Spot Light movieProjector
- Use the Spot Light named *movieProjector*.

2 Look through the Spot Light for positioning
- **Select** the Spot Light.
- Select **Panels → Look Through Selected.**

Track and tumble in this view to make any adjustments to the position of the Spot Light.

3 Add a Color Map to the Spot Light

- Open the Attribute Editor for the Spot Light.

- In the Attribute Editor, click on the **map** button to the right of the Color slider.

- In the **Create Render Node** window, click on **File** texture.

- In the Attribute Editor for the File texture, **select** the button beside the **Image Name** and browse in the *sourceimages* directory for a folder called *explosion*.

- Open the *explosion* folder and double click on *explosion.0*.

- Set **Use Frame Extension** to **ON** in the File texture's Attribute Editor.

- In the **Frame Extension** field type **= frame**.

  This simple expression will animate the image sequence.

4 Position the Image

- You can use the **Coverage** and **Translate Frame** attributes on the File texture's *place2Dtexture* node to position the image sequence on the movie screen.

  Some example values:

  Coverage: 0.6, 0.4;

  Translate Frame: 0.2, 0.32.

  You will notice that the circular region surrounding the image remains lit by the Spot Light. There are several things you can do to resolve this.

- On the File texture node, set the *Default Color* attribute to **Black**.

  At this point the circular lit region should disappear leaving only the image visible.

5 Or, use Barn Doors to clip the Spot Light

- Open the Attribute Editor for the Spot Light.

- Open the **Light Effects** tab and set **Barn Doors** to **ON**.

- Do a look through selected on the Spot Light.

- Press **t** to bring up the manipulators.

- Position the manipulators so they are in a rectangular shape inside the circle of light.

- Go back to your perspective view and render to see the effect.

6 Or, create a soft edge with an intensity map

Instead of using Barn Doors or simply changing the Default Color, you could also use a texture map on the intensity of the light to control the shape of the illuminated region and give it a soft edge.

- Map a **Ramp** texture to the **Intensity** channel of the light.
- Make the Ramp a **Box** ramp that is white on the inside and black on the outside. Use the interpolation to control the softness of the transition from black to white.
- Adjust the **Coverage** and **Translate Frame** attributes on the Ramp's *place2Dnode* to control the placement.
- Set the **Default Color** attribute to **Black** on the **Ramp** node.

Dropoff

Spot Lights also have **Dropoff**. Dropoff is similar to decay except that its function is to cause the light to diminish in intensity perpendicular to the light axis instead of along the light axis.

- **Select** the *light* and open the Attribute Editor.
- In the **Spot Light Attributes** section adjust the **Dropoff.**

You can watch the effect in the Spot Light swatch in the Attribute Editor or in the IPR window.

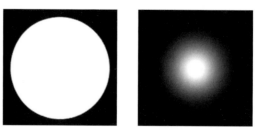

Spot Light Dropoff effect

Note: The results are computed as follows: Cosine raised to the power of Dropoff (where cos is the dot product of the light axis and the lighting direction vector).

Penumbra Angle

The penumbra is an area of diminishing intensity rimming the edge of the cone of light.

The intensity of the light falls off linearly between the cone angle and cone angle + penumbra angle. It is possible to enter negative numbers for **Penumbra Angle**. This will create a softening effect inwards from the edge of the cone of influence as shown below.

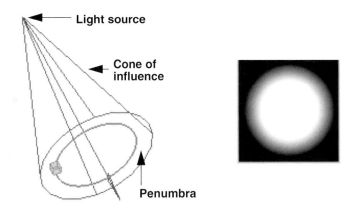

Spot Light Penumbra effect: The cone angle is 40 degrees. The Penumbra angle is -10. If you do the math, 40 + (-10) = 30. Therefore, the intensity of the spot would diminish to zero between the angles of 30 and 40 degrees.

LIGHT LINKING

Often when trying to solve specific lighting tasks, you will need to control which lights shine on which objects in your scene. This can be accomplished easily in Maya using several different methods. All of these methods will accomplish the same results so it is really just a case of which one is the easier workflow for what you are trying to setup.

1 Relationship Editor workflow

This method is the easiest to use when you are learning to use Light Linking, but it is not the fastest approach.

- Open the Relationship Editor by selecting **Lighting/Shading** → **Light Linking** → **Light-Centric...** from the main Maya menu.

    The Relationship Editor is automatically configured for a Light-Centric Light Linking task.

The Relationship Editor shows all of the light sets and individual lights in the scene on the left-hand side. On the right-hand side it shows all of the geometry sets and individual geometries in the scene.

Light-Centric Light Linking

- Click to select a light or light set from the list on the left.

  Geometry illuminated by the selected lights is highlighted on the right.

- Click on the right side to unhighlight or highlight geometry to be illuminated by the selected light(s). Unhighlighted geometry will not be illuminated by the selected light(s).

Or

- Change the Relationship Editor configuration to **Object Centric Light Linking** from the Options pop-up list.

Object-Centric Light Linking

- Click to select an object or set of objects from the list on the left.

  Lights illuminating the selected objects are highlighted on the right.

- Click on the right side to choose which lights will illuminate the selected objects. Unhighlighting lights will not illuminate the selected objects.

2 Menu Action workflow

This workflow is the fastest method for setting up Light Linking. By default, a new light added to a scene illuminates all objects in the scene. This means that there is a link between the light and each piece of geometry to start with. Menu actions provide a simple way to break/ make any of these links without needing to bring up an editor.

- **Select** the *light*.
- With the *light* still selected, **Shift-select** the object(s) you do not want the light to shine on.
- Select **Lighting/Shading** → **Break Light Links** to break the link(s).

  Now the selected light will not illuminate the selected geometry. This would also work with multiple lights selected. It does not matter which order you select the lights and geometry.

  You will notice that there is also a **Make Light Links** action in the menu. This can be used in the same way to recreate the light links at any time.

Note: It does not matter whether you select the lights first or the objects first.

Incorporating the Illuminates by Default feature

This workflow uses the menu actions described above and one additional feature: **Illuminates By Default**. This method is recommended when adding a light that needs to shine on only one or a few specific objects in a scene where there are many other objects and lights already set.

Using the Relationship Editor method would be time consuming to turn off all the objects you do not want illuminated by the new light(s).

Using the menu actions alone would also be time consuming because again you would need to select all the geometry you do not want illuminated in order to break all the links to the new light(s).

In this case, it is better to start out by telling the light(s) not to illuminate any geometry initially. Then it is just a matter of selecting the geometry you intend to illuminate with the new light(s) and making a link with the **Make Light Link** menu action.

Volume Primitives

A different way to add interesting fog or lighting effects to your scene is to use Volume Primitives. Volume primitives give you an object you can volume render much like Geometric Primitives give you an object for surface shading.

You can texture map the **Color**, **Transparency** or **Incandescence** to control the appearance of the volume. The attributes on these primitives also allow you to control the density of the fog in object space (maintaining the appearance of the object if scaled up or down), or world space (the fog appears denser as the scale increases). If **Illuminated** is turned on, then the Volume's brightness will be affected by the amount of Light Scatter for that primitive. This is also affected by the intensity of the light in your scene.

Point and Spot Lights are the only lights in Maya that have the ability to create "light based" fog effects. So, if you wanted to have a rectangular Area Light emit light fog, you could use the cube volume primitive for this effect.

LIGHTS IN MENTAL RAY FOR MAYA

All of Maya's lights will render with mental ray for Maya. However, some light types have mental ray attributes and support photon emission. Photon emission is necessary for effects such as Caustics and Global Illumination, which will be discussed in a later chapter. Lights that are capable of this include **Directional, Point, Spot,** and **mental ray Area Lights**. The other light types, **Ambient, Volume,** and **Maya Area Lights**, are supported but do not have mental ray for Maya attributes or support photon emission.

mental ray for Maya's Area Light

The mental ray for Maya Area Light is slightly different than Maya's Area Light. Maya's Area Light is only capable of being rectangular whereas mental ray for Maya's lights have a few more shape options.

1 Create a Point or Spot Light

- Open the Attribute Editor for the Spot Light.
- In the Attribute Editor, scroll down to the **mental ray** section and and open up the **Area Light Editor**.
- Select **Area Light**.
- Adjust the Area Light as desired. The icon will let you know the direction the light will be emitted.

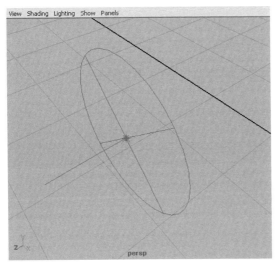

A disc-shaped mental ray for Maya Area Light emitting along the Z-axis.

Type

Type refers to the shape of the Area Light source. Shapes available from the drop-down list include **Rectangle**, **Disc, Sphere**, and **Cylinder.**

Sampling

Sampling represents the number of sample points emitted from the light (X and Y). The default values are 3 and 3. Values greater than 3 increase the quality by reducing graininess, but may increase render time.

Low Level

If this value is greater than 1, the light source will use the Low Sampling values instead as long as their sum is greater than the Low Level value. This affects reflection and refraction. The default is 0.

Low Sampling

The defaults are 2 and 2. In the case where a lit edge looks grainy, increasing this value may help. This value will then be used as the minimum sampling value while the Low Level value is greater than 1.

Visible

If you want the light object to be visible during a render, turn this on.

mental ray Export Options

This section is used to link a mental ray for Maya Light Shader to a Maya Light. To do this:

1 Create a Point, Directional, or Spot Light

- Open the Attribute Editor.

- Expand the mental ray section and open up the Export Options.

- In the Hypershade's Create bar, expand the Lights section of the Create mental ray Nodes menu and MMB drag the desired mental ray Light Shader to the Light Shader attribute in the light's Attribute Editor.

- Set the attributes in the mental ray Light Shader tab. The attributes in Maya's light attribute section are ignored and the mental ray Light Shader attributes are used. Adjust the Area Light as desired. The icon will let you know the direction the light will be emitted.

SUMMARY

Lighting is an important aspect of the rendering process and having a good understanding of it can help you establish mood and atmosphere in your scenes. Understanding the technical aspects of lighting can help you create impressive renders.

You have now completed and are aware of the following tasks:

- Introduction to lighting tools

- Lighting basics

- Decay Rates and Intensity Curves

- Color Curves, Color Mapping, Barn Doors

- mental ray for Maya's lights

4 Cameras

In Maya, the camera is very similar to a real world motion picture or still camera. It mimics real world settings to allow you to match images captured by real cameras.

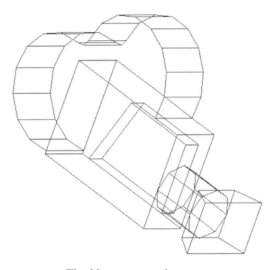

The Maya camera icon

In this chapter, you will learn the following:

- How to work with cameras in Maya

- Working with Film Gates and Film Backs

- Aspect Ratios

- Rotoscoping using D1 Images

- mental ray for Maya Camera Attributes

CAMERA BASICS

Creating a New Camera

The vast majority of your renderings will make use of Maya's Perspective camera. While there is nothing technically wrong with using this camera for all of your animation and rendering, it is advisable to create a new camera to work with.

Tip: The Persp camera is treated differently by Maya because it is a **static** node. It will be invisible to start with to discourage you from using it for your animation and rendering.

There are two ways to create a new camera in Maya:

Creating a new camera

- In the perspective modeling view, go to **Panels → Perspective → New.**

OR

- Go to **Create → Camera**.

   The create menu method will place the camera at the origin while the panels menu method will place it away from the origin like the default Persp camera. Other than the location at which it is created, there is no difference between these cameras.

Renaming the camera

- With the new camera selected, use the name field at the top of the Channel Box and give the camera a new name.

   This method of renaming will name both the **transform** node and the **shape**.

Working with Cameras

Once you have created a new camera or several new cameras, Maya makes it very easy to switch between them or change the view.

Switch between cameras

- In any modeling view, select **Panels → Perspective →** and choose from the list of cameras.

Changing the view from a camera

- The main workflow for positioning cameras is to use the following combinations:

  Alt +**LMB** to tumble the camera;

  Alt +**MMB** to track the camera;

  Alt +**LMB** + **MMB** to dolly the camera or **Alt** + **RMB**.

Additionally, Maya has a suite of camera tools which can be used to achieve precise control over your camera's position and behavior. These will not be covered as they are covered extensively in the Maya documentation.

- In the modeling window, select **View** → **Camera Tools.**

Stepping back and forth between camera views

It is possible to step back and forth between your present and past camera views.

- Use the **]** key to go forwards and the **[** key to go backwards though your recent camera views.

- The camera views are intentionally not included in the **Undo** feature. If you would prefer to have the camera views be included in the undo, you need to turn on the Journal Command flag in **Camera Attribute Editor**→ **Display Options** → **Journal Command.**

- Camera bookmarks can be very helpful when you need to return to a specific camera view. To create a bookmark, in the perspective window go to **View** → **Bookmarks** → **Edit Bookmarks...**

Selection and Frame Selection

To quickly dolly in on a selected object or group of selected objects, there are several methods.

- Use **View** → **Look at selection** to have the object centered in the window.

- Use **View** → **Frame Selection** to have the object centered in the window and close up to the camera.

These camera commands will also establish a new point of interest that the camera will orbit around. If you find that you cannot zoom in close enough on an object, try framing it with Frame Selection first.

Tip:	You can also do **Frame Selection** with a hotkey. Simply select an object and use the **F** key. To frame all objects in the scene press the **A** key.

Box dolly feature

To quickly dolly in on an area of the scene, use Maya's box dolly feature.

- **Alt + Ctrl + draw a marquee** around the objects you wish to dolly in on.

    Left to right dollies in.

    Right to left dollies out.

Dolly vs. Zoom

The difference between **dolly** and **zoom** is that when you **dolly**, you are physically moving the camera in space while **zoom** refers to changing the camera's focal length.

What is the difference between moving the camera and changing the focal length? Why would you choose one over the other? The answer is that when you move the camera, the perspective changes. Objects far from the camera change in relative size at a slower rate than objects close to the camera. This is essentially what you see through your human eyes; as you walk around your perspective changes.

When you **zoom**, you are changing the **focal length** of the lens; perspective does not change. This is something that your eyes cannot achieve which creates an unsettling quality when used for heightened effect.

Perspective could be thought of as the rate that objects change in size in the frame as their distance from the camera changes.

Tip:	In the camera's Attribute Editor, you can adjust the **Focal Length** in the **Camera Attributes** section to adjust the zoom or use the **Zoom** tool in the Camera tools.
	If you have all four modeling views open, and you can see your camera, you will see that the length of the lens is changing but the camera is not moving.
	Notice how this also changes the **Angle of View** attribute. It is not possible to animate the **Angle of View** but it is possible to animate the **Focal Length** attribute.

Hitchcock Vertigo Effect

Anyone who has seen the Alfred Hitchcock movie *Vertigo*, may be familiar with the eerie camera effect where some objects appear to move further away while others appear to move closer to the camera.

This is achieved by zooming in while dollying out OR by dollying in while zooming out.

Cameras for Batch rendering

For Batch rendering, you will need to specify which camera you wish to render from.

- For most purposes, use **Render Globals → Image File Output.**
  Then select the camera from the pop-up list.

Tip: For more advanced users who need to render more than one camera at the same time, it is possible to use the **Camera Attribute Editor→ Output Settings → Renderable** flag. In this case, Render Globals will show more than one camera marked as (renderable) in the Camera pop-up list.

ADVANCED CAMERA ATTRIBUTES

This section will cover the more advanced camera attributes.

Framing a Shot - Display Options

When you are trying to frame a shot to render, you need to be able to see what area will actually be rendered. Maya has some display mechanisms to allow you to see this area very clearly.

1 Display Resolution Gate

- With the Perspective camera's Attribute Editor open, go down to the **Display Options** section and set **Display Resolution** to **ON**.

2 Set the Overscan

- While in the Attribute Editor, find the **Film Back** section. Increase the **Overscan** attribute to **1.3** or **1.4**.

  This does not change the rendered image at all. Overscan is just a display feature to allow you see parts of the scene outside of the region that will be rendered.

Tip:	You can also modify the **Overscan** attribute for the camera to a value less than **1** to get a close up of your scene without disturbing your camera position.

Film Gates and Film Backs

The following describes a great deal about what Film Gates and Film Backs are in real life and in Maya. If you are creating an entire shot in Maya and have complete artistic license over the view from the camera, there is no reason to be concerned with Film Backs. As you have already seen above, the default settings will ensure that everything inside of your Resolution Gate will be rendered. If you are trying to match the look of a real shot, the use of Film Backs become important.

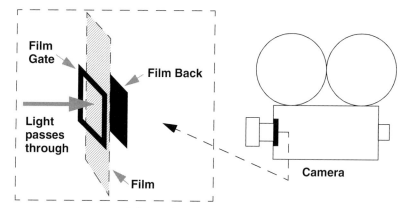

Film Back-Film Gate-Film relationship.

- In real cameras, the film negative is passed between two plates called the **Film Back** and the **Film Gate**. The film negative sits against the Film Back and is held in place by the Film Gate.

- The **Film Back** corresponds to the size of the film negatives and is measured in millimeters. Because of this, when people talk about a 35mm camera, they are referring to the size of the Film Back and the film negative.

- The **Film Gate** is a metal plate that sits in front of the film negative to hold it in place. The plate overlaps some portion of the film so only the region inside the gate is actually exposed to light. It is this region that you are simulating in Maya in order to match the real footage. It is expressed as the **Camera Aperture** attribute.

Note: There is no attribute to specify the entire size of the Film Back separately as this would just represent unexposed wasted portions of the film in real life.

The **Film Gate** attribute in Maya is presented as a list of presets. In the list you will see 5 different settings for 35mm. This is because, as you can see from the above discussion, for all 35 mm cameras the Film Back (and film negative) size will be the same. However, the size of the region inside of the Film Gate will differ depending on how big the opening is in the gate. Keep in mind that it is the exposed region of the film that you are simulating when you render an image in Maya.

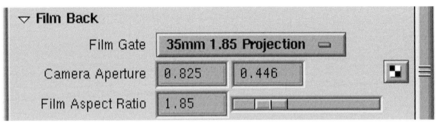

Film Back Attributes

Another attribute that is used to describe this region inside the Film Gate is the **Film Aspect Ratio**. The following diagram shows what is meant by film aspect ratio. It is simply the **Camera Aperture** attribute represented as a ratio.

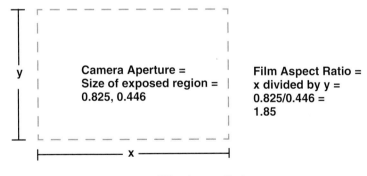

Film Aspect Ratio

How Film Back relates to Focal Length and Angle of View

1 Change the Film Gate presets

- Use the pop-up list of presets to switch between various different Film Gates.

  Notice that the **Angle Of View** changes but the **Focal Length** does not.

2 Adjust the Focal Length

- Adjust the **Focal Length** and notice that the **Angle Of View** changes.

  As you extend the focal length, the angle of view gets narrower. As you shorten the focal length, the angle of view gets larger.

The following diagrams illustrate these relationships.

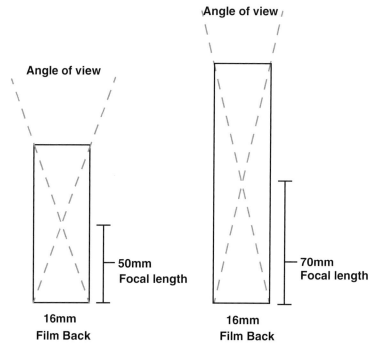

Effect of changing focal length without changing Film Back

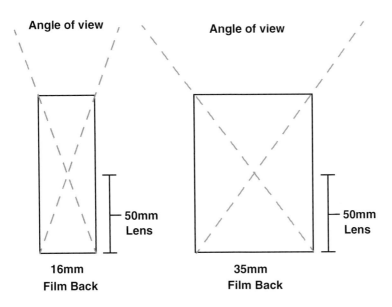

Effect of changing Film Back without changing focal length

Tip: The **Focal Length** of a lens is defined as the distance from the lens to the film plane. Lenses are identified by their focal length expressed in millimeters. By this you can see that a 50mm lens has a focal length of 50mm.

Most people are familiar with the effect of changing the focal length in real cameras. This amounts to switching to different lenses or adjusting the zoom to lengthen or shorten the lens you are using. You can see how this affects the angle of view in the first diagram above.

The second diagram above illustrates what will happen if you keep the same lens, but switch to a different size camera.

The process of switching to a different size camera while keeping the same size lens is exactly what you are doing when you switch the Film Back in Maya. The result is that the angle of view changes but the focal length does not.

Now you can see why changing to different Film Backs without changing the focal length seems to cause the camera to zoom in and out.

Note: The camera aperture relates to the focal length in that different Film Backs have different normal lenses. A normal lens focal length is not telephoto or wide-angle. It closely approximates normal vision. As the size of the camera aperture increases, a longer focal length is required to achieve normal perspective. That is why a 35mm camera uses a 50mm lens as a normal lens. On a 16mm camera, the same 50mm lens would appear to be telephoto in nature. A normal focal length for a camera is a focal length that equals the diagonal measurement of the camera aperture in millimeters (that means you'll have to find the hypotenuse).

How the Film Gate relates to the Resolution Gate

Now that you have looked at the meaning of **Film Backs**/**Film Gates**, you need to understand how this relates to the **Resolution Gate** for rendering.

1 Create a new file

2 Turn on Display Gates in Camera Options

- Set both the **Resolution Gate** and **Film Gate** to **ON** in the camera Attribute Editor.

  Notice that at this point the gates do not match. This is because they do not have the same aspect ratio; in layman's terms, they are two rectangles with different shapes. This will be addressed later in the lesson.

3 Change the Film Fit

The **Film Fit** attribute controls how Maya fits the Film Gate to the Resolution Gate. By default, the **Film Fit** attribute is set to **Horizontal**.

- In the camera Attribute Editor, change the **Film Fit** attribute to **Vertical**.

  Notice how the Film Gate is drawn differently relative to the Resolution Gate.

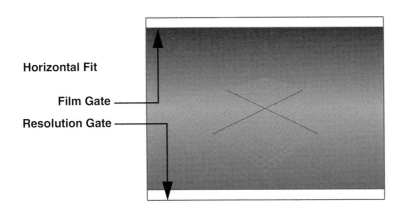

Horizontal Fit

Film Gate ——

Resolution Gate ——

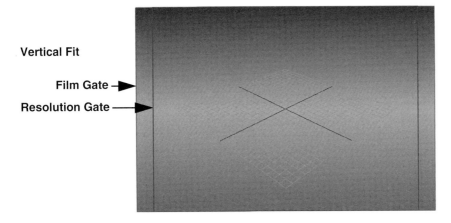

Vertical Fit

Film Gate —▶

Resolution Gate ——▶

Film Fit

Because the two gates have a different aspect ratio, Maya can only match them in one dimension - either horizontally or vertically but not both.

In the case of **Horizontal Fit**, the horizontal width of the Film Gate is matched to the Resolution Gate's horizontal dimension. This means that vertically the gates will not match.

In the case of **Vertical Fit**, this ensures that the vertical height of the Film Gate is matched to the Resolution Gate's vertical dimension. In this case, the horizontal width of the gates will not match.

Creating a Letterbox Look

The Film Fit can allow you to create a Letterbox look (where there is black at the top and bottom of the final image to simulate the way film looks if it has not been reformatted to fit a TV screen).

When Maya renders, the entire Resolution Gate is rendered. This means that regardless of the **Film Fit** method, what you see in the final render will always be whatever is within the Resolution Gate.

If the Film Gate is not filling the Resolution Gate in one direction, normally you will not be able to tell in the rendered image. This is because the **Ignore Film Gate** flag in the Render Globals is turned **ON** by default. However, if you turn this **OFF**, Maya will render black in the space between the Film Gate and the Resolution Gate.

- Go to **Window → Render Globals.**
- Open the **Render Options** and set **Ignore Film Gate** to **OFF.**

    You will notice that this creates black regions in the image that correspond to the gap between the size of the Film Gate and the size of the Resolution Gate as shown in the perspective view.

Tip: It is easier to see the Letterbox result if you **fcheck** the image because the Render View's black background makes it difficult to tell where the edge of the image is.

How to match the Resolution Gate and Film Gate

If you are working with Film Gates, chances are you are trying to match a real camera so you want your rendered images to match the real Film Gate exactly.

The only way that the Film Gate and Resolution Gate can match exactly in both dimensions is if they both have the same aspect ratio. This will be covered later.

Note: Again, this matching of aspect ratios is only required when aiming for the look of a specific real camera. Otherwise Film Backs do not need to be considered at all.

MATCHING LIVE ACTION

Image Planes

Image Planes are 2D texture-mapped planes connected to a camera - perpendicular to the lens axis. They can be used for several things such as creating environments or tracing concept sketches in the early phases of modeling. In this lesson, you are going to look at how to use them to match live action.

Matching live action refers to the process of positioning and animating objects in a scene relative to a background live action sequence of images. The specific case that will be covered involves working with NTSC digital video footage.

Note: NTSC is the only example that will be covered. Other examples, like PAL, will not be covered but the workflow itself is the same; only the specific numbers differ.

Non-square pixels

Using **NTSC Digital Video**, or **D1**, as it is commonly referred to in the industry, poses a unique challenge that is often misunderstood. The challenge surrounds the fact that digital video is generated by devices that typically use **Non-Square Pixels**. However, computer monitors display only square pixels. To compensate for this, Maya has a workflow to allow your objects to match-up correctly with the background plates.

Aspect Ratios

The key to successfully matching live action is to understand the meaning of several different **Aspect Ratios**.

Image Aspect ratio

This is the aspect ratio of the image you will render and is represented by the **Resolution Gate** in the UI. Image aspect simply represents the resolution of an image as a ratio.

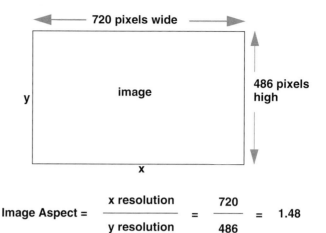

$$\text{Image Aspect} = \frac{\text{x resolution}}{\text{y resolution}} = \frac{720}{486} = 1.48$$

The above diagram illustrates how a digital video image does not satisfy the 1.33 aspect desired for television viewing, unless you take into account the **pixel aspect ratio** as described in the next section. This is the special case of image aspect differences you encounter when working with digital video that needs to match computer generated imagery.

Pixel Aspect Ratio

Each image is made up of pixels. The pixels themselves also have an aspect ratio called **Pixel Aspect Ratio**.

$$\text{Pixel Aspect} = \frac{x}{y} = \frac{1}{1} = 1.0$$

$$\text{Pixel Aspect} = \frac{x}{y} = \frac{1}{1.1} = 0.9$$

When you are dealing with digital video, the pixels have an **aspect ratio** of **0.9**. They are slightly taller than they are wide.

Device Aspect Ratio

Up until now, all of the aspect ratios you have looked at have followed the same equation of x divided by y equals aspect ratio. The device aspect ratio is calculated differently.

Device Aspect = Image Aspect x Pixel Aspect

= 1.48 x 0.9

= 1.33

Film Aspect Ratio

Another attribute that is used to describe the region defined by the Film Gate is the **Film Aspect Ratio**. It is simply the **Camera Aperture** attribute represented as a ratio.

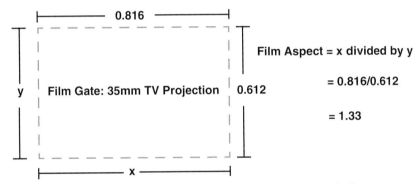

Film Aspect = x divided by y

= 0.816/0.612

= 1.33

You will see where these aspect ratios fit in as you go through the workflow.

Workflow to match live action digital video

1 Open a new scene
- Start with a new scene by selecting **File → New**.

2 Set the Resolution
- Open **Render Globals** and set the resolution to **CCIR 601/Quantel NTSC.**

  Notice that this preset automatically turns **ON** the **Lock Device Aspect Ratio**. This is important. Without this turned **ON**, Maya will render square pixels.

3 Set the Camera Attributes

- Open the **Display Options** in the Camera Attribute Editor and set the **Resolution** and **Film Gates** to **ON.**

- In the **Film Back** section, set the **Overscan** to **1.3.**

  Recall that this is only a display mechanism that will allow you to see the gates entirely.

- While in the **Film Back** section, chose the preset **Film Gate - 35mm TV Projection** which has a **Film Aspect of 1.33.**

  You would need to be given the information about which real camera the video footage was shot on in order to know which Film Gate to chose for an accurate match.

Tip: The important thing here is that the **Film Aspect is 1.33** which matches the device aspect of **D1** video. As long as these two aspect ratios match, the Resolution Gate and the Film Gate will match precisely.

---

4 Create the Image Plane

- In the **Environment** section of the Camera Attribute Editor, click on the **Create** button to create an **Image Plane.**

  This will build the nodes and the connections required for the Image Plane.

5 Bring in D1sphere.iff

At this point, you would bring in the D1 footage to use on the Image Plane. In this workflow example, you will simply bring in a D1 image of a sphere. The sphere makes it very obvious that you are seeing a distorted image due to the non-square pixels.

- In the **Image Plane** attributes, click on the small folder icon to the right of the **Image Name** attribute.

  This will open the file browser window and allow you to navigate to find the *Dsphere.iff* image.

- **Double click** on *D1sphere.iff* to load it into Maya.

  The image comes in looking slightly stretched horizontally.

- In the **Placement** section, set the **Fit** to **To Size.**

  The **To Size** Fit method on the Image Plane will alter the original aspect ratio of the *D1sphere.iff* image to make it fit the aspect ratio of the Film Gate (by default the Image Plane is Fit to the Film Gate).

You will notice that as soon as you Fit To Size, the sphere looks correct.

6 Animate the D1 sequence - expression method

If you had a sequence of images, you would need to animate them on the Image Plane. The easiest way to do this is to write a very simple expression.

- In the Image Plane attributes, turn **ON** the **Use Frame Extension**.
- Double click in the **Frame Extension** field and type:

```
= frame
```

- Hit the **Enter** key.

  This will create an expression that will sync up the D1 frame displayed on the Image Plane with the frame number in the Time Slider.

7 Animate the D1 sequence - keyframe method

If you want to animate images on the Image Plane but do not want to sync up the frame numbers with the Time Slider, you can keyframe the Frame Extension attribute. For example, if your D1 sequence is numbered frame 1 to frame 60, you might want to view this on frames 10 to 70 in Maya.

- Go to **frame 10** in the Time Slider.
- Double click in the **Frame extension** field and enter **1**.
- With the **RMB** on the **Frame extension** label select **Set Key**.
- This has now set a keyframe that tells Maya to display your D1 frame **1** at frame number **10** on your Time Slider.
- Go to **Frame 70** in the Time Slider.
- Double click in the **Frame extension** field and enter 60.
- With the **RMB** on the **Frame extension** label select **Set Key**.
- Now if you play back the scene, your 60 frame D1 image sequence will play from frames 10 to 70.

8 Match the live action

- At this point, you can go ahead and model, position, and animate your objects using the Image Plane as your guide.

9 Turn off the display of the Image Planes

- Once the animation is done, set the **Display Mode** to **None** in the Image Plane Attributes section.

This ensures that the Image Plane will not be rendered in your final images.

10 Render the Sequence

- In **Render Globals**, set the **Frame/Animation Ext** pop-up list to one of the settings that has a **#** in it.

  This will turn on animation.

- Set the **Start** and **End** frame numbers.

- Batch Render the sequence using **Render → (Save) Batch Render...**

11 Composite the images

Once the images are rendered, you will be able to composite them with the D1 footage and everything will match perfectly.

CLIPPING PLANES

Clipping Planes are used to determine what objects will be rendered in your scene. There is a near clipping plane and a far clipping plane and all visible objects between these clipping planes will be rendered. The position of these clipping planes is found under Camera Attributes in the Attribute Editor for the selected camera. The clipping planes are viewable in the modeling views if they are turned on.

- To turn on clipping planes in the modeling view, use **Display → Camera/Light Manipulators → Clipping Planes**.

- You can adjust them interactively or in the Camera Attribute Editor.

Maya outputs a **Z-depth buffer** which can be used to determine at which depth a pixel makes first contact with geometry in a scene. The z-depth values will be between **-1** and **0** depending on how far the geometry is from the near and far clipping planes. Those intersections clipped by the near or far plane will be given a depth of 0. If the clipping planes have a fairly large separation distance (in UNITS). Precision will be lost when comparing depths which are similar or close to one another.

For example, if your clipping planes are set far apart and you have a number of objects clustered together, each object will have a depth value that is very similar to the others. If these depth numbers are rounded-off, the values can become identical, resulting in artifacts.

These rendering artifacts will look like background objects appearing to be showing through foreground objects.

Auto Render Clip Plane

If you select a camera and open the Attribute Editor you will notice that **Auto Render Clip Plane** is **ON** by default. This allows Maya to automatically set the near and far clipping planes most optimally depending on where objects are in the scene. This tries to minimize the likelihood of the artifacts mentioned above.

- With **Auto Render Clip Plane** turned **ON**, the clipping planes can change from frame to frame in an animation. So, if you are outputting z-depth information for some other purpose, you may wish to turn the Auto clipping OFF.

- If you turn **OFF** the **Auto Render Clip Plane**, the values shown in the Camera Attribute Editor will be used in the render.

Optimizing Cameras for Rendering using Clipping Planes

- To see the camera's **Frustum** use **Display** → **Camera /Light Manipulator** → **Clipping Planes** or **Display** → **Show** → **Camera Manipulators.**

- Geometry that penetrates the **Near** clipping plane will be clipped to the near clipping plane. Any part of the geometry nearer to the camera than the near clipping plane will not be rendered.

- If a piece of geometry spans the **Far** clipping plane, it will be rendered in its entirety.

- If a piece of geometry is beyond the far clipping plane, it will not be rendered at all.

  The type of clipping occurring at the far clipping plane is at the object level, not at the triangle level.

The following diagram shows this clipping relationship. Geometry O1 will be cut by the near clipping plane so that only the portion beyond the near clipping plane is rendered. Geometry O2 will be completely rendered because part of it is nearer to the camera than the far clipping plane. Geometry O3 will not be rendered since it is beyond the far clipping plane.

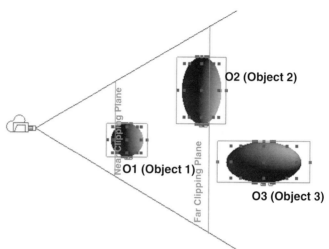

Near and Far plane clipping; O1 is partially rendered, O2 is rendered, O3 is not rendered

Camera Output Settings

The Camera Attribute Editor contains a section related to what the selected camera will output at render time. Switches can be found here that control whether the camera is a renderable camera and whether or not it will output mask, depth, or color (Image).

You can also select how the camera will derive depth information for use in post process rendering effects such as paint effects and depth of field.

The default setting for camera depth lookup is Furthest Visible Depth. This is the setting necessary for proper handling of camera to object depth sorting when working with Paint Effects element rendering.

The Furthest Visible Depth setting can have a detrimental effect on other depth based effects such as Depth of Field. If you find this to be the case, set this attribute to Closest Visible Depth.

MENTAL RAY FOR MAYA CAMERAS

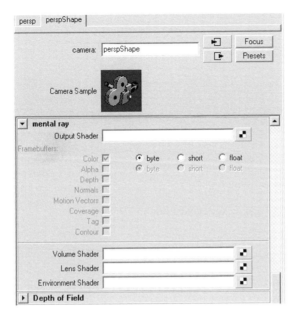

Geometry shaders

These are shaders that produce geometry procedurally at render time. Everything found in a scene file can be created procedurally (excepting the render statement) using geometry shaders.

Output Shader

Allow post-processing of a file prior to it being written. These are plug-ins written in C/C++ that allow custom compositing, motion blurring, DOF, halo, color correction and file grain. These custom effects may be preferable to what is in the base package.

Volume Shader

In the simplest case, this is a uniform fog that fades objects in the distance to white. It can also be used for smoke, clouds, and fur items that normally would be difficult to model. For GI, use the photon volume shader.

Lens Shader

By allowing modification of the ray direction and origin, more realistic paths through the camera can be achieved instead of passing through a precise path. It can be used to achieve custom DOF effects.

Environment Shader

This option attaches an environment shader to the camera and maps a texture on an infinite theoretical shape.

SUMMARY

Camera attributes are important in understanding the rendering process. In order to be able to use them effectively, it is important to have a complete understanding of the topics covered in this chapter.

In this chapter, you have learned the following:

- How to work with cameras in Maya
- Dealing with Aspect Ratios
- Matching live action with Maya rendered scenes
- mental ray for Maya attributes

5 Shadows

Some cinematographers say that the most important thing in lighting is what you don't light. They are referring to the relative effects of light and shadow. Shadows are involved in creating atmosphere and mood in a scene and help to define the look and feel of a scene.

In this chapter, you will learn the following:

- How Maya Depth Map Shadows work
- Different Light types and their Shadows
- Volumetric Lighting Effects
- Maya Raytraced Shadows
- mental ray for Maya's Shadow Maps
- Motion Blurring Shadow Maps
- mental ray for Maya's Raytrace Shadows

CHAPTER 5

SHADOWS

When working on lighting a scene you need to take into consideration the type of shadows you want. For example, the elevation and the direction of a light are important influences on the amount and shape of the shadow areas in the frame. Generally, shadows become more dominant as the angle of light-incidence increases and as the lighting moves from front to back positions. This, in turn, affects the overall mood of the image; if you want a dark and gloomy scene you would want the lights behind your objects so the shadows are being cast into the frame.

Shadows also play an important role in rendering texture. To maximize texture, you use side (cross) lighting. Side lighting creates long shadows that interact with the lit parts of the subject to yield good texture patterns. To minimize texture, you use frontal light as it will create a very flat look because there will be no shadow.

By default, all objects have the ability to cast shadows as well as receive shadows. Each are controlled separately from the Render Stats section of an object's Attribute Editor. The **Receive Shadows** attribute is not respected when IPR rendering.

When rendering shadows in Maya, you have the option to either **Raytrace** shadows or to use **Depth Map Shadows**.

Note: Use **Lighting → Shadows** to preview the position of your shadows in the hardware texture view. This function is only possible with Dmap shadows and only with certain graphics cards and drivers. See the documentation for more information on this.

When using Depth Map Shadows, the Depth Maps are computed as a first pass before rendering, while raytraced shadows are computed during the rendering phase.

MAYA'S DEPTH MAP SHADOWS

The shadow Depth Map computation in Maya is similar to shadow Depth Map computations for other renderers you may be familiar with. A "depth" rendering is done from the point of view of the light source, and later used during the rendering phase to determine if that light illuminates a given point.

In Maya, **Point, Directional, Volume, Spot,** and **Area Lights** are the light types that can produce Depth Map Shadows. Depth Map Shadows in the user interface are usually represented by the short form: **Dmap**.

How Depth Maps Work

Similar to a topographical map, a Depth Map is used to record distances between the Spot Light and objects in the scene.

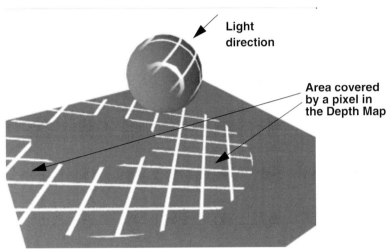

The Depth Map is a square grid of pixels in front of the light. This grid of pixels is projected over the scene from the light's point of view, dividing the scene into sections.

A ray is cast through the center of each pixel in the Dmap. When the ray intersects the nearest surface, Maya records the distance from the light to that surface. These depth measurements make up the Depth Map's pixel values. The Depth Map can be viewed with **fcheck** by hitting the **z** key. In this example it would look like the following image:

*Dmap viewed with fcheck using the **z** key*

This process takes place at the beginning of the render process. Maya later uses this depth information when creating the final rendered image from the camera view. This process is described below.

In the following diagram, Maya is computing the shading for points on the ground plane because the ground plane is visible to the camera. During this process, one of the necessary pieces of information is whether or not a point is in shadow.

In order to determine whether the point on the ground plane is in shadow or not, Maya does a comparison - it checks with all of the shadow casting lights to see if the point being shaded is closer or further from the light than the point stored in the Depth Map.

If the distance from the point being shaded (on the ground plane) to the light is greater than the stored depth value, then some other surface is closer to the light. This means that the point being shaded must be in shadow.

In this diagram, many points being shaded on the ground plane fall within the coverage region of a single pixel on the Depth Map. This means that all of these points would be compared to the same stored depth value and hence, would be considered to be in shadow. Obviously, some of the points do not look as though they should be in shadow. The next section of this chapter looks at ways to resolve this type of inaccuracy.

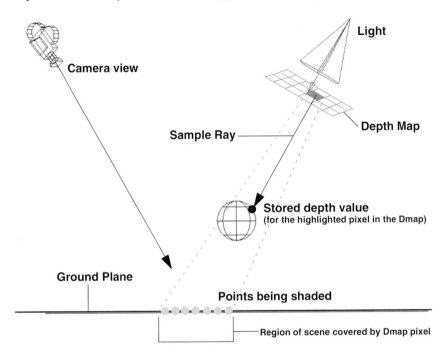

The points being shaded are further from the light than the stored depth value. This tells Maya that the points being shaded are in shadow from a surface closer to the light.

What is Self-Shadowing?

Self-shadowing refers to a surface shadowing itself. Those familiar with Depth Maps for shadowing know that there are self-shadowing artifacts that can occur simply due to the finite resolution of the Dmap - not necessarily due to the shape of the surface. Because only one depth value is stored per pixel, if you happen to be shading a point on a surface that lies between samples in the Depth Map, there is the possibility that the averaged depth from the Depth Map will incorrectly shadow the point being shaded. This self-shadowing will result in an undesirable moire pattern or banding on surfaces facing towards the light.

An obvious example of self-shadowing is shown below:

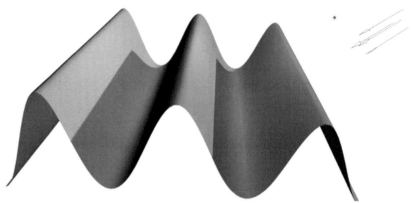

Obvious example of a surface shadowing itself

The self-shadowing from Dmap shadows can be somewhat puzzling at first because it can happen even when logic would suggest that it is not possible because there is nothing to cast a shadow. The following rendered image shows self-shadowing artifacts on a single ground plane:

Banding caused by self-shadowing

The diagram below explains how this happens in the case of the plane shown above:

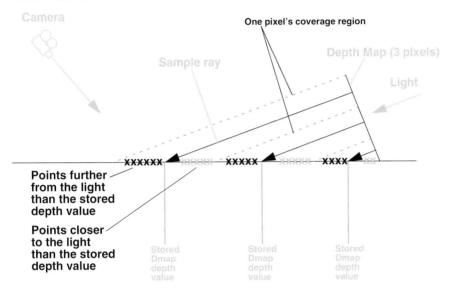

Even with a single plane, self-shadowing can occur due to the limited number of depth samples stored in the Dmap. Each pixel on the Dmap covers a large region of the ground plane. As the image is rendered from the camera, any points on the plane that are further from the light than the stored depth value on the Dmap will be incorrectly thought to be in shadow from the plane itself.

The image below shows the moire pattern that is also typical of self-shadowing:

Moire pattern caused by self-shadowing

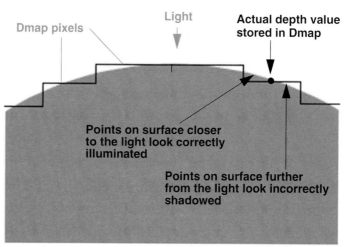

In the case of a curved surface such as this sphere, self-shadowing can still occur

In the examples shown above, the **Resolution** of the Dmap is intentionally low to exaggerate the self-shadowing artifacts. Increasing the resolution will not get rid of the artifacts, it will just make them smaller, sometimes giving a dull, dirty looking appearance to a surface.

Correcting Self-Shadowing with Dmap Bias

There are two shadow attributes available to help correct self-shadowing:

- **Use Mid Dist Dmap** which will be discussed later. This feature is turned **ON** by default and in many cases will prevent the self-shadowing artifacts shown above.

- **Dmap Bias** is another important Dmap shadow attribute that is used to correct self-shadowing.

The **Dmap Bias** attribute is very important when dealing with self-shadowing artifacts. The "Bias" is a value by which the camera ray's intersection point is moved closer to the light source to avoid incorrect self-shadowing. In other words, it is a value that can be thought of as a "fudge factor" that it is used, for shadow purposes, to move the point being shaded closer to the light to bring it out of self-shadow.

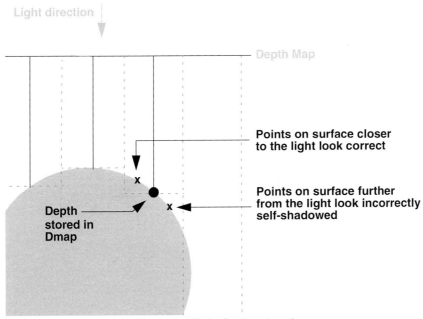

Typical self-shadowing situation

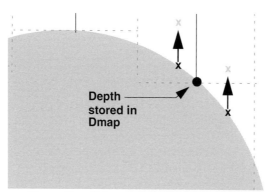

All points being shaded(x) are biased towards the light. This makes them(x) closer to the light than the stored depth value. This corrects the self-shadow problem.

Depth stored in Dmap

Dmap Bias "biases" the points being shaded towards the light to escape self-shadowing

While adjusting the Dmap Bias, care must be taken to find the right value. Using too small a value may result in self-shadowing artifacts on the surface as the previous images have shown. Using too large a value may lead to surfaces that should be in shadow not being in shadow or shadows that are detached from the shadow casting objects (as shown below):

With the correct Dmap Bias value, there is no gap between the chair legs and the shadow.

The chair appears to float when the Dmap Bias value is too high.

Note: The **Dmap Bias value** is not world units. Here's how it is applied: Spot / Point Light - multiplies the **Dmap Bias** with the current z-depth to arrive at a REAL bias value. The farther away it is from the light source, the bigger the REAL bias value. But it multiplies with the perspective Z-depth, so consider the user-entered **Dmap Bias** as a normalized bias value. Directional Lights are the same, except it does not multiply it with the Z-depth.

Correcting Self-Shadowing with Mid Distance

The **Use Mid Dist Dmap** feature in Maya is turned on by default to help prevent self-shadowing artifacts. It stands for "Use Middle Distance Depth Map", which is a variation on the Depth Map algorithm.

Note: If the Depth Map is to be used for purposes other than shadowing, it is best to turn this option off.

Use Mid Dist Dmap attempts to eliminate the need for the Dmap Bias attribute by storing the midpoint between the first and second surfaces visible to the light source (rather than simply storing the distance to the nearest surface). Because this midpoint is normally further from the light than any of the points on the surface itself, self-shadowing is less likely to occur. The diagram below shows how this works:

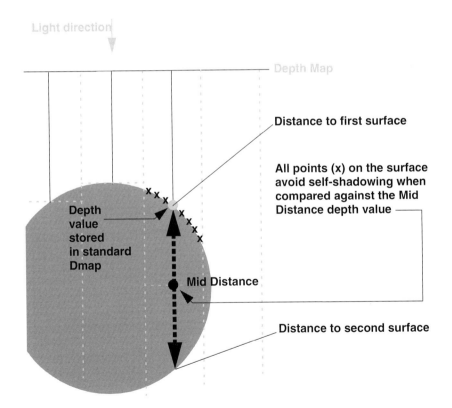

Because **Use Mid Dist Dmap** is turned **ON** by default, surfaces such as ground planes are not as susceptible to self-shadowing. The question often arises - what happens when there is only one surface that uses the Mid Distance algorithm? Answer - since there is only one surface, Maya stores the light's far clipping plane value which will always be further away than the surface being illuminated. Thus, the surface is correctly illuminated.

Tip: When **Use Mid Dist Dmap** is turned **ON**, there are actually 2 Depth Maps created - the standard Depth Map that stores the distances to the first surfaces and the Mid Distance Depth Map that stores the middle distances between the first and second surfaces. To see the difference, write the Dmaps to disk and **fcheck** them from your depth directory of your current project. **Be sure to press the Z key once you fcheck the images to see the depth channel**.

Dmap Bias and Use Mid Dist Dmap working together

The **Use Mid Dist Dmap** can prevent some self-shadowing artifacts. However, depending on the model and the angle of the lights, a small Dmap Bias is normally required as well (the default is 0.001). The reason for this is that when surfaces are modeled close together, the Mid Distance is not significantly far enough from the first surface to allow the first surface to escape self-shadowing.

The following diagram shows the previous example of the plane. This time, a second plane is added slightly below the original. Because the planes are close together, the mid distance does very little to reduce the self-shadowing.

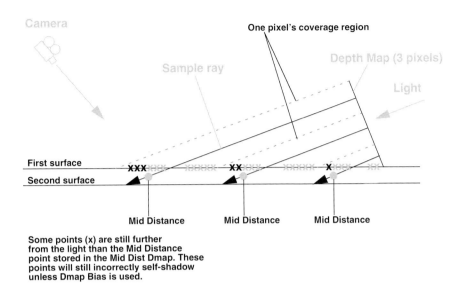

Camera

One pixel's coverage region

Sample ray

Depth Map (3 pixels)

Light

First surface

Second surface

XXX   **XX**   **X**

Mid Distance   **Mid Distance**   **Mid Distance**

**Some points (x) are still further
from the light than the Mid Distance
point stored in the Mid Dist Dmap. These
points will still incorrectly self-shadow
unless Dmap Bias is used.**

The following rendered images show the real effect of both **Use Mid Dist
Dmap** and **Dmap Bias** working together to effectively remove all self-
shadowing artifacts from the surfaces on a scooter.

Mid Dist Dmap OFF
Dmap Bias = 0.0

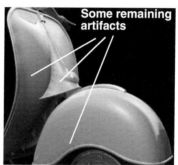

Mid Dist Dmap ON
Dmap Bias = 0.0

Mid Dist Dmap ON
Dmap Bias = 0.01

The Angle of Light affects Self-shadowing

The following diagram illustrates how the angle of the light directly affects the likelihood of self-shadowing on a surface. Surfaces that are at an angle to the light are most likely to show self-shadowing because a single pixel's depth value is forced to approximate the shadows for a much larger region, which results in greater self-shadowing error.

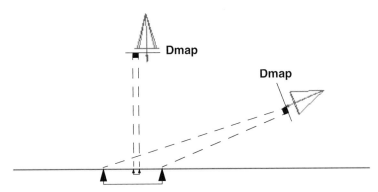

Angle of light impacts self-shadowing

Depth Map Resolution

Dmap Resolution defines the size of the Depth Map rendered from a shadow casting light. If it is set at 512, which is the default, the Depth Map will be 512 x 512 pixels. As mentioned earlier, from the light point of view the map is a square grid of pixels in front of the light. This grid is projected over the scene, dividing it into sections. As a result, each section of the scene is represented by one pixel on the Dmap.

Let's say you have a scene that is 100 grid units by 100 grid units. There is a Directional Light casting shadows in your scene and the **Dmap Resolution** is set to 100. Since the **Dmap Resolution** is set at 100, one pixel from the Dmap will cover approximately one entire grid square of the scene. If there is a sphere that is 1 grid unit in size, the shadow for it will be calculated with the depth value of as few as one pixel in the Depth Map. As you can see in the following image, there isn't enough information in the Depth Map to create a decent shadow.

Low Dmap Resolution

In the following diagram, the **Dmap Resolution** has been increased resulting in enough information in the Depth Map to create an accurate shadow.

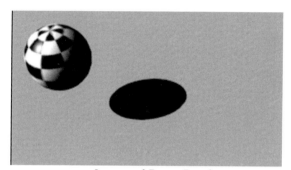

Increased Dmap Resolution

To automatically get the most detailed accurate shadows out of a Depth Map, there is an attribute called **Use Dmap Auto Focus** in the **Depth Map Shadow Attributes** section of the Attribute Editor. When this attribute's value is true, the renderer automatically computes the bounding volume for the objects in the view from the light source and uses the smallest possible field of view to render the shadow map. However, this can create artifacts over an animation if the bounding volume of the objects in your scene changes, possibly creating aliasing artifacts in your shadows, or unwanted softening or noise in the shadows.

Depth Map Filter Size

Dmap Filter Size helps control the softness of shadow edges. The softness of the shadow edge is a combination of the size of the shadow, the **Dmap Resolution** and the **Dmap Filter Size**. If you have an object casting a shadow and the shadow is a little rough around the edges, increase the **Dmap Filter Size** to soften the edge. The following image illustrates the difference between a low (left image) and high (right image) **Dmap Filter Size**. Increasing **Dmap Filter Size** will increase render time, especially in conjunction with an increase in **Dmap Resolution**. For really soft and fuzzy shadows, try lowering the resolution and using a medium Filter Size. Be aware that the lower the resolution, the lower the accuracy of the shadow; using too low a resolution can result in flickering shadows in animation.

Dmap Resolution 64   **Dmap Resolution 1024**

Dmap Filter Size 10   **Dmap Filter Size 10**

Effect of Filter Size with various Dmap Resolution

Shadow Color

A phenomenon of color vision is the tendency of the eye to perceive the shadows cast from a colored light source to be the complementary color. It is not there in reality, but it is an optical illusion or color impression within the eye.

Lightening the shadow color also increases the transparency of the shadow. The following rendered images show this effect:

Medium Blue shadow   **Black shadow**

Use Dmap Auto Focus

To avoid using very high resolution Dmaps wherever possible, it is important to keep the Dmap focused tightly on the shadow casting objects. The **Use Dmap Auto Focus** feature allows the light to automatically determine the most optimal coverage region for the Depth Map. The behavior of Auto Focus is shown in the Spot Light example below. The workflow when turning **OFF** the Auto Focus behavior is described in the Directional Light example following the Spot Light example. In all examples below, the **Casts Shadows** flag is turned **OFF** on the ground plane to help optimize the Auto Focus.

For **Spot Lights**, the **Cone Angle** limits the size of the Dmap coverage when the light covers an area smaller than the shadow casting objects. When the Cone Angle covers an area larger than the objects, Auto Focus keeps the Dmap tightly focused on the shadow casting objects. When **Use Dmap Auto Focus** is turned **OFF**, you need to set a specific angle to focus the Dmap. Care must be taken when setting this angle because if you set the **Dmap Focus** too small, the shadow may be cut off or may not appear at all.

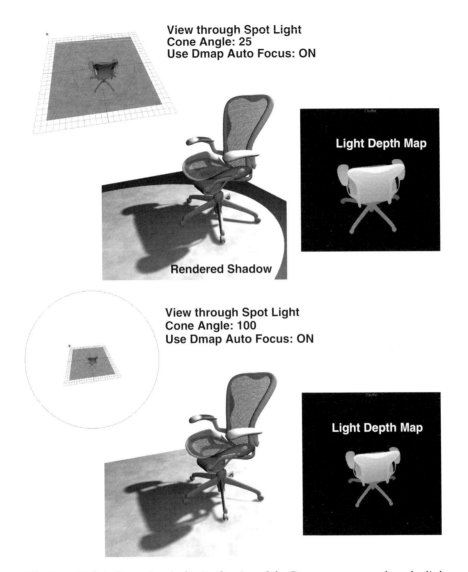

**View through Spot Light
Cone Angle: 25
Use Dmap Auto Focus: ON**

Light Depth Map

Rendered Shadow

**View through Spot Light
Cone Angle: 100
Use Dmap Auto Focus: ON**

Light Depth Map

The Spot Light's **Cone Angle** *limits the size of the Dmap coverage when the light covers an area smaller than the shadow casting objects (top above).*

When the Cone Angle covers an area larger than the objects, **Auto Focus** keeps the Dmap coverage focused on the shadow casting objects. Notice that the Dmap and the rendered shadow have not changed much compared to the one in the previous image, even though the Cone Angle is now much wider (bottom above).

For **Directional** Lights, if **Use Dmap Auto Focus** is **ON**, Maya will compute the vector for the light and the world bounding box based on all shadow casting objects. The Dmap coverage will be fit to the world bounding box width orthographic to the light. If you have a scene that scales a lot up or down or an object that crosses a large distance perpendicular to the light, the auto Dmap can cause flickering in animation. This is because the Dmap resolution remains constant but the coverage will keep changing, affecting the quality of the shadows. To avoid this, turn off **Use Dmap Auto Focus** and manually set the **Dmap Width Focus**.

To determine the value to use as the **Dmap Width Focus**, look through the selected Directional Light and track and zoom until the shadow casting objects are closely bounded by the view. Open the camera Attribute Editor for the "look through" camera. Under the **Orthographic Views** section, the **Orthographic Width** is the value you should use as the **Dmap Width Focus** on the light.

Tracking and dollying the "look through" camera changes the position of the light. Normally, the position of a Directional Light is not important, however, when turning **Use Dmap Auto Focus** off, you need to turn on **Use Light Position** on the light so that Maya knows the location from which you positioned the Dmap. Forgetting to turn on **Use Light Position** results in the default behavior where the Dmap is positioned at the origin. This may result in incorrect or offset shadows.

DEPTH MAP SHADOW DETAILS FOR EACH LIGHT TYPE

Directional

Directional lights have two possible behaviors when using Dmap shadows. Since Directional Lights are assumed to be at an infinite distance from the scene (hence the parallel light rays), by default Directional Lights will cast shadows on the entire scene. The bounding box of the scene is taken and an orthogonal Depth Map region is created, which contains the entire scene. This can result in shadow Depth Map resolution problems if the scene is very large, but only if a small section of the scene is being viewed, or if the scene changes size dramatically over an animation.

Use Light Position is provided to limit the number of objects that are involved in a Directional Light's Depth Map. Setting this attribute to **true** makes the Directional Light take its position (the location of the Directional Light icon in the modeling view) into account. Objects in the half space defined by the light's position and direction are illuminated by the Directional Light and are used in the creation of the shadow Depth Map.

Any objects "behind" the Directional Light are not lit and do not participate in the generation of the shadow Depth Map. The **Use Light Position** attribute is not on by default and can only be accessed when the **Use Dmap Auto Focus** is turned off.

Setting up good shadows with Directional Lights

1 Set the Depth Map options

- **Select** the Directional Light that you are using to cast shadows.

- In the Attribute Editor, go to the Depth Map Shadows section and set **Use Dmap Auto Focus** to **OFF**.

- Set the **Use Light Position** to **ON**.

2 Look through the Light

- Make sure that the Directional Light is selected, then select **Panels → Look Through Selected.**

- Zoom in and out and track in this view until all the shadow casting objects are closely bounded by the view.

  When you **Look Through Selected** on a light, Maya temporarily creates a camera node underneath the light transform node. When you change the panels view back to an orthographic or perspective view, the extra camera node is removed.

3 Note the Orthographic Values

- While looking through the Directional Light, select the **Camera** by going to **View → Camera Attribute Editor...**

- Open the **Orthographic Views** section and note the **Orthographic Width** value.

  The **Orthographic Width** value is the distance across the camera view. If you navigate around the scene until all the objects that will be casting shadows are contained within the view, the Orthographic Width will be the distance across the scene.

4 Set the Dmap Width Focus

- **Select** the light.

- Enter the value recorded from above into the **Dmap Width Focus**.

Tips for good Directional Light shadows:

- Render out the scene with **Disk Based Dmap** on **Overwrite Existing Dmaps** and **fcheck** the Depth Map for the light. It will be in the *depth* directory of the current project. This will help troubleshooting.

There is a *midmap* and the standard Dmap. You will need to press the **z** key to see the depth information in these files.

- To help set up accurate detailed shadows without using huge Dmap resolutions, background geometry or ground planes may be able to have the **Casts Shadows** flag in the **Render Stats** section of the Attribute Editor turned off so they will not be included in the auto focus. Another option is to use **Auto focus OFF** and **Use Light Position ON** to manually tighten the shot.

- In the case where you have a problematic scene (where the world bounding box changes size dramatically or an object crosses a large distance perpendicular to the light), you may have to sacrifice speed and use a very high resolution Dmap *and* manually set the **Dmap Width Focus** to avoid flickering shadows.

Point

By default, Point Light shadows are produced by casting up to 12 Depth Maps; a standard Dmap and a midmap are created in each of the cardinal axes directions (+X, -X, +Y, -Y, +Z, and -Z) from the Point Light's position in space. If there is no shadow casting object in a particular cardinal axis direction, Maya will not create a Dmap for that direction. Be aware that if you specify a large shadow Depth Map resolution, there can be 12 Depth Maps of that large resolution generated. Maya does try to compact the Depth Maps as much as possible, but large Depth Maps can still occupy a great deal of memory and take valuable time to render. To further optimize your shadow Depth Maps from Point Lights, you can turn individual directions off. For example, if there is nothing of interest to cast shadows on the ceiling of your room, you could disable the +Y Depth Map by turning **OFF** the **Use Y+ Dmap** attribute in the Depth Map Shadow Attributes section of the Point Light's Attribute Editor.

Spot

Spot Lights by default use only one Depth Map. Using only one Depth Map has limitations when the angle of the Spot Light exceeds 90-degrees; the resolution of the Depth Map must be increased dramatically to keep the shadow quality high. Maya allows you to use up to six Depth Maps for Spot Lights by turning **OFF** the **Use Only Single Dmap** in the Attribute Editor for Spot Lights. When this attribute is turned off, and the cone angle of the Spot Light exceeds 90-degrees, five or six Depth Maps are created around the Spot Light, tiling the faces of an axis-aligned cube with faces in each of the axis directions - much the same as for a Point Light. The only difference is that a Spot Light will only cast five Depth Maps if the Spot Light does not shine onto one of the six faces. Just as cubic reflection maps avoid aliasing at the boundaries between faces of the cube, the cubic shadow map is also filtered to avoid artifacts.

Motion Blur and Depth Map Shadows

Shadows themselves do not motion blur in Maya currently. To work around this limitation, render a shadow pass separately and process it to add blur before compositing. The other option is to use mental ray for Maya's shadow maps.

Working with Depth Map Shadows and IPR

There are some **Dmap Shadow** attributes that will update automatically in an IPR region while others that can only be previewed by selecting in the **Render View** window **IPR → Update Shadow Maps**. The Shadow Attributes are arranged in the light's Attribute Editor so that these attributes are grouped together.

Exercise: Casting Dmap Shadows with the SpaceJet

Open the file called *spacejet.mb*. The file does not include the entire diner scene as shown in the following images because, for the purpose of this shadow exercise, it is too slow to render. Instead, the file is simplified to contain only the spaceJet, two lights, ground plane, a cube to represent the diner, and a sidewalk.

The *moonLight* is the most dominant light source in the diner scene so it should definitely cast shadows. Because it is a Directional Light, this section will use the workflow steps that apply specifically to Directional Lights.

1 Turn on shadows for moonLight

- **Select** *moonLight* and set **Use Depth Map Shadows** to **ON**.

- IPR render the scene.

  You will notice that the shadows do not look very good. The shadow looks blockish and the image contains many self-shadowing artifacts.

2 Turn off Shadow Casting

In this scene, the shadows are looking extremely pixelated because the scene is large and the **Resolution** of the Dmap is at the default of 512. Before increasing the resolution of the Dmap, remember that the large ground plane does not cast shadows on anything so you can turn its shadows off (it will still receive shadows). This allows **Dmap Auto Focus** to reduce the area that the Dmap covers which improves the shadows from *moonLight*.

- **Select** the *groundPlane* and open its Attribute Editor. In the **Render Stats** section, set the **Casts Shadows** flag to **OFF**.

  Maya will not include the *groundPlane* geometry when it computes the world bounding box.

Tip: If you need to do this for many objects, use **Window** → **General Editors** → **Attribute Spreadsheet**... and look under the **Render** tab.

- Use **Render View** → **IPR** → **Update Shadow Maps** to see the change in the shadows.

  As you can see, the shadows have already tightened up considerably.

Shadows with ground plane shadow casting turned off

3 Manually set the Dmap Focus Width

In order to have even more control over how the Depth Map is fit to the scene, you can do it manually.

- Set the **Use Dmap Auto Focus** to **OFF**.

  You will notice that an attribute called **Dmap Width Focus** becomes available. The default value is 100 units but you will be entering a new value eventually.

- Set the **Use Light Position** to **ON**.

By default, Directional Lights do not have an origin. Turning this attribute on means that the physical position of the light in the modeling views becomes relevant and they will only shine on objects in front of the light. The **Dmap Width Focus** will be applied from this position.

■ With the *moonLight* still selected, go to **Panels** → **Look Through Selected** in one of your modeling windows.

You will be looking through a new camera that is orthogonal to the Directional Light.

■ Dolly and track this camera the same way you would any other camera until the view encompasses the *spaceJet*. Keep in mind that as you do this, you will be moving your light.

■ In this camera's Attribute Editor, open the section called **Orthographic Views** and notice the **Orthographic Width** attribute. Notice that as you dolly, this value changes.

■ Once you are satisfied with your setup, record the value of the **Orthographic Width** attribute.

■ Open the Attribute Editor for *moonLight*. Enter the value you recorded above in **Depth Map Shadow Attributes** → **Dmap Width Focus.**

■ Update the shadow maps in IPR or re-render to see the impact of the new Dmap Width Focus.

By doing this, you have manually set the width of the scene that *moonLight*'s Dmap will cover. You should see an improvement in the shadows.

Note: In a scene like this, it is a good idea to **lock** the Dmap focus in this way if the spaceJet is going to fly away beyond the diner buildings because this would cause the world bounding box to scale up and could cause the shadow quality to degrade.

Shadows with manual Dmap Width Focus

4 Increase the Resolution

Now that the **Dmap Width Focus** is optimized, you can see that the shadow quality is still blockish. The default resolution of 512 is not sufficient for this light shadowing the entire scene. You could just increase the **Dmap Filter Size** and have very soft shadows. However, some shadows from thin objects like the streetlights will be very faint and can flicker in animation with such a low resolution shadow map.

- In the Attribute Editor for *moonLight,* increase the **Dmap Resolution** until the blocky appearance is reduced and the level of shadow detail is to your satisfaction. Remember to use the **Update Shadow Maps** to see the results in IPR.

Shadows with high-resolution 2K Dmap

5 Adjust the Dmap Bias

At this point, the shadows are looking much better. However, you will notice that there are some self-shadowing artifacts. You will use the **Dmap Bias** attribute to correct this.

The default Dmap Bias value of 0.001 is too small for this scene.

- With IPR running, adjust **Dmap Bias** very slightly to values that are greater than **0.001**.

  By the time you get to a value of approximately **0.1**, the majority of the artifacts should be gone. There is a danger of using too large a value in that you may start to see surfaces come out of shadow that should be in shadow.

  These Dmap Bias changes will update in IPR automatically.

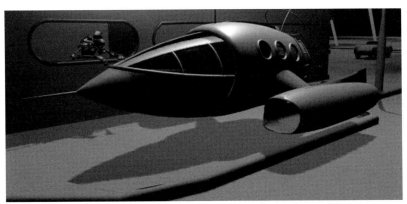

Shadows with self-shadowing corrected with Dmap Bias

6 Adjust the Depth Map Filter Size

The final step is to smooth the rough edges of the shadows.

- Increase the **Dmap Filter Size** until the shadows have a nice soft look.

  A value of **3** should be enough to give nice smooth edges on the shadows. The higher you set this attribute, the softer the edges will look but you will pay a significant price in the length of time it takes to render.

Tip: For very soft and fuzzy shadows, sometimes it is better to use a low-resolution Depth Map with some amount of filtering rather than very high-resolution Depth Maps with very high filter sizes.

Shadows with Dmap Filter Size of 3

Optimizing with Disk Based Depth Maps

The **Depth Map Shadow** section contains settings to allow you to **Overwrite Existing Dmap(s)/Reuse Existing Dmap(s)**. These settings cause the Depth Maps to be written to or read from disk and should be enabled when doing iterative render tests on a scene with shadows that are finalized, or when there is only a camera fly-by/ fly-through of the scene. Be aware that if you set these flags with animated moving objects, it will cause your shadows to remain stationary while the objects move.

To help lower render times with **Disk Based Dmaps**:

- Set **Disk Based Dmaps** to **Reuse Existing Dmap(s)**. Maya will calculate the Depth Map the first time you render and save it to disk. During each subsequent render, Maya will read the Depth Map from disk.

Volumetric Lighting Effects

Another feature of Depth Map Shadows in Maya is the ability to cast volume shadows through fog. This is a very popular effect in movies and television.

This effect is normally referred to as **Volumetric Lighting**. There is a scene file called *volumetricLightMoth.mb*. For an animated example of this effect, please see the movie file *fogLightMoth*.

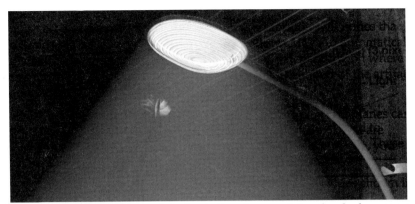

Technically, the shadowing of the fog is done by examining the shadow map a number of times across the fog volume.

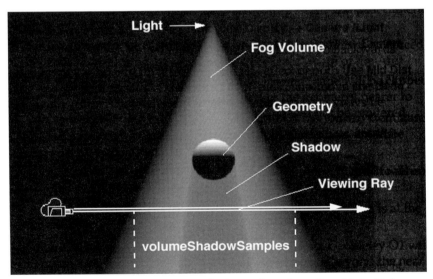

A side view of a ray penetrating a shadow volume for a Spot Light. Volume shadow samples (called **Fog Shadow Samples** *in the UI) are taken across the penetration interval.*

The number of times the fog is sampled is controlled by the attribute **Fog Shadow Samples**. The higher the number of samples, the higher the quality of the shadows in the fog. Keep in mind, though, that this will increase render times. Also note that, internally, Maya does not use **Mid Distance** when fog shadows are being rendered.

To darken the shadows in the fog, the **Fog Shadow Intensity** can be increased. The effect of increasing the **Fog Shadow Intensity** and the **Fog Shadow Samples** is shown in the images below:

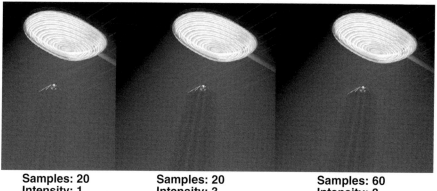

| Samples: 20
Intensity: 1
Faint and grainy
shadows | Samples: 20
Intensity: 3
More dramatic
shadows - still
grainy | Samples: 60
Intensity: 3
Dramatic and
smooth shadows |

RAYTRACED SHADOWS

Raytraced shadows are slower to render than Depth Map Shadows and generally have quite a different look than Depth Maps. However, there are several reasons you would need to use raytraced shadows:

- Rendering transparency-mapped shadow casting objects where you want to see the details of the texture map in the shadow.

- To have colored transparent shadows from objects with a material that has color on the transparency channel.

- Shadow attenuation where the shadow dissipates as it gets further away from the shadow casting object and for transparent objects, a shadow's tendency to be brighter in the center.

- Shadows from Ambient Lights because they have no Dmap shadows.

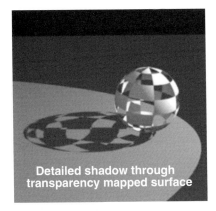

Detailed shadow through transparency mapped surface

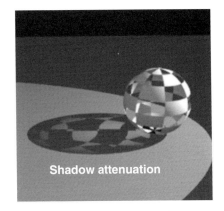

Shadow attenuation

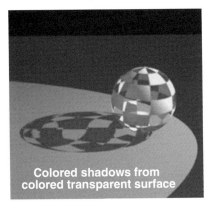

Colored shadows from colored transparent surface

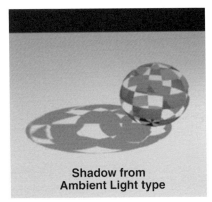

Shadow from Ambient Light type

How to get soft attenuated shadows

The raytraced shadow attributes **Light Radius** and **Shadow Rays** help control the final look of the shadow. Increasing the Light Radius to a non-zero value will cause the shadow to begin to dissipate as it gets further from the shadow casting object. The shadow of transparent objects tends to be brighter in the center, simulating a light's focus. On the material node of that object under the **Raytrace Options**, there is a **Shadow Attenuation** control to simulate this property. A setting of 0 results in a constant intensity of the shadow, whereas a setting of 1 results in brighter shadows focused in the center. This can be scen in the images below:

Tip:	To achieve a smooth appearance of raytraced shadows, the number of Shadow Rays will usually need to be increased. To increase the shadow ray resolution, increase the **Shadow Rays** attribute on the shadow casting light under the **Raytrace Shadow Attributes** section of the Attribute Editor.

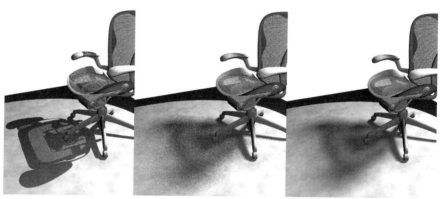

Light Radius: 0 **Shadow Rays: 1**	**Light Radius: 3** **Shadow Rays: 1**	**Light Radius: 3** **Shadow Rays: 10**

Self-shadowing Raytraced Shadows - Terminator Effect

To calculate raytraced shadows, Maya sends a ray from the camera and when this ray hits a surface, it spawns a secondary ray towards the light. This is a shadow ray which reports whether or not it hits any shadow-casting objects on its way to the light. If it does hit a shadow-casting object, then the point from which the shadow ray originated is in shadow. Because there is a shadow ray for each camera ray, raytraced shadows are very accurate leading to their characteristic sharp edges. This also explains why they take longer to render.

There is a common limitation when working with raytraced shadows that leads to a self-shadowing error known as the **Terminator Effect**. "Terminator" is the term for the transition point at which the illumination on a surface ends and the shadowed region begins. When raytraced shadows are used, artifacts may appear at this terminator point on the surface; thus, the name "terminator effect".

This type of artifact results from the fact that Maya uses flat triangles (polygons) at render time to approximate curved surfaces (in the case of NURBS). If the raytraced shadows were computed using the real position of the curved surface, there would not be any self-shadowing. However, because part of the polygon lies slightly below the actual surface, the shadow ray can intersect the surface itself on the way to the light (causing the self-shadowing artifact).

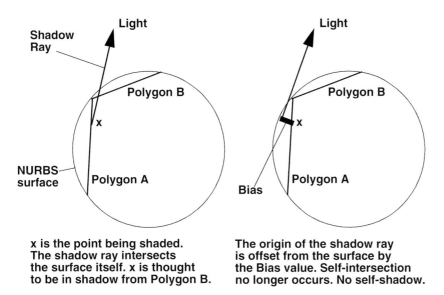

x is the point being shaded. The shadow ray intersects the surface itself. x is thought to be in shadow from Polygon B.

The origin of the shadow ray is offset from the surface by the Bias value. Self-intersection no longer occurs. No self-shadow.

There are two ways to correct this type of artifact.

- One way is to increase the tessellation on the surface. This results in triangles that more closely approximate the real position of the curved surface, thereby reducing or eliminating the self-shadowing artifact.

- The other way to correct these artifacts is to use the **Bias** attribute in the **Raytracing Quality** section of **Render Globals.** The bias is the amount Maya will offset any secondary ray from the surface generating the secondary ray so that it does not self-intersect.

The following images show the effect of increasing the tessellation or using the bias:

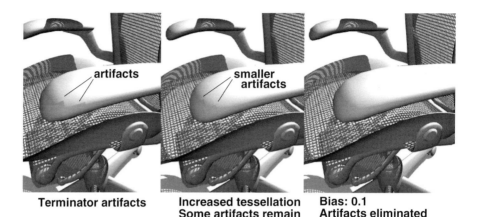

Terminator artifacts	**Increased tessellation** **Some artifacts remain**	**Bias: 0.1** **Artifacts eliminated**
		No tessellation increase

Note: Raytraced shadows will not work properly in almost every motion blur instance.

MENTAL RAY FOR MAYA'S SHADOW MAPS

The shadow map computation in mental ray for Maya is similar to Maya's Depth Map shadow computation. Like Maya's Depth Map Shadows, this type of shadow can be imprecise, yet it is faster to compute than raytraced shadows.

In mental ray for Maya, **Point, Directional, Spot,** and **Area Lights** are the light types that can produce Shadow Map shadows.

Creating mental ray for Maya Shadow Maps

- Select a light and turn on **Use Depth Map Shadows** in the light's Attribute Editor.
- Scroll down to the mental ray section of the light's Attribute Editor and under the Shadow Maps section turn on **Shadow Maps**.
- Make sure that **Shadow Maps** is turned **ON** in the Shadow Maps section of the mental ray Render Globals.

Depth Map Resolution

Dmap Resolution under mental ray for Maya's Shadow Maps Attribute Editor is the same as Maya's Depth Map Resolution. It defines the size of the shadow map rendered from a shadow casting light. The larger this value, the more accurate the shadow map, resulting in more accurate shadows. However, increasing this value will increase your render time.

Softness

Softness under mental ray for Maya's Shadow Maps Attribute Editor works the same as Maya's Dmap Filter attributes in that it control the softness of the shadow edge.

Samples

Samples represent the number of samples the renderer will take to alleviate artifacting. The higher the samples, the longer the render will take.

Softness: 0

Samples: 0

Softness: .3

Samples: 0

Softness: .3

Samples: 30

Self-Shadowing and Shadow Maps

mental ray for Maya's shadow map algorithm attempts to resolve self-shadowing artifacts without user interaction. Therefore, parameters such as Maya's **Use Mid Dist Dmap** and **Dmap Bias** are not necessary and will not be used when **Take Settings from Maya** is selected.

AutoFocus and Shadow Maps

The mental ray for Maya's shadow map algorithm employs an autoFocus feature similar to Maya's to keep the shadow map focused tightly on the shadow-casting objects. Unlike Maya, however, a user cannot edit the placement of these maps.

Reusing Shadow Maps

You can re-use shadow maps to help speed up render times. Normally, mental ray for Maya will compute one shadow map per frame for an animation. If the light or shadow doesn't change over the course of an animation, you can reuse the shadow map over and over, saving computation time and speeding up the render process. To reuse a shadow map:

- Open up the mental ray for Maya Render Globals and under the Shadows section, make sure the **Rebuild Shadow Maps** flag is **OFF.**

- Open the Shadow Map Editor under the mental ray section of the light's Attribute Editor.

- Type a name for the shadow in the Shadow Map File Name field. This will be the name of the shadow map that is saved to disk.

- Do a render to generate that shadow map. The file will be saved in the *mentalRay* sub-directory of your current project directory under *shadowMap*.

- Leave the name in the field and mental ray for Maya will automatically re-use this map for every frame of an animation.

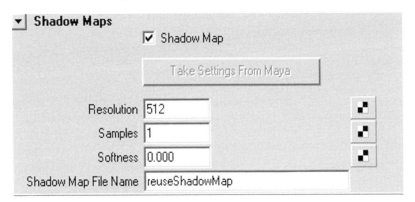

Motion Blur and Shadow Maps

In the real world, a photographer selects a camera with specific properties (such as a wide-angle lens), adjusts the camera's settings (for example, the shutter speed) for the shot he wants to make, positions the camera to compose the shot, then photographs the three-dimensional real world to produce a two-dimensional photograph. One of the properties the 3D camera will attempt to reproduce is motion blur - the phenomena of an object to look blurred as it moves quickly across a frame. With mental ray for Maya, if an object has motion blur, we can also motion blur its shadows. This is something not possible with Maya's shadow types.

Exercise: Creating Motion Blurred Shadow Maps

Open the file called *moblurShadowMap.mb*. The file is very simple, consisting of a plane of light and an animated sphere.

1 Turn on Depth Map Shadows for the Directional Light

- **Select** *shadowLight* and set **Use Depth Map Shadows** to **ON**.

- **Scroll down** and set **Shadow Maps** to **ON**.

- Do a render in the Render View window and save it.

2 **Turn on motion blur for the scene**

- **Open** the mental ray for Maya Render Globals and under **Motion Blur** → **Calculation,** choose **Linear** from the **Motion Blur** pull-down menu.

- Set **Motion Blur by** to **3** to increase the amount of blur.

- Make sure that **Motion Blur Shadow Maps** under the shadow section of the mental ray for Maya Render Globals is **ON.**

3 **Render a frame.**

- Go to frame 15 and do a render into the Render View window.

- Save this image and compare the shadows from the first image which has no motion blur on them, to the current image.

4 **Edit the motion blurred shadow**

- If you find that your shadow exhibits artifacting or that the shadow itself is not soft/blurred enough, you may want to go to the shadow map settings under the light's Attribute Editor, and increase the **samples** and **softness** parameters.

Tip: If the blur on the object is relatively small, you may want to use only the softness attribute to give the illusion of a motion blurred shadow.

Volumetric Shadow Maps

In order to cast shadows through a fog volume, you can use either mental ray for Maya's shadow maps or raytrace shadows. If you use the raytrace shadow option, you will be able to cast transparent information through the shadow volume. Capturing transparent information through a volume is something that is not possible when using Maya's shadows.

Exercise: Creating Volumetric Shadow Maps

Open the file called *volumeShadowMaps.mb.* The file is very simple, consisting of a Spot Light and a sphere.

1 **Turn on shadows and fog for the Spot Light**

- **Select** *fogLight* and set **Use Depth Map Shadows** to **ON.**

- **Scroll down** and set **Shadow Maps** to **ON.**

- Select the map button next to Light Fog under the Light Effects section.

2 Edit the shadows

- You may find that you either can't see your shadows or there may be some artifacting. To get rid of this, turn up the **Samples** attribute under the mental ray section of the Attribute Editor to 2. Then, slowly increase the value for the **Volume Samples Override** on the light's *coneShape* node as needed.

- To further alleviate artifacting, turn on **Jitter**. This will randomize the samples of the volume by replacing banding artifacts with noise.

MENTAL RAY FOR MAYA'S RAYTRACED SHADOWS

Raytrace shadows in mental ray for Maya are the same to setup and use as in Maya. If you are using the mental ray for Maya renderer with raytrace shadows, you will need to make sure raytracing is turned **ON** in the mental ray for Maya Render Globals. Other reasons to use mental ray for Maya's raytrace shadows include:

- Capturing transparency-mapped detail in a shadow that is cast through a volume.

- Rendering motion blurred shadows. Note that you can also use mental ray for Maya's Shadow Maps for this effect.

Shadow Methods

Under the Shadow section of the mental ray for Maya Render Globals, there is a **Shadow Methods** drop-down menu. This section mainly pertains to raytrace shadows and controls how occluding objects that cast shadows are found. For more detailed information about mental ray raytrace shadow methods, see the mental ray reference guide. The various methods are:

- **Off**: No shadows, raytrace or otherwise, will be calculated for the scene. This method is good for previewing a scene without having to calculate shadow information.

- **Simple**: The default. This shadow method calculates raytrace shadows in the usual way.

- **Sort**: Is used only if there is a custom shader that requires it, otherwise sorted is the equivalent of Simple (except less efficient).

- **Segment**: This is the most sophisticated way of calculating shadows. This method is used for shadowing volume effects such as software rendered particles.

SUMMARY

Shadows are an important part of creating mood and atmosphere in a scene. There are a number of important concepts to understand in order to achieve the best shadows possible without compromising your render times.

In this chapter, the following concepts were covered:

- How Maya Depth Map Shadows work
- Different Light types and their Shadows
- Volumetric Lighting Effects
- Maya Raytraced Shadows
- mental ray for Maya's Shadow Maps
- Motion Blurring Shadow Maps
- mental ray for Maya's Raytrace Shadows

Lobby Project

Global Illumination, Final Gather, and HDR, raytrace shadows.

Gold Ring

Final Gather render with an environmental HDR image. No lights were used.

Global Bicycle

This image was created using the mental ray for Maya Global Illumination setting. There are no direct light sources in the scene, just one spotlight emitting photons.

Audi A4 Headlight

The geometry is a mixture between polygon and NURBS surfaces imported from a CAD/CAM system. It is rendered with the Maya Software Renderer using raytracing.

BMW F1

The geometry was modelled in Maya with NURBS. An additonal light was used to get the specular highlight on the tires. HDRi by SpheronVR, www.spheron.com.

Caustic Cognac

This image illustrates mental ray for Maya caustics in the cognac and glass. Caustics are light patterns formed by reflected or refracted light.

HDRI Car

HDR image rendered out with Z-depth. Depth of Field was added in compositing.

Caustic Animation

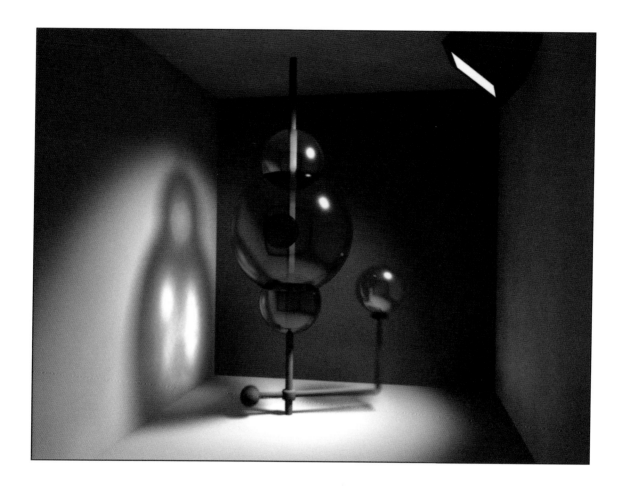

*This scene is a still of an animation that explores caustics in animation.
Global Illumination, Caustics, 1 mental ray Area Light, and mental ray linear
motion blur were used.*

Seawolf

This submarine model was rendered with the Maya software rendering engine. Fluid Effects was used for the ocean and Paint Effects for the water spray in the area where the submarine's hull meets the water.

Arch & Furniture

mental ray Renderer was used to lighten the scene with an HDR image. The HDR image was assigned to a large NURBS sphere around the room. In the Render Globals, Production Quality and Final Gather was set to ON. All other settings are default. Two mental ray area lights were used, with Decay set to Linear. The shaders are Blinn shaders with Texture Bump Maps.

Audi A4

The silvermetallic is a Layered Shader which uses two Ramp Shaders and a Phong E, rendered with the Maya Software renderer using raytracing.

Chair Interior

Architectural scene using one Area Light , Final Gather, and Global Illumination. Notice the blue color bleeding in the background.

Space Jet

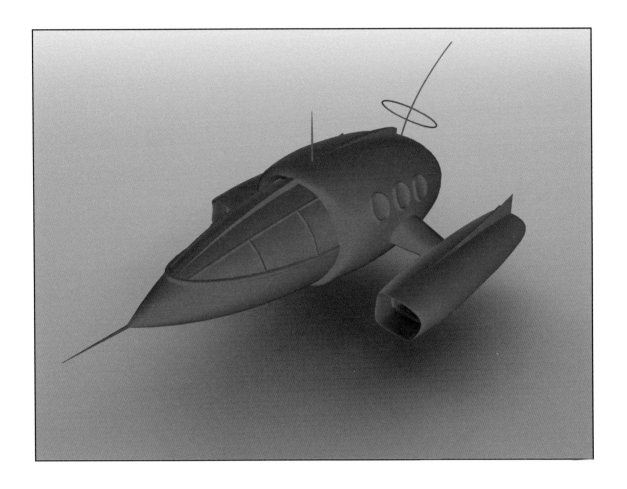

Final Gather render with no lights. Notice the color bleed.

Volumetric DGS

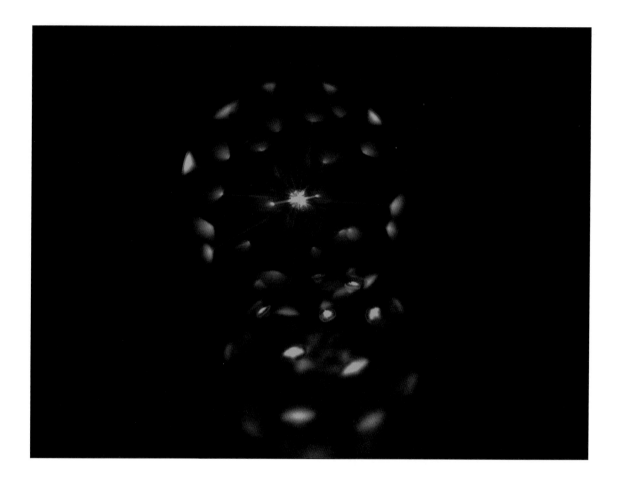

Volume effect using mib_volume MR Volumetric material.
The ground is a DGS material with glossy reflection.

Sunset Napa Valley

HDRi by SpheronVR, www.spheron.com

Crystal Ball Volume

This image uses a number of mental ray for Maya shaders and illustrates Volumetric Caustics. The Caustics are scattered from the fog volume within the crystal ball.

6 Raytracing

Raytracing is a method of rendering in which rays originate from the camera/eye and are sent out into the scene. Depending on what they encounter, they can spawn other rays. For instance, if a ray hits a reflective surface it will spawn another ray that will bounce off of the surface, and if it encounters another object then you will get a reflection.

Raytracing enables you to cast accurate shadows through partially transparent surfaces and allows you to see real reflections. If you don't raytrace, you can still get the look of reflections through the use of texture maps on the reflected color attribute. However, this can amount to a lot of work and still cannot produce important self-reflections. Raytracing also enables your scene to have refractive surfaces.

In this chapter, you will learn the following topics:

- How Raytracing works in Maya
- Reflection/Refraction/Shadow limits
- Memory Requirements

How Raytracing works in Maya

The Maya rendering architecture is a **hybrid** renderer. It uses an **EAS (Exact Area Sampling)** or **A-buffer algorithm** for primary visibility from the eye, and then raytraces any secondary rays.

When an object is encountered that requires raytracing to compute some component of its shading (raytraced shadows, reflections, and/or refractions), the raytracer is invoked. An important distinction to make here is that not all objects in a scene will need to be raytraced. If you had a transparent surface with a **refract index** of **1.0** (meaning no bending of light will occur), you would simply leave the **Refractions Flag** turned **OFF** for that material. To use raytracing in Maya, you will need to enable it through the Render Globals window. Keep in mind that raytracing is memory intensive and will increase rendering time.

1 Enable the Raytracer

- Select **Window → Rendering Editors → Render Globals** and open the **Raytracing Quality** section.

- Click the **Raytracing** check box to turn it **ON**.

   You have now enabled raytracing for the entire scene.

2 Set which Objects will not be raytraced

There is a further level of control in choosing which objects you want raytraced in a scene. By default, all objects created in Maya have raytracing turned on. You will want to turn off raytracing for objects which do not need to be raytraced to cut down on rendering time.

- **Select** an object you do not want raytraced and open the **Attribute Editor.**

- Open the **Render Stats** section.

- Turn **Visible in Reflections** to **OFF**.

- Turn **Visible in Refractions** to **OFF**.

Note: If you are opening Maya files from versions before Maya 2.0 then all objects will have **Visible in Reflections** and **Visible in Refractions** turned **OFF**.

---

3 Start rendering

- You can now render into a view or batch render the scene file.

Reflections, Refractions, and Shadows

Once you have turned **Raytracing** to **ON** in the **Render Globals** and the appropriate **Render Stats** are set, when you render a scene it will have *reflections* and/or *refractions* depending on the materials assigned to the surfaces. If you have turned **Raytrace Shadows** to **ON** for the lights in your scene then you will also get raytraced shadows. Notice when you turned raytracing on in the Render Globals that there are three sliders; **Reflections**, **Refractions**, and **Shadows**. These sliders correspond to limits that are associated with the rays being used in raytracing. Because shooting many *reflection*, *refraction* or *shadow rays* increases rendering time, there is a way to limit the number of such rays being shot. There are two locations where these limits are available. The first is available in the *Render Globals*, which affect everything. The other is in the material's Attribute Editor for *reflections and refractions* and in the lights Attribute Editor for raytraced *shadows*. The lower of the two sets of values will determine the limit for each surface. Where limits are concerned, if you have your limits set too low you won't get the desired results. For example, if you have light passing through a transparent sphere off of a plane and back again, you need to make sure that you have enough reflection rays to pass through all those surfaces. The same goes for shadows. If you have the shadow limit set at one and you want to cast a shadow through a transparent surface, you will not see a shadow. You would need to increase the shadow limit on the light.

Reflectivity

In the case of transparent surfaces such as glass, the level of Reflectivity depends on the angle at which the glass is viewed. Standing in front of a storefront window looking straight in, you will see a very faint reflection. However, if the viewer is to look at the window from an angle, the reflections will be more pronounced. This is controlled by the *Specular Roll Off* attribute on the Blinn material.

There is a physical property called *Total Internal Reflection* (TIR). This is when light tries to pass from a dense medium to a less dense medium at too shallow an angle and the light bounces off the boundary of the two mediums. This effect is the basic mechanism behind optical fibers. Light bounces along the inside of the optical fiber unable to escape because whenever it tries to leave, TIR occurs.

Refractions

There is an additional control for refractions called **Refraction Index.** This can be defined as the ratio of the speed at which light is travelling in the object versus in a vacuum. If the index of refraction is 1.0, then there is no distortion or bending of the light as it travels through the surface, e.g. water (20-degrees Celsius) has a refraction index of 1.33.

Tip: To make objects viewed through refracting surface less jagged, try increasing the shading samples (on the refracting object). If it is just a single object which causes you trouble, you should increase the shading samples on a per object level.

An important feature to be aware of with reflections and raytracing is the ability to map the **Reflected Color** of a material and also get reflections from objects in the scene. This means reflection maps and raytraced reflections can be used together. Basically, if a reflection ray coming off a surface strikes an object, it will *reflect that object*, and if the ray goes off to infinity, it will use the *reflection map*. This can be used to get the environment to show up on a reflective surface.

Reflection Specularity

This helps control the contribution of the specular highlights in reflections. Sometimes you can encounter some artifacts in the reflections of highlights.

Light Absorbance

This will describe how light-absorbing a material is. Transparent materials usually absorb an amount of light which passes through them. The thicker the material, the less light gets through.

Surface Thickness

This simulates a surface thickness (in world space) of transparent objects, created from a single surface. This works well when the edges of the surface aren't visible (i.e. a car windshield).

Chromatic Aberration

Different wavelengths of light refract at different angles when passing through a transparent surface during raytracing. Chromatic Aberration only affects light rays as they pass through the second surface of a transparent object.

1 Create a Reflective Material

- **Create** a **Blinn** Material.
- Set **Reflectivity** to **1.0**.
- Assign *Blinn* to a sphere.

2 Create an Image Plane

- **Select** the camera and open the Attribute Editor.
- Go to the environment section and click **Create** beside **Image Plane**.
- On the **Image Plane**, map a **Granite** texture.
- Change **Color1**, **Color2**, and **Filler Color** to black.
- Change **Color3** to white.

3 Position camera and Render

- Make sure you have turned **ON** the **Raytrace** in the Render Globals.
- Add a **Light** to your scene.
- **Render** the scene.

  You will notice that none of the stars are reflecting off of the sphere.

4 Map the Starfield onto the Shader

- **Select** the *Blinn* material and open the Attribute Editor.
- Drag the **Granite** texture onto the **Reflected Color** of the *Blinn* shader.

5 Render the Scene

  You should now see stars reflected in the sphere.

6 Add other Objects to the Scene

- Add a **Cone** to your scene.
- Render your scene.
- Notice that the other objects will be reflected in the sphere as well as the stars.

Note: If you have a number of objects in your scene that need to reflect the environment, you will need to map the environment texture onto each one. Another work around for the above problem is to create a large sphere and map your environment texture onto it. Then place all your objects inside of it. When you raytrace, the reflections of the environment will come from the large sphere.

Memory and Performance Options

In the Render Globals, if you open the **Memory and Performance Options** tab, you will find a **Raytracing** section. This section has several controls that Maya uses to define what will happen when you start a render with **Raytracing** enabled.

The first thing you need to know is when a raytrace is invoked, it breaks the bounding box of the scene up into cubes that are called voxels. The **Recursion Depth**, **Leaf Primitives**, and **Subdivision Power** attributes are used to determine the size and number of the voxels used. If there are too many objects in a voxel, Maya subdivides the voxel into smaller voxels all contained in the big voxel.

Why does the renderer voxelize space? One of the primary performance problems in raytracing is *surface intersection*. If the renderer can limit the number of objects participating in the calculation, it can speed up the algorithm. As a ray is traced through the scene, the renderer can immediately and efficiently know which voxels are intersected and which ones are not. The renderer can safely ignore those objects which are contained in voxels which *don't* intersect the ray. That way, the renderer has limited the number of objects participating in surface intersection.

Recursion Depth

With a fixed resolution for voxels, it is possible that a voxel may contain many triangles, thus raytracing will be very slow if this voxel is hit, because the ray will need to intersect against many triangles. When there are many triangles, Maya can further subdivide the voxel into another 3D array of voxels occupying the space of the parent voxel. Thus, each of those voxels should contain pointers to fewer triangles, reducing the amount of work for the raytracing. The **Recursion Depth** attribute determines the number of levels that this occurs on. It is recommend that this stay at **2**, because there is a trade-off of voxel *traversal time* vs. *triangle intersection time*. Larger does not mean better. Larger also means more memory used by the voxels.

Tip: In cases where the raytrace is running out of memory to the point where it cannot complete the render, it is possible to lower the **Recursion Depth** to **1**. This will take much longer to render but will use less memory.

Leaf Primitives:

This attribute determines the number of triangles in a voxel before you recursively create voxels.

Subdivision Power:

This determines the (x,y,z) resolutions of the voxels. So, when it is determined that a voxel needs to be subdivided, the **Subdivision Power** is used to determine how many voxels will be created.

A problem that arises when raytracing is that of the "big floor". If you have a large plane in a scene with a small concentration of detailed surfaces in one area, it will be slow to render with raytracing. The problem here is that the entire bounding box of the scene will be used to create evenly sized voxels. What you get is a bunch of voxels that are empty or have only one surface in them and you get one voxel with the bulk of the geometry. Even if the voxels are recursively subdivided, you still end up with lots of geometry in few voxels. This will slow down the renderer. One way around this is to turn raytracing **OFF** for the big floor. With the big floor out of the way the bounding box for raytracing is centered around the concentrated geometry and you get a much better *voxel/geometry* distribution.

SUMMARY

Some interesting effects can be achieved using the built-in raytracer in Maya. With a general understanding of limits and memory requirements, you will be able to optimize raytracing and achieve desired results.

This chapter covered the following topics:

- How raytracing works in Maya

- Reflection/Refraction/Shadow limits

- Memory Requirements

Controlling Renders

An important consideration when rendering in production is
the amount of time it takes to render a frame. Fortunately,
there are a number of options that allow you to get the best
performance from the Maya renderer. This chapter will focus
on how to set up renders to get the best quality and shorter
render times.

```
=======================================
Resource Usage At End Of Frame
=======================================
      3308         Page faults
192.912 Mb         Max resident size
539.869 Mb         Peak total size(Estimated)
450.757 Mb         Peak arena size
=======================================
 22.856 Mb         Heap
  0.655 Mb         Transforms
  3.146 Mb         NURBS AG
  0.226 Mb         Render Geometry Arena
  1.966 Mb         Data Blocks
  2.376 Mb         Pixel Map
  0.262 Mb         NURBS Surface Shapes
  9.175 Mb         MEL
  0.262 Mb °       Noise Table
 24.543 Mb         Render Cache
  0.328 Mb         NURBS Geometry Cache
  0.131 Mb         Keys
=======================================
```

In this chapter, you will learn the following:

- Maya's Anti-aliasing
- Tessellation in Maya and How to Control it
- Memory Requirements and Optimizations
- Render Diagnostics
- mental ray for Maya's Sampling Quality
- mental ray for Maya's Approximation Editor

CHAPTER 7

ANTI-ALIASING

How Anti-aliasing Works

Part of the philosophy of the Maya renderer is that it attempts to solve each part of the rendering process independently, using the best method for each rendering problem. For this reason, when it comes to *anti-aliasing*, (geometric) edge anti-aliasing is solved completely before the shading is solved. Let's take a closer look at what this means.

Note: Anti-aliasing is the smoothing of jagged or stair-step effects in images by adjusting pixel intensities so that there is a more gradual transition between the color of a line and the background color.

In some renderers, including PowerAnimator, both the *Edge anti-aliasing* and the *Shading anti-aliasing* are affected by the same controls. In Maya, these two processes are controlled separately. There is a significant benefit to separating the anti-aliasing controls, which will become clearer as they are defined.

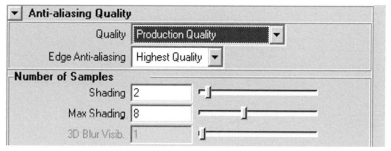

Separate controls for Edge Anti-aliasing and Shading Samples

Edge Anti-aliasing

When Maya goes to render a pixel, one of the things it needs to know is what geometry is visible in that pixel. This visibility of objects is determined by a method that is analogous to the pushpin array of nails novelty toy you often see in science or games stores.

Note:	The pushpin novelty toy consists of an array of blunt nails pushed through a plastic board with a Plexiglas front shield to prevent the nails from being pushed all the way out of the board. You press your hand or face into the blunt end of the nails, and the nails on the other side of the board take on the shape of your hand or face.

When Maya uses this *pushpin* approach to determine what geometry is visible in a pixel, it pushes the triangles (tesselation triangles) into a digital pushpin array. The digital pushpin array is many times more dense than the pixel, which gives very accurate information about the visibility of objects within the pixel. Maya uses this information to compute **Edge Anti-aliasing**. The algorithm used to determine edge anti-aliasing is called **Exact Area Sampling**; or EAS for short.

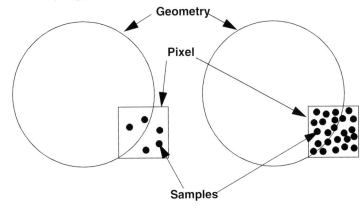

Edge Anti-aliasing

As you can see in the diagram above, a small number of *visibility samples* will not provide very much information about the edge of the geometry in the pixel. However, if there are many visibility samples, there is a lot more information and the renderer can much more accurately determine the object's edge in a pixel. The appearance of the edge becomes much cleaner and smoother in the rendered image as the number of visibility samples increases.

The number of visibility samples Maya looks at in a pixel is controlled by the **Edge Anti-aliasing** attribute in the Render Globals.

1 Adjust the Edge Anti-Aliasing

- Open the scene file called *control_antialiasing.mb*.

- Open the Render Globals and in the **Anti-aliasing Quality** section, set the **Edge Anti-aliasing** to **Low Quality** and render the scene.

Notice how the edges of the NURBS plane look rough and jagged.

- Use the **Keep Image** feature in the Render View.

- Repeat the above steps with the Edge Anti-aliasing set to **Medium** and **High Quality**. Keep the image after each render.

2 Compare the Results

- Use the arrows on the far sides of the slider at the bottom of the Render View to step through the images for comparison.

  Notice how the edges of the NURBS plane get smoother as the quality is increased.

The actual number of visibility samples used at each quality level is as follows:

- **Low Quality** - Fastest anti-aliasing setting. For each pixel being rendered, **2 samples** are analyzed producing low quality edge anti-aliasing. This setting is mostly used for quick test renders of complex scenes as it produces very low quality anti-aliased edges.

- **Medium Quality** - For each pixel being rendered, **8 samples** are analyzed producing medium quality edge anti-aliasing. This quality is a little slower and gives moderately good edge anti-aliasing.

- **High Quality** - For each pixel being rendered, **32 samples** are analyzed producing high quality edge anti-aliasing.

- **Highest Quality** - This quality setting also uses **32 samples** per pixel. However, it also enables something called *adaptive shading* which leads to the discussion of shading anti-aliasing which will be covered later in this lesson.

Small Geometry Edge Anti-aliasing

Often in animation, the edges (silhouette) of very small objects will appear to flicker due to inaccuracy of visibility determination. In this scenario, the 32 samples Maya uses on **High** or **Highest Quality** is not sufficient to prevent this flickering. However, there is a way to solve this problem.

1 Set Edge Anti-aliasing to High or Highest

- In the Render Globals window, set the **Edge Anti-aliasing** to **High** or **Highest**.

  The Geometry **Anti-aliasing Override** does not take effect unless the **Edge Anti-aliasing** is set to **High** or **Highest** Quality.

2 Turn ON Geometry Anti-aliasing Override

- **Select** the flickering geometry.
- Open the Attribute Editor and go to the **Render Stats** section.
- Turn **ON** the **Geometry Anti-aliasing Override** flag.

  You will notice that the *Anti-aliasing Level* attribute becomes un-greyed.

Note: The Geometry Anti-aliasing Override switch and the Anti-aliasing Level are also available from the Rendering Flags Window and from the attribute spreadsheet.

---

3 Set the Anti-aliasing Level

- Set the **Anti-aliasing Level** to **2**.
- Re-render to see if the flickering has stopped.
- If the flickering remains, increase the **Anti-aliasing Level** to **3** and re-render. Keep increasing the level until you are happy with the results.

There are currently *5 different anti-aliasing levels* defined with **1** being the **default** (Maya's highest quality Edge Anti-aliasing in the Render Globals), and **5** being the **Best** anti-aliasing quality. A higher the anti-aliasing level setting will take longer to render the object. *Anti-aliasing level 2 or 3 should be sufficient for most problems.*

The following are **Geometry Anti-aliasing Override** level settings:

Level 1 takes **32 visibility samples** per pixel;

Level 2 takes **96 visibility samples** per pixel;

Level 3 takes **288 visibility samples** per pixel;

Level 4 takes **512 visibility samples** per pixel;

Level 5 takes **800 visibility samples** per pixel.

One important thing to note is, the cost to render the rest of the image does not change. It is only more expensive to render the geometry with the **Geometry Anti-aliasing Override** turned **ON** and with higher anti-aliasing levels. So it is important to switch on the **Geometry Anti-aliasing Override** for only the flickering geometry.

This feature is useful only for non-3D motion blurred objects. If 3D motion blur is ON and there is no camera animation, a non-moving object's anti-aliasing level can be overridden and set to some higher value. A moving object's anti-aliasing level setting will be ignored. If moving object's edge anti-aliasing is a problem, try increasing the **Max 3D Blur Visibility** samples in Render Globals when rendering on **Highest Quality** mode.

Tip: One thing to note, if the flickering is caused by small geometry that is a few pixels in size, it is best to switch on *multi-pixel filtering*. Sometimes it is theoretically impossible to fix the flickering problem without multi-pixel filtering. This is because without the filtering, the edge anti-aliasing is done with respect to **1** pixel and roping artifacts will appear even if the most accurate answer for that pixel's edge anti-aliasing is given. Multipixel filtering takes into account and filters more than **1** pixel's results (the ideal pixel width being **2**). Also note that sharp television cameras have the same problem - even though each pixel is resolved completely, thin, high contrast lines (such as the white lines on sports fields) can exhibit the same artifacts, so the problem is not isolated to CG. The best multi-pixel filtering options can be one of the default *3x3-width gaussian filter* or use *3x3-width quadratic* but if it's too soft, try *2x2-width triangular filter*.

Shading Anti-aliasing

As you may have noticed, working with the *Edge Anti-aliasing* has allowed us to clean up the edges of our NURBS plane, but what about the rough looking circle of light on the plane? The "jaggies" at the edge of the circle of light are affected by **Shading Anti-aliasing**.

When it comes to shading, the Maya renderer tries to shade each object only once per pixel. However, this is not always a high enough sampling frequency to properly anti-alias some shading events like *thin specular highlights*, *shadow edges*, or *complex* textures.

In the Render Globals, there is a section that deals with **Number of Samples**. This allows you to control the *shading anti-aliasing*.

Notice that when the **Edge Anti-aliasing** is set to *High Quality*, the **Max Shading** attribute is greyed-out. This means that whatever value the shading attribute is set to will determine the number of *shading samples* per object per pixel. The **default** is **1**. This means only *one shading sample* per *object* per *pixel*.

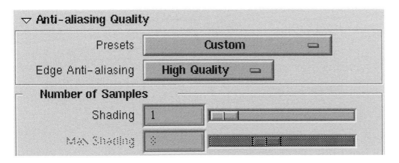

Let's look at how changing the shading samples will affect our image. Focus on the region illuminated by the Spot Light on the plane.

1 Set Edge Anti-aliasing to High Quality

- Continue working with the scene file called *antialiasing.ma*.

- Render the file with the **Edge Anti-aliasing** set to **High Quality** and the **Shading** set to **1**.

- Keep the image.

- Change the **Shading** value to **8**.

- Render the image again.

  Notice how this time the image takes a lot longer to render.

- Compare the images.

  The images should look like this:

Edge Anti-aliasing set to High Quality - Shading samples set to 1

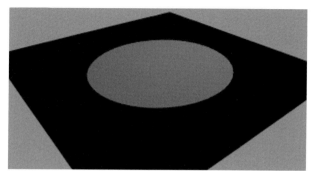

Edge Anti-aliasing set to High Quality - Shading samples set to 8

By setting the **Shading Samples** to **8**, the edge of the lighting on the surface had been smoothed *but* rendering time increased significantly. For this reason, increasing this value is not recommended because it will increase the number of shading samples globally for *every* pixel, whether it needs it or not. This can amount to a lot of wasted render time.

A more efficient approach to improving shading anti-aliasing is to use **Adaptive Shading**. This adaptive feature is enabled by setting the **Edge Anti-aliasing** to **Highest Quality**. Notice that the Max Shading attribute becomes un-greyed.

Note: As discussed earlier, the **Edge Anti-aliasing** is resolved separately and ahead of the *shading* anti-aliasing. Setting the **Edge Anti-aliasing** to **Highest Quality** is the switch that enables the adaptive shading capabilities.

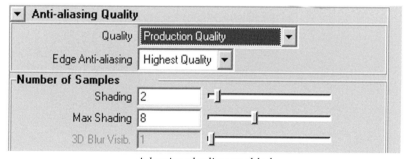

Adaptive shading enabled

Both **High** and **Highest Quality** will use **32** visibility samples to compute the edge anti-aliasing so the edges of the NURBS plane will anti-alias the same whether on **High** or **Highest**. Render again to compare the differences in **Shading Anti-aliasing**.

2 Set Edge Anti-aliasing to Highest Quality

- Set the **Edge Anti-aliasing** to **Highest Quality**.

- Set the **Shading** attribute back to a value of **1**. The **Max Shading** attribute should be showing a value of **8**.

- Render the scene again.

  You should notice that this time the circle of light is looking very smooth but the render time did not increase as much as before.

The image should look like this:

Edge Anti-aliasing set to Highest Quality - Shading samples set to 1 & 8

The reason why the shading quality looks much better but did not take longer to render is that Maya only used more shading samples on the pixels where it needed it around the edge of the circle of light. Because Maya was able to adapt to the needs of the shading, it is called **Adaptive Shading**.

How adaptive shading works

To do this adaptive process, Maya examines the contrast between a pixel and its five already-computed neighboring pixels (the next scanline in a tile is not yet rendered so all 8 neighboring pixels cannot be examined). The following diagram shows the five neighboring pixels involved in the contrast computation:

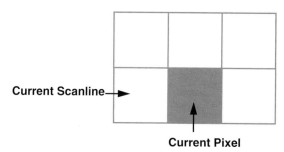

The 5 neighboring pixels used to compute contrast

Once Maya knows how much contrast there is between a pixel and its 5 neighbors, it compares this value to a **threshold** value specified in the Render Globals.

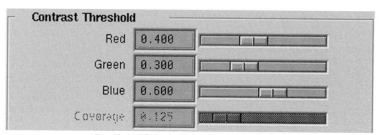

Render Globals Contrast Thresholds

If the contrast between the current pixel being shaded and any of its neighbors exceeds the **Contrast Threshold** in the Render Globals, then additional shading samples are used.

The number of additional shading samples used is determined by a simple linear function. The following diagram shows a chart of how this mechanism works:

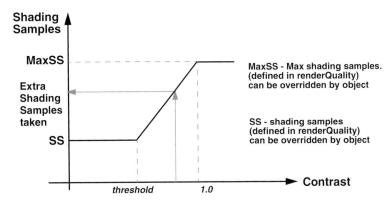

Graph showing how the number of extra shading samples for highest quality is computed

The number of samples starts at the **Shading** value (SS) and remains at that number until the contrast threshold is exceeded. At this point, as the distance above the threshold increases, so does the number of shading samples taken until the full contrast of 1.0 is reached and **Max Shading** samples are taken.

There are several examples of how you can use this mechanism to your advantage:

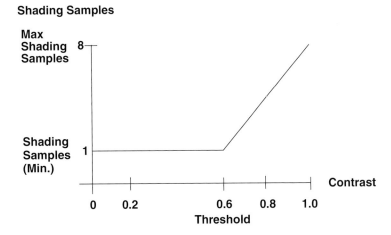

Example: Low Contrast Scene

Suppose there is a low contrast scene - either all low-lighting or all evenly brightly lit. When Maya looks at the difference between 2 pixels, it will likely find very little contrast. When this difference is compared against the threshold in Render Globals, it is very likely to slip under the threshold (i.e. - the contrast between the 2 pixels is less than the contrast threshold).

The result is that the minimum number of shading samples will be used to shade the current pixel.

If you look at the default **Contrast Threshold** settings in the Render Globals, you will see that they are:

> **Red** to **0.4;**
>
> **Green** to **0.3;**
>
> **Blue** to **0.6.**

These settings were chosen because they roughly correspond to the human eye's responsiveness to these wavelengths of light. The human eye is very sensitive to changes in green, but not very sensitive to changes in blue.

Shading Samples Override

In cases where there is a particular object that requires a very high number of shading samples, it is possible to override the adaptive shading range set in the Render Globals.

Overriding Shading Samples

- **Select** the object.
- Open the Attribute Editor and go to the **Render Stats** section.
- Turn **ON** the **Shading Samples Override** flag.
- Enter the required **Min** and **Max** shading samples for that object in the Shading Samples and Max Shading Samples fields.
- **Render** the scene.

This is much more efficient in rendering than increasing the shading samples in the Render Globals.

Image Plane Aliasing

If your Image Plane appears aliased, increasing the **global shading samples** will not help. The only way to improve the anti-aliasing of the image planes would be to increase the values of the **shading samples** and **max shading samples** in the Attribute Editor of the Image Plane. If the image of the Image Plane matches the resolution of the rendering, additional anti-aliasing will not be required.

TESSELLATION

Tessellation is the process of approximating a NURBS surface with triangles. Tessellation is a required step because the renderer only knows how to render triangles and volumes, not NURBS surfaces. Tessellation generally applies only to NURBS surfaces, but in the case of displacement mapping, it can also apply to polymeshes.

You need to be aware of tessellation since it determines how smooth an object will look when you start getting close to it. When an object is poorly tessellated and close to the camera it will look faceted (image below on right). If an object in your scene never approaches the camera then you could probably leave the tessellation controls at a lower setting. In the following diagram, there are three images of the same object at different positions. The tessellation settings are the same for each image and you can see that the closer you get, the more it is a factor in the smoothness of your object. If the object never gets any closer then the small image on the left then you can leave the tessellation at its default setting. As it comes closer to the camera, you need to start increasing the amount of tessellation to smooth out the surface. At its closest position, the tessellation controls will need to be set quite high to ensure that the surface is smooth.

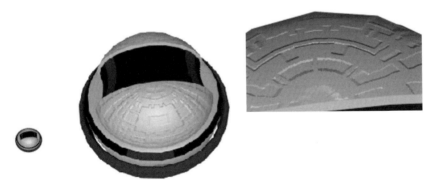

Object approaching camera

In the pre-production phase of a project, the models that will be needed in the scene will be decided upon. Based on storyboards, you will know their positions in the scene and distance to the camera. You need to determine which objects will never get close to the camera and which ones will. Once that information is determined, it is easy to define what the tessellation controls need to be set at. If an object is far from the camera at all times, leave it at the default. If an object is mid-distance to the camera, increase the tessellation slightly. If the object gets very close to the camera, increase the tessellation more. The only way to determine how much tessellation is needed is to do some test renderings. These test renderings can be done very early in the process since tessellation has nothing to do with the material that is assigned to the surface (unless the surface has a displacement map). As soon as an object is modeled you can set the tessellation attributes.

Note: If you are tessellating a surface that will have a displacement map on it, you need to have the displacement map assigned to the surface to determine good tessellation levels.

The next image has the same objects as the previous image but the tessellation has been improved so the surfaces appear nice and smooth.

Improved Tessellation

Tessellation in Maya

Tessellation is dealt with on a per object basis. To access the tessellation controls you need to **Render → Set NURBS Tessellation**.

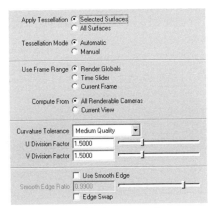

Tessellation controls

If you choose **Automatic**, Maya will evaluate the tessellation based on coverage and distance of the surface from the camera. Because of the manner in which this is evaluated, if the surface or camera is animated, this relationship will change over time. When the surface is closest to the camera, you will require the best tessellation. Maya will compute this for you for a specified frame range set under **Use Frame Range**. The tessellation will be evaluated at each frame, and the tessellation attributes will be adjusted to provide optimal tessellation.

If you choose **Manual**, you can use a number of controls that will allow you to evaluate the best tessellation. There are two levels of tessellation control, the first level is **Basic**.

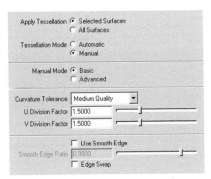

Basic Tessellation controls

This first level of tessellation control is a good starting point in determining the tessellation of your surfaces. It allows you to change the tessellation of your surfaces from a pull-down menu. The first thing you should do is go to the object Attribute Editor and turn on **Display Render Tessellation**. This is an invaluable tool in helping you to determine tessellation. If you are in wireframe mode and turn on this control, it will put you in shaded mode so you will be able to visually see how the surface will be tessellated when it is selected.

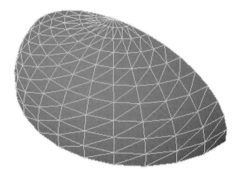

Surface with Display Render Tessellation on

Curvature Tolerance has a pull-down menu that allows you to change tessellation criteria from **No Curvature Check** up to **Highest Quality**. When you are changing these values, the software is actually changing the **Explicit Tessellation Attributes** for you. Maya is trying to give you one menu where you can control a number of different settings that affect tessellation.

The **Curvature Tolerance** setting in the top part of the tessellation section has several settings. These settings correspond to the **primary** and **secondary tessellation** attributes. For the **primary tessellation** Attributes, modes U and V are set to **Per Surf # of Isoparms in 3D**. The **secondary tessellation** attribute that affected by the settings is the **Chord Height Ratio**. They correspond to the following:

- **Curvature Tolerance - Low Quality** = Chord Height Ratio of **0.987**
- **Curvature Tolerance - Medium Quality** = **0.990**
- **Curvature Tolerance - High Quality** = **0.994**
- **Curvature Tolerance - Highest Quality** = **0.995**

U Divisions Factor and **V Divisions Factor** allow you to further increase the surface tessellation. These numbers act as a multiplier on the **Per Surf # of Isoparms in 3D** as per the following equation:

```
Number U/V = U/V Divisions Factor* ((#spans U/V) + 1)
```

where the *#spans* information can be found at the top of the NURBS shape's Attribute Editor.

Turning on Display Render Tessellation

1 Create a NURBS Plane

- Set **2** spans in **U direction** and **2** spans in **V direction**.

2 Turn on Display Render Tessellation

- In the Attribute Editor for the *plane*, open the Tessellation section and set **Display Render Tessellation** to **ON**.

3 Change U and V Divisions Factor

- Set **U Divisions Factor** to **1**.

- Set **V Divisions Factor** to **2**.

  According to the above equation, the surface should have 6 isoparms in the V direction and 3 in the U direction.

  number U = 1 * (2 + 1) = 3

  number V = 2 * (2+1) = 6

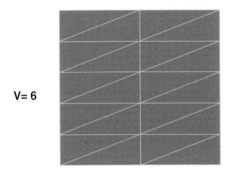

V= 6

U=3
Plane with Display Render Tessellation on

Smooth Edge

Depending on the surface you are tessellating, you will often have sections that are over tessellated. This happens when you are trying to increase the tessellation to improve the smoothness of one area and the control causes another area to be over tessellated. One way to control the tessellation of edges without affecting the surface is to use **Smooth Edge**. It allows you to increase the tessellation along the edge of a surface without having to add extra tessellation over the entire surface. This can help keep tessellation values down for a surface when extra tessellation is only needed along the edge. For example, you might trim a hole out of a plane. When you render the object you might need to use Smooth Edge in order to increase the tessellation along the trim edge. By using Smooth Edge, you avoid having to increase the tessellation for the entire surface. In the following images, the surface is a plane with one corner pulled up. The image on the left has Smooth Edge **OFF** and the image on the right has Smooth Edge **ON**. You can see that along the curved edge there is more tessellation on the image on the right but the flat areas of the surface have the same tessellation.

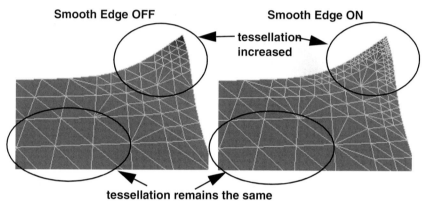

Smooth Edge

The **Smooth Edge** option lets you increase the tessellation quality (number of triangles) only along the boundary of an object (to avoid faceting artifacts along the edges), without incurring the high rendering time cost of increasing the tessellation level uniformly across the entire object.

To control Smooth Edge and how finely it tessellates a boundary, there is an attribute called **Smooth Edge Ratio**. It is a ratio between the length of the tessellated triangle and the curve of the boundary. The closer this value approaches 1, the more triangles will be tessellated along the boundary.

There are some situations when the **Smooth Edge** attribute shouldn't be used. In the following diagram, when Smooth Edge is turned on you will notice some artifacts in the highlights along the curved parts of the surface. What has happened is the surface was tessellated normally everywhere except the edge, where more triangles were used to get a smooth edge. This caused the curvature in the surface to be slightly different closer to the edge.

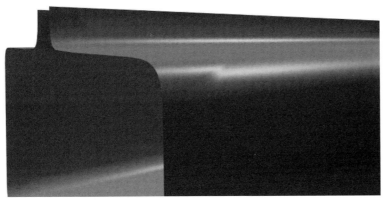

Smooth Edge ON - Causing Artifacts

To correct the above problem, you need to turn Smooth Edge **OFF**, and rely on tessellating the entire surface. This ensures the same number of triangles are used along the entire curved section. This will give you an even highlight.

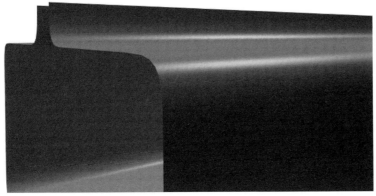

Smooth Edge off with Explicit Tessellation Attributes

Note: When using Smooth Edge, it is important to notice that when you increase tessellation along the edge, it can also increase tessellation further into the surface to prevent cracking and T-junctions within the surface.

Explicit Tessellation Attributes

If you have set **Curvature Tolerance** to it's highest setting and are still not satisfied with the smoothness of your surfaces, then you need to turn **ON** the **Explicit Tessellation Attributes**. The explicit tessellation attributes is broken down into **Primary Tessellation Attributes** and **Secondary Tessellation Attributes**. The primary tessellation attributes describe how the overall surface will be tessellated. There is **Mode U** and **Mode V** which tells Maya how to tessellate the surface. The U and V values represent the U and V parametric dimensions of the NURBS surface. These values can be set differently so you could have different tessellation happening for each direction of your surface.

There are four settings for Mode U and V:

- **Per Surf # of Isoparms** lets you specify the number of isoparms you want to create on your surface, ignoring the surfaces isoparms. This lets you get a sparser number of isoparms on your surface than there are number of spans on your surface.

- **Per Surf # of Isoparms in 3D** also lets you specify the number of isoparms you want on your surface, but attempts to space the isoparms equally in 3D space (as opposed to parametric space). Good for converting NURBS to polygons. This mode produces more evenly distributed triangles than other modes.

- **Per Span # of Isoparms** lets you specify the number of subdivisions that will occur between each span, no matter how large or small. Therefore, very small spans are divided into the same number of subdivisions as very large spans. This is the most common mode. The default setting is 3. The per span settings are important as this can help a lot in avoiding cracks between joined surfaces where the spans match. This is particularly important for character building with multiple surfaces.

- **Best Guess Based on Screen Size** creates a bounding box around the NURBS surface, projects it into screen space, and calculates the number of pixels in the space. Maya uses this number to guess at the per surface # of isoparms. The maximum value is 40. The more screen space the object uses, the higher the number that is set by using this mode. This mode would not be ideal for animation if the camera or the object is moving, since the bounding box would be changing constantly. If the bounding box changes, so does the tessellation and this will cause textures to jitter. You may also experience problems with specular highlights.

Note: Be careful when using Best Guess Based on Screen Size when Display Render Tessellation is on. If you have a complicated NURBS surface it can take some time to update the display.

Secondary Tessellation Attributes give you the best control for fine-tuning the tessellation of your surfaces. The Secondary Tessellation Attributes allow you to have adaptive tessellation. This means you can have more tessellation on a curved part of your surface than the flat parts. There are three options to choose from:

- **Use Chord Height** is the first option and it is a physical measurement based on units. A surface curve will have triangles that will try to approximate the curve. The chord height is the perpendicular distance at the center of a triangle edge to the curve that defines the surface. If the actual distance measured is greater than the Chord Height Value, then the triangle is subdivided again. Once it is subdivided, it will be checked against the same criteria again and if it still doesn't meet the criteria, then it will continue to be subdivided until it does. Since Chord Height is based on a default unit, it doesn't always work well for very small models as the Chord Height Values on a small model will be smaller still.

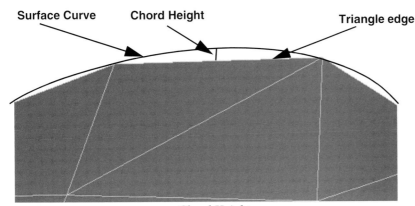

Chord Height

- **Use Chord Height Ratio** is the second option and is the option used by the Curvature Tolerance. It is a ratio based on the chord height divided by the triangle edge length and subtracted from 1.

Chord Height Ratio = 1 - chord height/triangle edge length

If you look at the Chord Height diagram above you can see what the Chord Height is. The triangle edge length is the length of the edge defined by the two points on the triangle that intersect with the surface curve. The default value is 0.983, which means the chord height is very small compared to the triangle edge length. The closer this control is to 1, the tighter the fit of the triangle to the surface.

- **Use Min Screen** is the third option. It bases the tessellation on a minimum screen size (default 14 pixels). All triangles created during tessellation must fit within this screen size. If they don't then they are further subdivided until they do. This option is good for still images with a setting of 11.0 for Min Screen. It will render out nice and smooth surfaces. It is not recommended for animations, because the tessellation will constantly be changing when an object is moving. This will cause textures to jitter or jump, because the shading for a particular pixel will have different tessellations to deal with on each frame. Be careful when Display Render Tessellation is on and you are using Min Screen, as the display can take a few seconds to update.

Note: It is possible in the Secondary Tessellation attributes to turn on more than one option. Do not turn on more than one option as the renderer will go through each option and check the tessellation of the surface. This will cause the renderer to slow down with no gain in visual appearance.

Set NURBS Tessellation Window

The Set NURBS Tessellation window allows for automatic optimization of the NURBS surface tessellation throughout an animation range. This tool runs through the intended frame range and determines what the worst case tessellation requirements are. It then sets all of or just the selected surfaces to receive this optimal tessellation.

This method of tessellation setting is exceptionally powerful for scenes in which the camera is moving and changing distances from NURBS objects. If you dynamically tessellate objects based on camera distance, this can result in nickeling artifacts as tessellation changes from frame to frame. By locking down the tessellation for best (near camera) results, you can also save memory and enhance performance by not "over tessellating".

From the main rendering menu set, select **Render → Set NURBS Tessellation -** ❐.

Tessellation and Displacements

Displacement maps are a special case since the surface does not know how the displacement map will displace it. It is very difficult to effectively detect curvature changes based on the displacement, so a higher initial tessellation is needed. By default, when you add a displacement map to a surface the tessellation is increased by a factor of 6. You should also avoid using the Secondary Tessellation attributes as you want to make sure the surface is evenly tessellated all over for the displacement map.

Note: It is possible that you will have a surface that is hard to smooth out using the tessellation controls. One possibility is to rebuild the surface with more isoparms and use the setting **Per Span # of Isoparms**.

Multipixel Filter

Multipixel filtering blurs or softens the entire rendered image to help eliminate aliasing or jagged edges in rendered images, or roping or flickering in rendered animations. Maya does this by blurring each pixel in Render Diagnostics.

In the render menu, there is a command called **Rendering Diagnostics.** This is a good command to run before you do any rendering as it can help you look at your scene very quickly. When executed, feedback is given in the history section of the Script Editor.

Scene Optimization

To help optimize your scene, there are two commands you can run. In the Hypershade window, select **Edit → Delete Unused Nodes** and from the main Maya window select **File → Optimize Scene Size**. These commands can help optimize the size of your scene by cleaning up unused nodes and other things.

Edit → Delete Unused Nodes will delete any unused nodes in the Hypershade window such as duplicate shading groups that aren't being used, extra placement nodes, extra utility nodes, etc.

File → Optimize Scene Size will clean up the following:

- Invalid NURBS surfaces and curves

- Empty sets, partitions, and transforms

- Unused animation and NURBS curves, cached data, deformers, expressions, group ID, rendering, snapshot, and unit conversion nodes, locators, point constraints, and referenced items

It is recommended that you make a habit of optimizing scene size before you save. Optimizing your scene size before saving can:

- Improve the overall performance of renderers (the improvement can be significant)

- Improve Maya's use of memory
- Reduce unnecessary waste of disk space

Use the following steps to optimize scene size:

1 Optimize Scene

- Select **File → Optimize Scene Size → ⬚**.

    The Optimize Scene Size options window opens.

- **Select** the items you want optimized.

- Click **Optimize**.

2 Save Settings

- Click **Save** in the window to save the settings.

- When you select **File → Optimize Scene Size**, the saved settings are used.

Pre-Render Optimization

There is a command you can run that will create a smaller and more efficient Maya binary file reserved for rendering. By deleting information not relevant to the renderer, the new "leaner" file can help reduce overall memory usage and decrease render times. When the command is invoked, your file is run through **Optimize Scene Size** with all flags checked on, and then additional information is deleted (history, UI settings, datablocks, static actions, and animation caching). BOT files are also created and relinked to existing textures. It is a good idea when using file referencing to **Export All** first, otherwise some optimizations may be missed. The usage for this pre-render setup is straightforward. See the *maya -optimizeRender -help* message for a list of flags to use with this.

Note: You will get optimal results when using BOT files for large resolution textures. When using the *-botRes* flag, you will specify the resolutions that will be relinked with BOT files. If you specified *-botRes 1024*, all textures bigger than 1024x1024 will be relinked to use BOT files.

This script searches for the following scenarios:

- Motion blur limitations
- Output image file format restrictions
- By frame of 0 causing hang

- Fractional by frame requiring modify ext
- No renderable cameras
- Ortho camera rendering artifacts

The following Warnings may be issued:

- No lights warning
- Composite rendering warning

Warnings for the following scenarios which affect performance:

- Suggestion of using 2D motion blur instead of 3D motion blur
- RT warning and RT limits
- High shading sample warning

mental ray for Maya Sampling

Sampling in mental ray for Maya is adaptive, meaning that the algorithm attempts to use the fewest number of samples to achieve the best quality image. mental ray for Maya will only take extra samples or oversample when appropriate to compute high resolution, anti-aliased details. Sampling performance and quality is controlled by the **Sampling Quality** parameters in the mental ray for Maya's Render Globals.

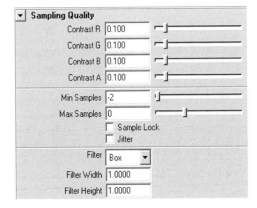

Contrast

Contrast is an important tuning factor. Starting with the minimum level of sampling specified, an image is broken into blocks and sampled at their corners. The resulting samples are then compared with neighboring blocks. If the contrast between the sampled blocks is higher than the RGBA threshold values, further subdivisions are made. The process is repeated until either the contrast between each block is lower than the threshold values or the maximum sampling value has been reached.

For best results, in terms of render time, use the high threshold values with lowest possible sampling levels. The default values for RGBA are 0.1. Most usable values are in the range of 0.2 and 0.05. The A (alpha) value is an average of the R, G, and B contrast values. If alpha is not necessary, it's recommended to set that value to 1.0.

Time Contrast

Time Contrast controls temporal contrast. This is similar to contrast but is used solely with moving geometry's motion blur.

Note: Motion blur may need a higher sampling limit.

Samples

Control the Minimum amount of samples that will be taken as well as the Maximum. If the sample limit is less than 0, there will be fewer samples taken than there are pixels. This is called **infrasampling** and is useful because of *edge following*. If the sample limit is greater than 0, there are more samples taken than there are pixels. This is called **oversampling** and occurs on an adaptive basis based on the minimum and maximum sampling value.

The sampling limits are specified in powers of 2. The sampling levels determine the size of the blocks:

- -2: block will contain 4x4 pixels with 1 sample
- -1: block will contain 2x2 pixels with 1 sample
- 0: block will contain 1 pixel with 1 sample
- 1: pixel will contain 4 blocks with 1 sample for each block
- 2: pixel will contain 16 blocks with 1 sample for each block

The useful sample limit range lies between -3 and 4. Typical Sample Values:

- -2, 0: low quality preview render
- -1, 1: medium quality render
- 0, 2: high quality render
- 0, 3: highest quality render

Jitter

Jitter slightly randomizes sample points which alters underlying sample point clustering. This can be used to reduce regular sampling artifacts such as **Mach** banding without having to increase sample rates. Jitter is more effective with raytracing.

Note:	If aliasing occurs, lower the contrast threshold values before increasing the sample limits. Lowering these threshold values will cause more samples to be taken in the problem areas while the rest of the image will be sampled at the lower rate. Sometimes values below 0.05 will be necessary to avoid artifacts. If this doesn't help, add jitter before increasing sample rates.

Filters

Once block samples are calculated, they are combined into pixels using a filter. Large filter sizes tend to blur the image and can slightly increase render times.

Tessellation in mental ray for Maya

In mental ray for Maya, **Approximation Nodes** are used to control how finely the renderer tessellates surfaces into triangles for rendering.

Approximation nodes can be used to specify separate tessellation settings for surfaces, trim curves, and displacement maps. The different kinds of approximation nodes give users control over all aspects of the tessellation process, allowing them to produce tessellations that capture the important aspects of their surfaces without over-tessellating and slowing down the renderer. For example, consider a simple flat NURBS surface with a complex trim curve. For such a case, users would specify a low-quality surface approximation in conjunction with a high-quality trim curve approximation. mental ray would then ensure that the surface is approximated with only a few triangles except around the trim curves, where many triangles would be used to ensure a smooth edge.

The same analogy applies to a simple surface with a complex displacement map. For that case, users might apply a low-quality regular surface approximation in conjunction with a high-quality displacement approximation, to ensure that triangles are added only to areas where they are needed to capture the complexity of the displacement map.

Note:	Currently, there is no equivalent to Maya's Display Render Tessellation in mental ray for Maya. Also, you cannot assign approximation nodes when multiple pieces of geometry are selected.

The Approximation Editor

The **Approximation Editor** provides users with the ability to create approximation nodes which can be assigned to geometry on a per object basis. Approximation nodes contain information on how that surface will be tessellated at render time. Depending on the surface topology, certain geometry may require various forms of tessellation.

The Approximation Editor is found under **Windows** → **Rendering Editors** → **mental ray** → **Approximation Editor.** The default approximation settings in the editor are *DeriveFromMaya*.

mental ray for Maya's Approximation Editor

- **Surface Approximation** calculates the tessellation of a NURBS surface.

- **Trim Curve Approximation** calculates the tessellation of a trimmed NURBS surface.

- **Displacement Approximation** calculates the tessellation of a NURBS or POLY surface that is influenced by displacement maps. If the Displacement Approximation is set to **DeriveFromMaya**, mental ray for Maya will use the **Fine** setting and triangles will be placed only in areas where they are needed. If a Displacement Approximation is created with the Fine tessellation method, the user will have access to the Fine attributes enabling greater control.

- **Subdivision Approximation** controls render time smoothing of polymesh surfaces.

Note:	The Subdivision Approximation feature is available if the mental matter™ library is loaded. Please see the Maya documentation for details.

With a surface selected, the 3 options to the right of the editor become active.

- **Create** will generate a new approximation node. Any geometry that is selected will use this approximation node.

- **Assign** will assign a new approximation node from the drop-down options to the selected geometry. Assigning an approximation node to a surface is done automatically at creation time.

- **Edit** will open the Attribute Editor for the selected approximation node.

Approximation Presets

The **Presets** drop-down menu provides some useful tessellation settings. Selecting an entry from this list will load the preset values for the approximation node's attributes. These settings can be used as is, or taken as useful starting points for tweaking.

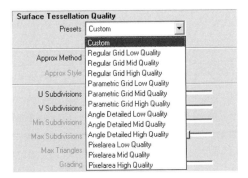

- **Regular Grid** means the user has control over all approximation attributes. This is the default.

- **Parametric Grid** subdivides each patch (area between an isoparm) into a fixed number of triangles. Use this when triangles are distributed roughly according to the spacing of isoparms on the surface, with closer isoparms producing a higher number of triangles (this setting is good for patch models).

- **Regular Grid** subdivides the surface as a whole into a fixed number of triangles. This method will ensure even triangulation over a surface even if the spacing of the isoparms is uneven.

- **Angle Detailed** is an adaptive form of tessellation where more triangles are placed in areas of high curvature. This method is good for capturing sharp features, while still using as few triangles as possible to describe a large, flat area.

- **Pixel Area** tessellates surfaces based on their size (in pixels) in the final rendered image. Surfaces that are close to the camera will receive more triangles, whereas surfaces that are further away will receive fewer.

Approximation Methods

The **Approximation Methods** drop-down menu determines the criteria the tessellator uses for determining when to subdivide a part of the surface. Some methods will place a fixed number of triangles evenly over a surface, while others are more adaptive and place triangles over a surface where needed based on a set condition.

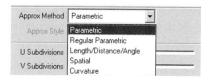

- **Parametric** subdivides a surface based on U and V. Each patch is subdivided into N triangles, where:

  ```
  N = (U Subdivisions) * (V Subdivisions) * degree^2 * 2
  ```

  Thus, with U Subdivisions set to 1.333 and V Subdivisions set to 4 on a degree-3 NURBS surface, each patch will be subdivided into 1.333*4*3*3*2 = 96 triangles.

- **Regular Parametric** also subdivides a surface based on U and V except when the entire surface is subdivided into N triangles, where:

  ```
  N = (U Subdivisions) * (V Subdivisions)
  ```

  Unlike the Parametric method, which tessellates each patch independently, the number of triangles will be constant over the entire surface.

- **Length/Distance/Angle** are adaptive, which means the surface is tessellated until certain criteria are met. The 3 criteria are:

  Length which means that a triangle is subdivided until no triangle has an edge longer than a certain length. If **View Dependent** is **ON**, the value is specified in pixels.

Distance will subdivide triangles until they are not further than a certain distance from the NURBS surface. If **View Dependent** is **ON**, the distance is expressed in pixels.

Angle will subdivide until the normals of neighboring triangles form an angle of less than a certain tolerance. Small values can cause the number of triangles to increase. A recommended value is 45-degrees. 0 is ignored by the tessellator.

The **Any Satisfied** flag will determine when subdivision stops. It will stop when any one of the criteria is satisfied (i.e. triangles are smaller than a certain size **OR** distance from the surface is less than a certain amount).

- **Spatial** is the same as the **Length** criteria as described above.

- **Curvature** is the same as the **Distance** and **Angle** criteria as mentioned above. This method is included for backwards compatibility only.

Approximation Styles

The **Approximation Style** drop-down menu determines the general framework that the tessellator uses to subdivide the surface into triangles.

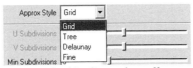

- **Grid** works on a grid of isolines that allows subdivisions by adding more isolines. This produces regular triangle meshes which can sometimes contain more triangles than necessary.

- **Tree** uses a hierarchical subdivision style that allows local subdivisions without affecting other areas.

- **Delaunay** attempts to maximize triangle compactness and avoid thin triangles. This style is supported only for NURBS surfaces. The "Max Triangles" and "Grading" attributes can be used to fine-tune tessellations using the Delaunay style.

- **Fine** subdivides surfaces into a large number of uniformly-sized small triangles in order to guarantee a smooth result. To deal with the large amount of triangles, mental ray for Maya breaks the surface up into independent sub-objects that are each tessellated and cached separately. This allows the tessellator to generate a large number of triangles without a huge memory cost.

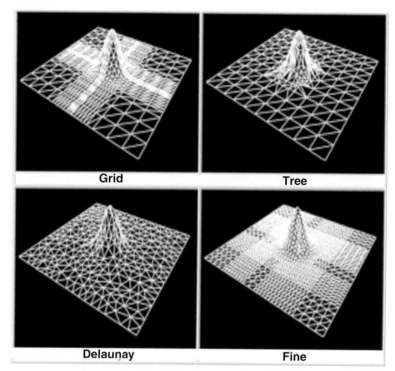

Approximation Styles in mental ray for Maya

U, V Subdivisions

These values are used by Parametric and Regular Parametric methods. They specify how many times each patch (Parametric) or surface (Regular Parametric) will be subdivided in the U and V directions.

Min, Max Subdivisions

When using the Length/Distance/Angle method, these attributes can control the minimum and maximum number of times that triangles are subdivided. You can get good results with a maximum value as low as 3. As a rule of thumb, each subdivision level can increase the triangle count by a factor of 4. Therefore, raising the maximum subdivisions from 3 to 4 can produce 4 times as many triangles.

Grading

Setting this value to non-zero enables a more smooth transition from the surface's interior triangle density to its edges. Values less than 20 are recommended.

Sharp

Will use the surface normal to create the impression of a sharp edge (Sharp = 1) or a rounder edge (Sharp = 0). Use a high value when trying to capture sharp details in a displacement.

SUMMARY

When everything else is completed in a scene and you are ready to render, you need to be aware of how to control the render. This means paying attention to image quality, memory requirements, and render times.

This chapter covered the following topics:

- Maya's Anti-aliasing
- Tessellation and How to Control it
- Render Diagnostics
- mental ray for Maya's Sample Quality
- mental ray for Maya's Approximation Editor

8 SFX and Compositing

Once you have modeled, textured, and added lights to your scene, there are a number of effects you can add to enhance the quality of your render.

In this chapter, you will learn the following:

- How to control Maya's Light Glow and Shader Glow
- What to expect with Maya's Motion Blur
- mental ray for Maya's Motion blur
- Rendering for Compositing

LIGHT EFFECTS IN MAYA

Maya's OpticalFX lets you add glows, halos, and lens flares to Point and Spot Lights which can be used to create explosions, rocket thrusters, and other special effects. Maya also has Shader Glow which can be used to create lava, neon lights, etc. When using Light Glow or Shader Glow, the following factors can dramatically affect the results:

- Image resolution
- Anti-aliasing quality

Image Resolution

Light Glow and **Shader Glow** are post-processes in Maya. This means that they are calculated and added after the image is rendered. The amount of glow you see is affected by the total number of glowing pixels so the size of the rendered image will affect the look of the glows. For this reason, it is essential to render glow tests at the final resolution that you will be rendering to.

Note: In keeping with the above information, when using Render Region or IPR, you will not see an accurate preview of your glows.

Anti-Aliasing Quality

Along the same lines, changing the anti-aliasing quality settings will also affect the results when rendering glow. This may make it necessary at times to do final render tests at the quality level of the final output renders.

Light Glow

In the real world, when light shines directly into an observer's eye or into a camera's lens, the light source may appear to glow. If the light passes through a mesh (for example, a star filter on a camera) or through hair or eyelashes, the light will refract, producing a star-like glow. In some cases, the light may reflect off the surfaces of a camera's compound lens and produce a lens flare. These are all examples of optical light effects.

When lights appear to glow, it is purely a retinal effect in the eye. To see this, look up at a light source such as a street light and squint. You will see a glow around the light. Now use your finger to block only the light source; the glow disappears. Notice also that if you cover only part of the light source, the glow is still visible and will in fact appear in front of your finger. Maya's Light Glow simulates this real world effect and the effect of blocking the light source is called **occlusion**.

Controlling Light Glow Occlusion

The most common issue that comes up when working with Light Glow in Maya is the need to control the **Light Source Occlusion**. Often people will animate the position of objects that pass in front of glowing lights and will find that the glow shows right through the objects. This is because the light needs you to specify how big or small the light source actually is in order to know when it is completely covered by an object.

1 Create a Light Glow

- Open a Point Light's Attribute Editor.

- In the **Light effects** section, click on the **Map** button beside the **Light Glow**.

  Maya automatically creates an optical FX node, connects it to the light node, and displays the Attribute Editor.

  In the modeling view, you will notice that a new icon has appeared surrounding the light.

2 Set the size of the Light Source

Now that you have created a glow effect, you need to consider how you want this glow to behave. Recall that the Light Glow is only going to shut off completely if the entire light source is occluded. If the light is going to pass behind an object, the size of this sphereShape icon relative to the size of the object will determine whether you see the glow though the object or not.

- **Select** the Light Glow icon in the modeling view.

  Notice that a new tab appears in the Attribute Editor called **sphereShape**.

- Click on the *sphereShape* tab in the Attribute Editor.

- Select **Render Sphere Attributes** → **Radius**.

- Use this **Radius** attribute to adjust the size of the icon in the modeling view.

Note: Adjusting this Radius attribute will not affect the appearance of the Light Glow. It is only used to determine occlusion.

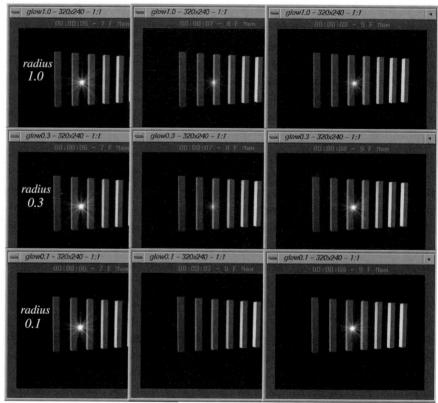

Comparison of radius values of 1.0, 0.3, and 0.1

In the images shown above, a glowing Point Light moves from left to right behind the columns. In the middle images, the glow is partially dimmed with a radius of 1.0, increasingly dimmed with a radius of 0.3, and fully occluded with a radius of 0.1.

Tip: There is an attribute on the opticalFX node called **Ignore Light**. Turning this **ON** means that the Light Glow visibility (*sphereShape*) is ignored. So if your Light Glow is completely blocked by another object between your camera eye and the Light Glow, Light Glow will still be at full intensity. If Ignore Light is **OFF**, that completely-blocked scenario will show no glow.

Shader Glow

How to correct flickering Shader Glow

Glow from one object can affect the intensity of another object's glow. For example, a large glowing object that enters a frame may appear to cancel the effect of, or alter, the glow of a smaller object in the frame. This phenomenon is caused by the Shader Glow's Auto Exposure control.

In order to control the scene's Shader Glow and prevent flickering as an object enters or leaves the frame, follow the procedure below.

1 Set the Glow and Halo Intensities

- Make sure the **Automatic Exposure** control is turned **ON** in the Shader Glow's Attribute Editor (this is the default setting).

- Select a frame in which the glow and halo effects have the look you want.

- **Render** the scene into a new window.

2 Manually set the values

During the render, the glow and halo intensity normalization factors are printed in the output window. They are displayed at the bottom of the text. The first value represents the glow normalization and the second represents the halo:

```
intensity normalization factor = 0.0110171

intensity normalization factor = 0.0243521
```

- Enter these glow and halo intensity normalization factors in the **Glow Intensity** and **Halo Intensity** attributes in the Glow and Halo attributes sections of the Shader Glow Attribute Editor.

3 Turn off Auto Exposure

- Turn **OFF** the **Auto Exposure** in the Shader Glow Attribute Editor.

- **Render** the scene again.

Adding Shader Glow

Note: Remember that tweaking Shader Glow intensity on a material can require a great deal of effort because one glowing surface can affect the look of another glowing surface. Also note that all Shader Glow in a scene is controlled by a single Shader Glow node in the Hypershade window under the Materials tab.

Creating glowing engine cores

The engine cores inside the engines of the spaceJet are simple cylinders mapped with a Lambert shader.

1 Create a Material Node

- **Create** a **Lambert** material and assign it to the *cylinder*.

- Map a **Checker** texture to the **Incandescence** channel. Adjust the *place2DTexture* **Repeat U** to **1.0** and **Repeat V** to **8.0**.

- Set the **Color** to **Black** and the **Diffuse** to **0.0**.

  When using Shader Glow, the lighting on the surface can influence the result of the Shader Glow. Incandescence is independent of lighting so this will allow you to control the Shader Glow more easily.

2 Add a Glow Effect

- In the Attribute Editor for the Lambert material, open the **Special Effects** section and set **Hide Source** to **ON**.

  The Hide Source attribute will allow you to render the Shader Glow without the geometry. For the engine cores, this gives a far more interesting result, as shown below.

- Adjust the glow intensity as required. Remember that a render region will not give the same results as a full image render.

Shader Glow using Hide Source for engine cores

Creating Neon Effect

Neon tubes are the quintessential Shader Glow example. Try this to create a realistic pink neon effect.

- **Create** a **Surface Shader** material and assign to an object.
- Set the **Out Color** attribute to a bubble-gum pink.
- Set the **Out Glow Color** to a dark burgundy.

  Notice how you are able to set the glow color.

With other material types, there is no attribute to control the Shader Glow color. It is derived from the glow color on the Shader Glow node and the color of the material. With this Surface Shader material it is possible to experiment with different combinations of glow color and surface color. Also, because the Surface Shader has no sense of a shading model, it renders as though it is self illuminating - perfect for neon tubes, L.E.D. displays, etc.

DEPTH OF FIELD

Image rendered with Depth of field

Focus Distance 8, F Stop 11, Focus Distance Scale 1.0

1 Setting up the camera for Depth of Field

- Select **Windows** → **General Editors** → **Connection Editor**.

- Open the Hypershade and locate the icon for the camera you are using to render.
- **Drag** this camera icon into both sides of the **Connection Editor**.
- Connect the **Center of Interest** to the **Focus Distance**.

    This allows you to position the **Center of Interest** using the camera's manipulators to designate the point in the scene that you want to be in sharp focus.

- Set the **Camera Manipulators** to **ON** and place the **Center of Interest** to the location you want to remain in focus.

Tip:	Another alternate but equally useful workflow in setting up Depth of Field is to use the **Distance** tool. This can be found under **Create → Measure Tools → Distance Tool**. This will allow you to measure the distance between the camera and the point in your scene that you want to use as the Focus Distance.

2 Turning on Depth of Field

- In the Attribute Editor for the camera, open the **Depth of Field** section.
- Set the **Depth of Field** flag to **ON**.
- Adjust the **F stop** to control the amount of depth of field.

    The F stop value represents the distance in front of and behind the Focus Distance that will remain in focus. A low value will represent a short distance that will be in focus; a very high value F stop will result in very little blur because there will be a deeper range that is in focus. In essence, the lower the F stop value, the smaller the region in focus will be.

Tip:	It is possible to use Render Region to test render depth of field.

Limitations of Depth of Field

Transparent surfaces can cause problems with depth of field. The technical reason for this limitation is that the transparent surface is at a certain depth from the camera. Maya only stores one depth per pixel, and it chooses to store the nearest point to the eye. For transparent surfaces, the depth of the transparent surface will determine the blur, so the background will show through, un-blurred. The background, when seen through the transparent object, will be blurred at the same depth as the transparent surface. This limitation is not limited to Maya and has led to the industry accepted practice of rendering components separately and compositing.

Environment Fog cannot be used with Depth of Field at this time. The environment fog is a volume that Maya evaluates from the near clipping plane to the far clipping plane. For this reason, all of the depth samples will be at the near clipping plane and the resulting image will be completely blurry at all times.

MOTION BLUR

In Maya, there are two different types of motion blur: **2D** and **3D**. Both will simulate how a real camera works if some objects are moving while the camera's shutter is still open. This technique is very common in the entertainment industry to create photorealistic images and animation involving quick motions.

Understanding the Shutter Angle attribute

Whether using 2D or 3D motion blur, it is important to understand the shutter angle. The motion blur algorithm uses a **shutter open**, **shutter mid**, and **shutter close** sample for every frame to determine the change in position of a given triangle.

Note: Triangle refers to a tessellation triangle on a surface.

The shutter angle that you specify for motion blur will determine the amount of blur that results according to the following:

- Take the Shutter angle value and divide it by 360 (degrees). You will get a decimal value. For example, the default is 144. 144/360 = 0.4.

- 0.4 represents the interval in time between the shutter open and shutter close samples. Shutter mid is always the frame time itself. For example, for motion blur at frame 1, shutter open would be at frame 0.8 and shutter closed would be at frame 1.2.

- From frame 0.8 to frame 1.2 = 0.4.

By this, you can see that a shutter angle of 360 degrees would give shutter open and close samples that are exactly one frame apart, i.e. 360/360= 1.

You will notice that by setting the shutter angle to 360, the amount of motion blur increases. This is because the longer the shutter is open (i.e. the further apart the shutter open and shutter close samples are taken), the blurrier a moving object will appear to be.

Setting the Shutter Angle

- Open the Attribute Editor for the camera.
- Open the **Special Effects** section.
- Adjust the **Shutter Angle** attribute.

2D vs. 3D Motion Blur

The decision to use 3D or 2D motion blur is really a matter of determining which one is more appropriate for a given scene and the time available to render the animation.

3D motion blur is usually slower and memory intensive. However, there will be times where 3D motion blur is required due to some limitations of 2D blur. In general, it is recommended that you try to use 2D motion blur because it is very fast and produces excellent results in most cases.

All of the motion blur attributes, other than Shutter Angle, are found in the Render Globals under the **Motion Blur** section. If it is desirable for motion blur to be off for some objects, open the Attribute Editor for those objects and toggle **OFF** the motion blur in the Render Stats section. The following are some examples that compare the results of 3D vs. 2D motion blur.

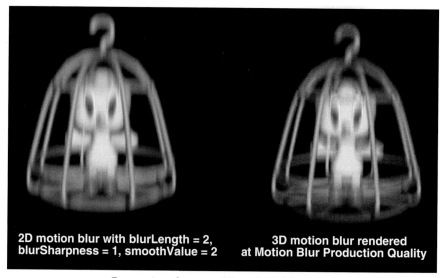

2D motion blur with blurLength = 2, blurSharpness = 1, smoothValue = 2   **3D motion blur rendered at Motion Blur Production Quality**

Comparison between 2D and 3D Motion Blur

Also note the difference in rendering time for the above images. The 2D motion blur image took 5 minutes to render and generate the motion vector file and 12 seconds to do the blur or redo the blur, while the 3D motion blur image took 30 minutes to render.

Tip:	The motion vector files can be used by other programs to generate blur.

Limitations of 2D Motion Blur

The 2D Motion Blur does not work well in these situations:

- **Moving transparent objects with a background**
  The background will also be blurred in this case. The solution is to blur the transparent object separately and composite with the rest of the scene.

- **Detailed background behind moving objects**
  Some details might be lost since Maya has to make assumptions on the background area occluded by the moving objects. The solution is to blur the moving objects without the background and then composite the results.

- **Rotating objects**
  The following image shows a case where the 2D motion blur breaks down with rotation.

The birdcage is falling vertically and rotating from back to front around the vertical axis. The motion vector thinks the movement is from side to side because it does not know about the points in between the position of the pixel at the back and the position at the front.

- **Objects entering from outside the image or leaving the image**
  Maya does not know the object color outside of the image and has to make assumptions. The solution is to render a slightly larger image which covers the original image and then crop it to the desired size.

- **Volume objects (particles, fog) and Image Planes**
  Motion vectors are only calculated for moving triangles (tessellated results for NURB surfaces and poly meshes).

Note: The rendered results from 3D and 2D are quite different. It is not a good idea to mix the rendered images from these two different kinds of blurring operations.

MENTAL RAY FOR MAYA MOTION BLUR

In mental ray for Maya, there are also two different types of motion blur: **Linear (transformation)** and **Exact (deformation)**. Motion blur in mental ray for Maya will blur everything: shaders, textures, lights, shadows, reflections, refractions, and Caustics. It is important to note that motion blur in mental ray for Maya is calculated as forward only. The Shutter Angle in Maya determines the blur path length, but this can be adjusted by the mental ray for Maya motion blur attributes in the Render Globals.

To turn on motion blur in mental ray for Maya, you will need to go to the mental ray for Maya Render Globals and open up the Motion Blur section and select an option from the Calculation drop-down menu.

Blurred shadows and reflections using mental ray for Maya

Linear vs. Exact Motion Blur

Like Maya's motion blur, the decision to use Linear or Exact motion blur depends on the type of motion of your object's as well as the time available to render the animation. Linear motion blur is faster to calculate than Exact motion blur.

Linear motion blur only takes into account an object's transformation, rotation, and scale. The object's deformation will not be considered. For example, if you have Blend Shapes or a skeleton that deforms a piece of geometry, the resulting motion wouldn't be considered when calculating this type of motion blur.

Exact takes into account all the transformations as well as the object's deformations. This type of blur is more expensive to render than linear.

Note: Turning off an object's blur in its Render Stats will NOT turn off motion blur for that object. You will have to render those objects without blur as a separate pass and then composite afterwards.

Editing mental ray for Maya Motion Blur

Shutter represents the length of time the camera's shutter is open. The longer a shutter is open, the more blurry an object will be. However, unlike a real camera, the shutter value does not affect the brightness of an image. If the shutter is set to 0, there will be no motion blur. Larger values increase the length of the blur.

Shutter Delay represents the normalized time that a shutter remains closed before opening. For instance, if the shutter delay is set to 0, the shutter opens at the beginning of the frame. If the shutter delay is set to .5, then it opens halfway through the frame.

Note: If the Shutter Delay is set to 1, it is expected that the frame will render black as this implies that the shutter doesn't open. However, mental ray for Maya will simply render without any blur.

There are 4 separate controls for **Time Contrast: Red, Green, Blue, and Alpha.** If you find that your motion blur is grainy, you can smooth it by decreasing your time contrast values. The lower the time contrast values, the greater your render times.

Note: When adjusting the quality of motion blur, be sure to adjust the **Time Contrast** attributes in the **Motion Blur** section rather than the **Contrast** attributes in the **Sampling Quality** tab.

Depth of Field

Depth of field in mental ray for Maya is set up the same way as in Maya. This is not a post-process effect in mental ray for Maya, but true depth of field.

Reasons to Render for Compositing

Compositing is the process of merging multiple layers of image information into one image to create a final look. A common misconception is that compositing is for large productions with many artists. However, smaller production facilities and individual artists can also benefit from the opportunities and advantages offered by compositing. For example, with compositing you can:

- Have the flexibility to re-render or color correct individual elements without having to re-render the whole scene.

- Increase creative potential and achieve effects with the 2D compositing package that are not possible with the renderer, such as blurred reflections or shadows.

- Take advantage of effects which are faster and more flexible in 2D such as depth of field and glow rather than rendering them in 3D.

- Combine different looks from different renderers such as hardware and software particle effects.

- Combine 3D rendered elements with 2D live action footage.

- Save time when rendering scenes where the camera does not move; you only need to render one frame of the background to be used behind the whole animation sequence.

- Successfully render large complex scenes in layers so that you don't exceed your hardware and software memory capabilities.

Setting up a render for Compositing

Rendering in layers refers to the process of separating scene elements so that different objects or sets of objects can be rendered as separate images. The first step is to determine how to divide the scene into layers. This may be very simple or incredibly complex and will depend entirely on your needs for any given project. Once you have decided how you want to separate your scene elements, there are several workflow approaches you can use to render them separately.

Rendering with Render Layers

Another approach to separating your scene elements is to use **Render Layers**. You can assign objects to Render layers using the same workflow as you would when working with Display layers.

The Render layers allow you to organize the objects in your scene specifically to meet your rendering needs. The most basic approach might be to separate objects into foreground, midground, and background layers. Or, you may decide to divide the scene elements by specific objects (or sets of objects) such as the Helmet, Liner, and Goggles shown below.

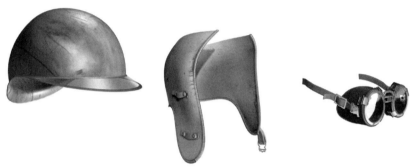

Objects rendered as separate images.

If you need to have very precise control over the color of your rendered objects separate from the shadows on them, you can further break down your shot by rendering separate passes within any Render layer. The term Render "passes" generally refers to the process of rendering various attributes separately such as color, shadows, specular highlights, etc. The Render Layers spreadsheet in Render Globals allows you to set this up. The following images show the objects rendered in two passes: Color and Shadow.

Note: The shadow pass renders the shadows on the object, not the shadows cast by the object onto other surfaces.

Color and Shadow rendered as separate Render Passes.

You can also further break up the color pass elements to **diffuse** and **specular**.

The role of the Alpha channel

When rendering objects for compositing, one of the most important requirements is an **alpha channel**. The alpha channel, sometimes called a **mask** or **matte**, contains information about the coverage and opacity of objects in an image. This information is later used by the compositing application to combine the images.

The images below show the RGB channel and the alpha channel for each object. You can see that where the helmet's visor is semi-transparent, the alpha channel is gray and where the goggles' lenses are fully transparent, the alpha is black. The opaque regions of the objects are white in the alpha channel.

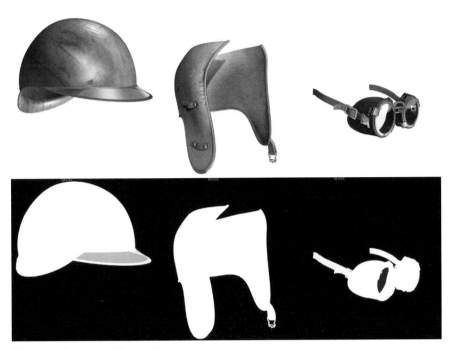

Using Matte Opacity

There are many cases where compositing the separate elements of even a simple scene can be tricky and can require careful planning. The following image depicts the compositing phase where the three separately rendered objects would be layered together. A problem exists where, for example, the back of the helmet will show in front of the liner. This is because the alpha channel does not contain any information about what part of what object goes in front or behind other objects. For this reason, the compositing application doesn't know which part of which object goes in front or behind the other objects.

Maya's **Matte Opacity** feature provides one way to resolve this dilemma.

Note: In some cases, it is also possible to affect the alpha channels later in the compositing application to allow images to composite correctly. A third possible approach is to render the images with a depth channel for use in compositing packages with depth compositing capabilities. However, there are limitations to depth compositing techniques so it is a good idea to learn these other methods as well.

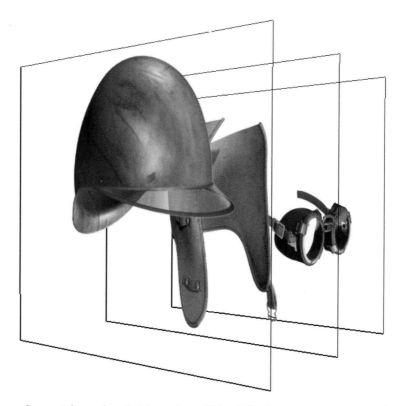

Separately rendered objects that will be difficult to composite correctly.

To ensure that the helmet, liner, and goggles will composite properly, you can use an attribute called **Matte Opacity** found in the Attribute Editor for all materials. This allows you to manipulate the rendered alpha value on a per-material basis.

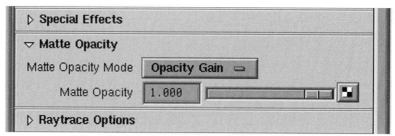

Matte Opacity found in Materials' Attribute Editor

The **Matte Opacity** feature has three modes:

Black Hole

To solve this particular compositing problem, the **Black Hole** mode is useful. This mode will set the RGBA values to exactly (0,0,0,0) resulting in images with cutout regions that allow the objects to fit together correctly. The diagram below shows how the images would fit together.

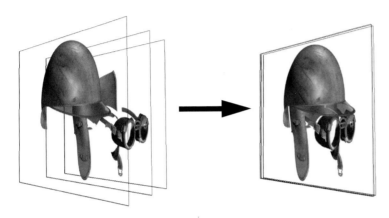

Black Hole used to knock out parts of the objects

Opacity Gain

This is the default mode for Matte Opacity. Alpha values are calculated in the normal way then multiplied by the Matte Opacity value. Because the Matte Opacity attribute has a default value of 1.0, the rendered alpha values remain unchanged (1.0 * x = x). However, you can adjust the Matte Opacity value to achieve the following effects:

- Animate the Matte Opacity value from 0-1 or vice versa to create fade-in or fade-out effects when composited.

- Texture map the Matte Opacity attribute to create interesting compositing effects, especially if you use an animated texture or sequence of images.

Solid Matte

When Matte Opacity is in Solid Matte mode, the normally calculated alpha values are ignored in favor of the Matte Opacity setting. The entire matte for the object is set to the value of the Matte Opacity attribute. This can be useful if you need an object to have a specific alpha value. For example, if you have a transparent object, the normal alpha value calculated by the renderer will be 0. Solid Matte can be used to set a non-zero value for the alpha on the transparent object. If you were rendering a view through a window and wanted to composite this into another scene, setting the Matte Opacity value to 1.0 (in Solid Matte mode) on the window's material would help you achieve this.

Note: Opacity Gain and Solid Matte modes will not change the RGB component of your image. They will only change the alpha value generated by the shader.

Altering the mattes in the compositing application

Depending on what effects will be used at the compositing stage, it is sometimes important to render the whole object rather than having parts cut away with black hole. This gives you greater flexibility for effects such as blur, or overcoming moire patterns on edges. Under these circumstances, you would need to use some techniques in the compositing application in order to composite the elements correctly. This can involve manipulating a combination of the alpha values themselves or creating custom masks to reveal/conceal objects as they are layered together.

Rendering Shadows and Reflections separately

Maya also provides a way to create custom reflection and shadow passes. You may need to do this, for example, if you want to blur the reflections or shadows or adjust the shadow color in a compositing package.

Setting this up involves the **Use Background Shader** which acts as a shadow and/or reflection catcher. In the images below, a ground plane under the goggles has a Use Background shader assigned and the Primary Visibility is turned off for the goggles.

Below is an image rendered normally:

Normal render - No Use Background shader - Shadows and reflections visible

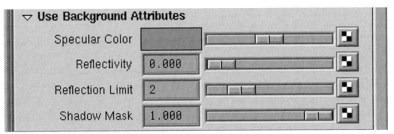

Use Background Attributes

To Render only the Reflections

- **Assign** a **Use Background Shader** to the ground plane.

  The ground plane is the reflection-catching object in this case.

- Turn **OFF** the **Primary Visibility** on all objects other than the ground plane. The easiest way to do this for multiple objects is to use **Window → General Editors → Attribute Spread Sheet**...

  This will ensure that the goggles are not visible but they will still show up in the reflections on the ground plane.

- Turn **OFF** shadows temporarily.

  If you are working with **Depth Map Shadows** on multiple lights, the easiest way to turn them off temporarily is to go to the **Render Options** section of Render Globals. Turn the **Enable Depth Maps** flag off. If you are working with **Raytraced** shadows, you can set the **Shadows** to **0** in the **Raytracing Quality** section of Render Globals.

- In the **Use Background Shader** Attribute Editor, set the **Reflectivity** to the desired value between **0** and **1**.

  This value should be set to the same value as the Reflectivity on the original material assigned to the ground plane.

- **Render** the scene.

This rendered reflection pass shows the reflections in the RGB channels and a white mask in the alpha channel. In some cases, the alpha channel would not be used in the final composite because reflections are normally added to the background image. However, if the background image is a light or white color, adding the reflections will not be visible; in this case, the alpha is needed.

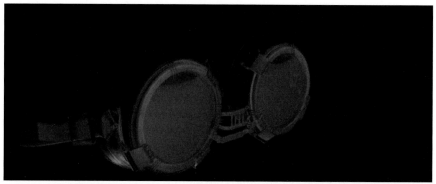

Use Background Shader - RGB channels showing reflections only

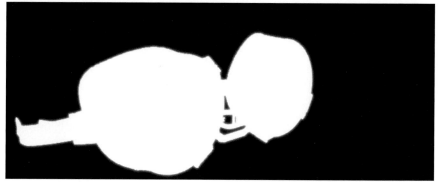

Use Background Shader - alpha channels showing reflections mask

To render only shadows

- **Assign** a **Use Background Shader** to the ground plane.

  The ground plane is the shadow-catching object in this case.

- In the Attribute Editor for the Use Background Shader, make sure the **Shadow Mask** is set to **1.0**.

- Turn **OFF** the **Primary Visibility** for all objects other than the ground plane.

- Set the **Reflection Limit** to **0** on the Use Background Shader.

  This will ensure that no reflections are visible in the rendered results. If you are not raytracing shadows, you can simply turn off raytracing altogether.

Composite Rendering

If you find yourself in a situation where you are rendering an object over a background that is any color other than completely black (0,0,0), you should set **Composite Rendering** to **ON** in the Render Globals under the Render Options section.

What this feature does is prevent the edges of geometry from being anti-aliased against the background color. For this reason, the RGB component of the image will look badly aliased. However, the mask channel is perfectly anti-aliased. The **mask channel** is what is used to blend the rendered element into the background of choice at the compositing stage. Because the composite rendering flag prevented the edges from including any of the rendering background color, you will not get an unsightly rim showing in the rendering background color after compositing.

Composite Threshold is mainly a games feature. This is a normalized [0,1] alpha threshold; the foreground is registered only if the alpha value is above the Composite Threshold.

Use Background Shader

You can also use the Use Background Shader to make 3D geometry look like it is part of a real image. For example, placing a model of a car over a background shot of a road in the desert. To do this, you would follow these steps:

- **Open** the scene with the 3D model of the car.

- **Create** an **Image Plane** with the image of the road.

- Model a surface that approximately matches the perspective and shape of the road (stand-in object).

- **Assign** a **Use Background Shader** to the road geometry.

  This will make the stand-in geometry disappear seamlessly into the background image.

- Place the *car* model on the *road* geometry.

- Turn **ON** shadows for the **lights** shining on the *car*.

- **Render** the scene and the stand-in geometry will receive shadows, creating the illusion that the car model is actually part of the image.

Tip: The same approach can be used to make a 2D image on an Image Plane look like it is part of a 3D scene. Use the same technique of modeling stand-in geometry. Assign a Use Background shader to the stand-ins. With the stand-in geometry casting shadows and raytraced reflections of other geometry in the 3D scene, it is very convincing.

Camera Projection

The Use Background technique described above reaches its limit in a case where, for example, you decide you want to be able to animate something that is getting its color from part of a 2D Image Plane. This might be a case of making a dog talk or a cat's eyes bulge wide open where the dog and the cat exist in a live shot behind stand-in geometry. In this case, you can use a **Camera Projection** method of texture mapping to project the 2D image onto the stand-in geometry (instead of using an Image Plane). Then you would do a **Convert Solid Texture** to create parametric texture maps on the surfaces. Once this is done, you would be able to animate the stand-in geometry. Once the geometry is rendered, it will be composited over the original live footage and voila! You have a talking dog.

SUMMARY

Adding effects enhances a scene's quality and produces some interesting results. Compositing involves rendering a scene in separate components which will later be composited together. In this chapter, you have learned the following:

- How to control Maya's Light Glow and Shader Glow

- How to add Depth of Field

- What to expect with Maya's Motion Blur

- mental ray for Maya's Motion Blur

- When to Render for Compositing

- Using a Background Shader

Hardware Rendering

Maya's new Hardware Renderer is used to create high quality bitmap images. These images are created using the hardware features of the graphics card. In previous versions of Maya, this method was mostly used to create a low quality preview of the animation or to output hardware rendered particles. Because modern graphics cards support advanced render features, a new Hardware Renderer has been introduced with Maya 5. The new Hardware Renderer delivers superior image quality.

Barrow image using hardware renderer

In this chapter, you will learn the following topics:

- Hardware renderer basics
- How to adjust and optimize the hardware renderer output

Hardware Rendering

The term hardware rendering is known from computer games or applications for real-time visualization. When people talk about hardware rendering they usually mean a real-time display of geometry and textures for interactive use. In this case, the graphics card displays the objects in the computer's screen but it is not captured for later reuse.

In Maya, the Hardware Renderer is used to create bitmap images. It uses the power of modern graphics cards to create images using the hardware features of the graphics card, rather than using the computer's processor to compute images. Using this method has the potential to be much faster than software rendering due to its inherit parallel architecture.

In previous versions of Maya, this method was mostly used to create a low quality preview of the animation or to output hardware rendered particles. Modern graphics cards now support more advanced features. The Hardware Renderer can take advantage of this to deliver a much better quality than could be achieved in the past.

There are two ways of doing a hardware render: using the Hardware Render Buffer or the Hardware Renderer. Both methods use the speed of the graphics cards to create bitmap images. The biggest difference is the quality of the resulting images. The Hardware Renderer delivers a much better quality then the Hardware Render Buffer.

If you select the Hardware Renderer, you can output features like shadows, per-pixel specular highlights, bump maps, and reflections for materials. Also, the quality of particles is much better than with the Hardware Render Buffer. For a full list of supported Hardware Render features, check the documentation of the current release.

In addition to the better quality output, the new Hardware Renderer gives you another workflow advantage - it can output images in batch mode. This means you can create images in the background (or offline) and work parallel in Maya or other applications to continue other work. This is not possible with the Hardware Render Buffer. There, everything which is displayed in the framebuffer is part of the resulting image. This means if you render and work in a another application or a screensaver starts, this content is visible in the stored image. So, if you work with the Hardware Render Buffer your workstation is locked, but with the Hardware Renderer it's not.

How to control the Hardware Renderer

The speed and quality of the hardware rendered image is scene dependent. When starting the Hardware Renderer for the first time, you may detect a period of time were the Hardware Renderer seems to do nothing. The reason for this is that the Hardware Renderer must translate the scene into a data structure which is optimized for the graphics hardware. This is done in software by the CPU and includes the translation of geometry into a format optimized for drawing, the loading of File textures, and the evaluation and baking of shading networks, if necessary. The data is cached for subsequent frames, provided it has not changed, and is the reason why the first frame may take longer than the other frames to compute.

You can control image quality and optimize your scene by doing the following:

- For the best control use Lambert and Phong materials. Using other shading models will work, but Lambert and Phong are the best to control because their appearance in the Hardware Renderer is closest to the appearance in the Software Render. Note that this won't actually speed things up but rather make tweaking easier.

- Model with polygons or tessellate NURBS manually using the **Modify → Convert → NURBS to Polygons** command. If you don't like to do this manually, keep in mind that the Hardware Renderer uses the same tessellation settings as for the Software Renderer. You can check and optimize the settings in the Attribute Editor of the object's shape node. Further details about this process are available in the chapter "Controlling Renders".

- Take care about the UV mapping of your polygon. In some cases, you may detect a poor quality for the specular highlight. A reason for this can be the UV space mapping. Try to avoid thin triangles or triangles which cover a small UV area. These things don't necessarily speed things up, but will impact image quality. Note, however, that UV coordinates are required if the surface is going to have a texture map (unlike software rendering). If UV coordinates are not specified, the hardware renderer will create some on the fly for the purposes of specular highlights and bump mapping. It will take some time to compute this, although it's usually quite small. For more details about UV mapping, see the chapter "Texturing Polygons".

- Bake your textures using the **Edit → Convert to File Texture** command in the Panel menu of the Hypershade or the **Lighting/ Shading → Batch Bake** command in the Render menu. This gives you better control about the quality of a baked 3D texture.

Another important thing to check is which graphic cards are installed in your computer. Check out the qualification charts on the Alias I Wavefront home page to see which card is supported and which driver is recommended. This has significant impact to the final image quality and rendering speed. New video card drivers are released frequently and we encourage you to upgrade to the latest qualified A I W driver. We have constant contact with the hardware vendors, and we are pushing them for better performance and stability.

Render Globals

Control of the renderer's settings is another important step to get a good image quality within a short render time. To achieve this, as with any other renderer in Maya, open the Render Globals and switch to Maya Hardware. Now you see two sections in the Maya Hardware tab, Quality and Render Options, where you can have global control about your scene.

Quality settings

- **Enable Edge Anti-Aliasing**: The Number of Samples attribute only has effect if this option is turned on. If it's turned off, the rendered pixel is only sampled once.

- **Number of Samples**: Defines the number of samples per pixel. This attribute influences the render time dramatically. The higher the value, the better the Anti-aliasing, but the longer it takes to calculate.

- **Transparency sorting**: This attribute defines two different ways to detect and draw transparent objects.

- **Per object**: Objects are sorted from furthest to closest in depth to the camera. The objects bounding box is used to determine its position related to the camera position. If an object has different shaders assigned to it, each part of the object gets its own bounding box with respect to the assigned shader. This option provides faster results but may not render complex transparent objects correctly because each object's polygons are drawn in arbitrary order. However, in most cases this option, gives you a proper result.

- **Per polygon**: Each object's polygons are sorted and drawn from furthest to closest in distance from the camera. This option provides more accurate transparency representation, but takes longer to process. Only use this option if Per object delivers incorrect results.

- Color Texture Resolution: The Hardware Renderer automatically bakes 3D textures into 2D textures. This process is comparable to the Hypershade command **Edit → Convert to File Texture**, but processed automatically. The baked channels may include color, diffuse, bump, incandescence, specular color, cosine power, and ambient color.

Render Options

- **Culling**: This option controls how the rendered polygon is rendered, dependent on its normal direction to the camera.

- **Per object**: The setting in the Render Stats section of each individual object is used by the Hardware Renderer. (You find the RenderStats section in the Attribute Editor of each object's shape node).

- **All Double-sided**: Both sides of the polygons in the scene are rendered. This is a global effect.

- **All Single-sided**: Only polygons which normals are facing to the camera are rendered. This is a global effect.

- **Enable Motion Blur**: The Hardware Renderer supports MotionBlur if this option is on. If you render particles with motion blur, it is recommended to create a particle disk cache for proper calculation and to bake simulations before rendering. Failure to do so will result in incorrect particle positions. Motion blur requires the scene to be evaluated both forward and backwards in time; if there is no disk cache for dynamics, the image will be rendered with the wrong particle positions when the scene is evaluated backwards in time.

- **Motion Blur by Frame**: The Hardware Renderer calculates the motion blur by evaluating the object at different positions and blending them. With the Motion Blur by Frame option, you can modify the start and end point of the motion blur calculation. This attribute is related to Number of Exposures and the Shutter Angle attribute in the Camera Attribute Editor.

- **Number of Exposures**: This attribute defines how many samples are calculated to create a smooth motion blur. It divides the given time range into specific frames. The final image is the accumulated average of all the exposures.

Exercise

In this exercise, you will learn some methods to manipulate the output settings and the general look of your hardware rendering.

1 Changing the output filename

- Load the file *barrow_HW.mb*.

- Go to the **RenderGlobals** window and change the option **Render Using** to Maya Hardware. In the Common tab, you see in the pull-down menu of the Frame/Animation Ext only one choice available: *name#.ext*.

If you type a new name in the attribute File Name Prefix, you can check at the top of the window how the name will change. If you need a dot between the name and the number, simply type the dot into the Frame/Animation Ext text field.

Note: If you need to mask geometry for later compositing, you need to set a hidden attribute. Go to the Script Editor and type: *setAttr "hardwareRenderGlobals.enableGeometryMask" true.* This is a global attribute, it affects all objects in the scene. Keep in mind that if objects are transparent, they will be ignored as geometry mask, which means they will not show up in the resulting image. To disable geometry masking, type: *setAttr "hardwareRenderGlobals.enableGeometryMask" false.*

---

2 Light Linking

- Enable the attribute **Use Depth Map Shadow** in the Attribute Editor of the *mainLight*.

You will notify that all objects in the scene cast shadows, including the particles. To avoid this, break the light link for the particles. Pick the light and the particle objects and select **Render → Lighting/Shading → Break Light Link**.

By default, particles cast shadows. In this scene, the fire casts a shadow.

3 Performing a batch command

To render an animation, define the frame range in the **Render Globals** as usual. Now you can start a batch render from the Render menu. (**Render** → **Batch Render**).

To batch render outside Maya, you have to run Maya from the command window. The command is:

maya -prompt -proj myproject -file myfile -command hwRender

In this case, you can type:

maya -prompt -file barrow_PAL.mb -command hwRender

If you need to specify additional options, such as frame range, use the setAttr command to set attributes on the hardware Render Globals node before running the hwRender command. Multiple commands can be specified in the -command flag by enclosing the commands in quotes and separating the individual commands by semicolons.

4 Rendering with motion blur

- Open the scene *podCrash_hardware.mb*.

This scene contains an animation including particles. If you render frame 78 of the scene, you may notice that the motion blur looks incorrect. For the speed of motion, there are not enough numbers of exposures set for this scene. You can increase the number of samples, but this will slow down rendering. Set the attribute Number of Exposures with care, try first with low numbers like 4 - 6. Another way is reducing the length of the motion blur. You can do this in the Camera by decreasing the Shutter Angle or in the Render Globals by lowering the value for Blur by Frame. A value of 0.2 in this scene gives you a better look for the motion blur.

Default settings for motion blur. Artifacting is noticeable.

Blur by Frame set to 0.2. Less artifacting.

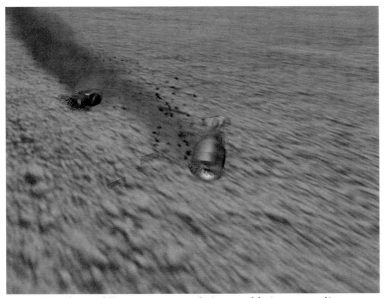

Numbers of Exposures set to 6. Acceptable image quality.

5 Caching particles

If you like to render with motion blur and your scene contains particles, it can be necessary to create a particle cache before rendering the entire scene. To do so go to **Dynamics** → **Solvers** → **Create Particle Disk Cache**. It is a good idea to cache one frame before and one frame after the animation. The reason is, when calculating frame 1 with motion blur, e.g frame 0.8 is used to calculate an exposure at this point.

10 Vector Rendering

BITMAP FORMAT VS. VECTOR FORMAT

In computer graphics, you can differ between two principal concepts of storing graphic elements: **Bitmap images** and **Vector images**. Both techniques have advantages and disadvantages and are used for different needs.

Bitmap Images

Bitmap images are mainly used to display photographs or computer generated photorealistic images. A bitmap image has two main attributes that define its quality: the resolution and the number of bits per pixel. The resolution is defined by the number of pixels in the X- and Y-directions. The number of bits per pixel defines how much information can be stored per pixel. Both attributes together define the file size of an image. The advantage of bitmaps is their ability to carry the necessary information to display photorealistic content. The biggest disadvantage is that the resolution directly affects image quality. Scaling a bitmap image always impacts the image quality. Another potential problem is that high quality bitmaps need a lot of disk space and memory. These drawbacks limit the use of bitmaps.

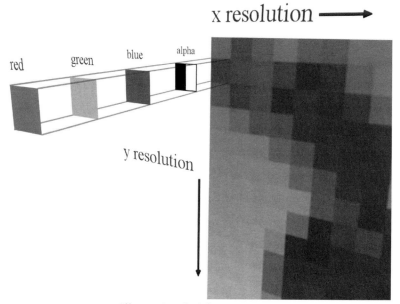

Illustration 1: A bitmap image

The most common type of image format output by a renderer like the Maya Renderer or mental ray, is 32-bit (24 bits for the color information (red, green, blue) and 8 bits for the alpha channel (rgba)). This means you have 24 bits of color information per pixel = 2 to the exponent 24 = 16,777,216 colors. The alpha channel contains an additional 8 bits of information that are used for compositing.

Vector Images

Vector images deal with curves and closed shapes which can be filled with solid colors or color ramps. A vector graphic is described by two color properties: **outline** and **fill**. These two properties are a mathematical description for the shape and color. Because of this, the main advantage of a vector image is that its quality is independent of the resolution. That means you can scale a vector graphic to any size you like without losing detail and quality. Also, vector graphic formats don't take up as much disk space as bitmap images.

Vector graphic formats are mainly used for print publishing, especially diagrams, logos, and typography. Web vector formats are also very common because they have a relatively small file size and are scalable. Also, the individual elements can be easily animated and used for interaction with the user. The disadvantage is that it is hard to get realistic results with a vector graphic.

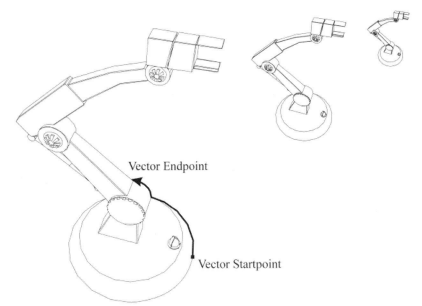

Vector Endpoint

Vector Startpoint

Illustration 2: A scaled vector graphic

This image shows a vector graphic in three different scales. The arrow indicates one vector which describes an outline. For this illustration, the original output from the Maya Vector Renderer was imported in a vector graphics software. The look of the line, which means the square at the Startpoint and the arrow at the Endpoint, was modified later.

Why Vector Rendering?

In 3D computer graphics, bitmap images are mainly used as textures. In previous versions, Maya only output bitmap images. With Version 5, it is possible to output the most common vector formats in addition to the existing bitmap formats. This expands the value of Maya for people working in the print and web publishing industry.

Maya's Vector Renderer is based on RAViX® Technology (Rapid Visibility Extension). This technology detects the lines and vertices that make up a 3D model and converts 3D models into 2D vector-based imagery. Because of this, animated objects like menus and characters can now easily be done in Maya. All of this animation can now be rendered in a Vector format and later reused and edited in software packages like Macromedia Flash® MX or Adobe Illustrator®.

To have best control about the Vector Renderer, it is recommended to work with polygonal objects. However, you're not limited to polygons as NURBS and Subdivision Surfaces are supported as well.

The Vector Renderer supports the most common vector formats: Macromedia Flash (.swf), Encapsulated Postscript (.eps), Adobe Illustrator (.ai), and Scalable Vector Graphics SVG (.svg).

You can use software like Flash MX, GoLive, Freehand, Illustrator, or CorelDraw to open and edit these formats.

Additional to the vector formats, the Vector Renderer outputs a bitmap version of the vector graphic in different bitmap formats. These formats are Alias Pix (.pix), Cineon (.cin), GIF (.gif), JPEG (.jpg), Maya (.iff), Quantel (.yuv), RLA (.rla), SGI (.sgi), Softimage (.pic), TGA (.tga), TIF (.tif), and Windows Bitmap (.bmp). With these image formats, you can create nonrealistic effects and compose them with your software or hardware generated renderings.

The Vector Renderer is not designed to create a vectorized copy of the software rendering. Because of this, the Vector doesn't support all features that are available with a traditional renderer like the Maya Render or mental ray. For a full list of unsupported features, check the online documentation of the actual release you're working with.

RENDER GLOBALS

This chapter describes the options in the Render Globals window and their impact on the output image. It is important to understand the attributes because they have the most impact to render time, file size, and the image quality. In addition to that, you find in the online docs some common methods for reducing the file size of the final image.

Open the Render Globals and under Render Using select Maya Vector from the pull-down menu. If you don't see this option then you'll need to go to your **Windows → Settings/Preferences → Plug-in Manager** and load *VectorRender.mll*.

Image Format Options tab (swf)

Under the Common tab in the Image File Output section, notice the default Image Format is Macromedia SWF format. If you choose the Maya Vector tab, you'll get attributes that relate to this format.

Frame Rate

The frame rate measured in frames per second.

Flash Version

The version of the rendered Flash Player file.

Open in Browser

If enabled, the vector image or animation is displayed in your default browser after it is rendered. In the Maya Render View window, you see a bitmap version of the vector image. The Browser gives you information about the image name and location, the file size, and the time it took for rendering.

Combine Fills and Edges

When Combine Fills and Edges is **ON**, outlines and fills for a surface are a single object. When Combine Fills and Edges is **OFF**, outlines and fills for a surface are separate objects. The size of the rendered file is smaller when Combine Fills and Edges is off.

This option can usually remain deselected. The optimization of the file size typically happens in Flash. Inside Flash, it is more important to have easy access to all parts of the vector graphics. This flag really only includes fills and outlines. If you add Highlights and Reflections, these effects are treated as separate objects in Flash.

Image Format Options section (svg)

Frame Rate

The frame rate measured in frames per second.

Svg Animation

If Svg Animation is **Native**, Maya creates one SVG file containing the frames of your animation and the scripting that drives it. If Svg Animation is **Script**, Maya creates an SVG file containing the frames of your animation and an HTML file containing the JavaScript that drives it.

If your animation is long, file size increases when Svg Animation is **Native**.

Compress (SVG only)

Only use this option if you plan to publish the rendered SVG file directly to the web. If you plan to import the SVG file into another application like GoLive or Illustrator, the Compress attribute must be disabled, because you can't edit a compressed SVG file.

Appearance Options section

Curve Tolerance

A value from **0** to **10** determines how object outlines are represented. When Curve Tolerance is **0**, object outlines are drawn by a series of straight line segments (one segment for each polygon edge). This produces an outline that exactly matches the outline of polygons, but also produces larger file sizes.

When Curve Tolerance is **10**, object outlines are represented by curved lines. This produces an outline that may appear slightly distorted compared to the original object's outline, but also produces smaller file sizes.

Detail Level Preset

Predefined settings for the Detail Level Attribute.

Detail Level

Determines the level of detail in the rendered image. A High Detail Level produces a more detailed image and a more accurate render than a Low Detail Level, but takes longer to render and increases file size.

A value of **0** sets Detail Level to Automatic to allow Maya to choose the appropriate level of detail for your scene.

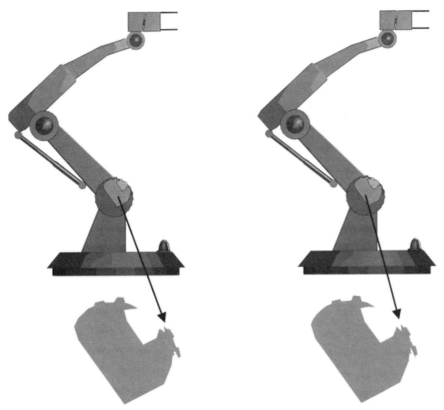

Illustration 3: Detail level comparison

With a higher Detail Level, the Vector Renderer generates more edit points for the single objects. The best way to see this is to open Adobe Illustrator or CorelDraw and the file *robot_compare.ai* provided in the support files.

The left robot was rendered with a curve tolerance of **7.5** and a Detail Level of **10**. The file size is 81.7 KB. The right robot was rendered with a curve tolerance of 7.5 and a Detail Level of **50**. The file size is 124.64 KB. The extracted part shows some additional details in specific areas, but the influence to the overall look for this object is not so dramatic. So, in this example, there is no benefit when using a higher setting for the Detail Level.

Fill Options section

The choice to use the Fill Object attribute has a main impact to the file size, as well as the render time. Keep in mind that if you really need a photorealistic rendering, a bitmap format is the better choice.

All fill styles, except Single Color, respond to Point Lights and get the final color from the Color attribute in the assigned material of the object. All other light types and most of the material attributes are ignored by the Vector Renderer. If your scene does not contain Point Lights, a default Point Light is automatically created which is located at the camera and will be deleted after rendering. There is no Enable Default Light attribute available in the Render Globals Common tab if the Vector Renderer is selected. Also, Light Linking and all attributes (except Primary Visibility) in the Render Stats section of the object's shape node are ignored by the Vector Renderer.

In the following description of the attributes, the terms face, surface and triangle are used. Face is used to describe a polygonal face. Surface represents a single NURBS surface. The term triangle is used to describe the triangulated version of a polygonal face or a NURBS surface.

Single Color

If single color is selected, the fill color behaves similarly to Maya's Surface Shader. The objects appear flat shaded and independent from lighting. They get the color from the Color attribute of the assigned shader. Internally, an Ambient Light is calculated to shade the surfaces, so the final color may vary slightly from the material Color attribute.

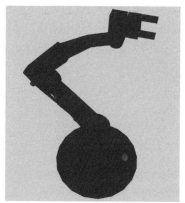

Illustration 4: The robot with a Single Color fill

Two Colors

This attribute uses two solid colors to achieve a shaded, 3D-like look on the surface. This doesn't mean that the final image only contains two tones of a color. An object with a blue material can have various tones of blue, depending on the view angle and the lighting.

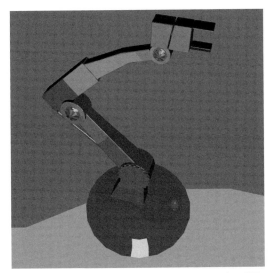

Illustration 5: The robot with a Two Color fill

Four Colors

Works like the attribute Two Colors, but uses four solid colors to shade a surface.

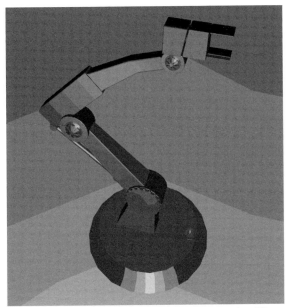

Illustration 6: The robot with a Four Color fill

Full Color

Shades each triangle with a solid color. You can achieve a similar look when using **Shading** → **Flat Shading All** in the panel menu of the perspective view. This option creates a huge file size and takes a long time to render because the color must be calculated for each triangle. This means that the tessellation for NURBS objects is also taken into account.

Illustration 7: The robot with a Full Color fill

Average Color

When selecting Average Color, each face and surface is shaded with one solid color. The definition of a face is driven by the smoothing angle between them. By making edges hard with the **Edit Polygon** → **Normals** → **Soften/ Harden** command, you can influence the look of the shaded object.

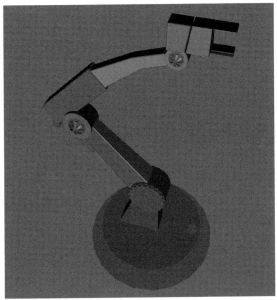

Illustration 8: The robot with an Average Color fill

SWF and SVG options

These attributes are only available if SWF or SVG as the output format is selected.

Area Gradient

This attribute fills each face and surface with one radial gradient. This attribute can create a nice 3D effect with a small increase of the file size. Flat faces and surfaces get a more even fill, smooth surfaces and faces a gradient fill.

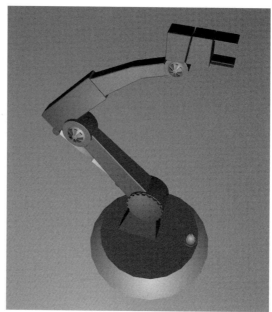

Illustration 9: The robot with an Area Gradient Color fill

Mesh Gradient

This is the most expensive option available in this section and creates the biggest files. However, it gives you a vectorized look which is the closest to a regular software rendering.

It fills each triangle with a linear gradient based on the material color and the lighting. The look is comparable to Gouraud shading without respect to the highlights. A similar look can be achieved inside Maya when selecting **Shading → Smooth Shade All** from the panel menu in the perspective view.

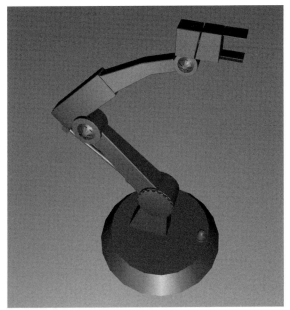

Illustration 10: The robot with a Mesh Gradient Color fill

Show Back Faces

If this option is enabled, the Vector Renderer also renders faces whose normals are facing away from the camera. This option is equivalent to the attribute **Double sided** in the Render Stats section of the object's shape node. Disabling this attribute reduces the file size in some cases.

SWF options

The next three options are only available when Macromedia SWF, or a bitmap format, is the selected output format. Different from the other Maya renderers, these three options have a global influence to the scene. As mentioned above, the Render Stats in the Attribute Editor are ignored. You can only control the shadows, highlights, and reflections for the whole scene, not on a per object basis.

If you render with these attributes enabled, each feature appears as one part in the vector graphic. If you import it into FlashMX, you will get the whole image on one layer. But, each part is separate and you can select it as one piece, making it easier to apply each "feature" to one layer.

Shadows

If selected, it enables all objects to cast and receive shadows. Both Dmap and raytrace shadows will work. When raytraced shadows are used, the

Light Radius attribute in the Lights Attribute Editor is also ignored. Only shadow-casting Point Lights are rendered.

There are two other restrictions when rendering shadows with the Vector Renderer - Transparent objects cannot receive shadows and the shadow color is ignored.

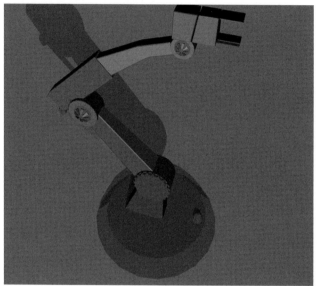

Illustration 11: The robot with an Average Color fill and a shadow

Highlights

This option is only available when Fill Style is Single Color, Average Color, or Area Gradient. With this attribute, a highlight is calculated. The highlight appears as a number of concentric solid color regions. The number of rings is driven by the Highlight Level attribute. The highlight is a separate, semi-transparent layer which lies above the fill and edges. Therefore, objects appear brighter than without the highlights.

The following material attributes influence the look of the highlight:

AnisotropicRoughness;

BlinnEccentricity;

PhongCosine Power;

PhongERoughness.

If the specular color is mapped with a texture, the materials default color is used to compute the color of the highlight.

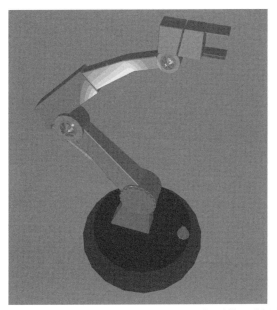

Illustration 12: The robot with an Average Color fill and highlights

Reflections

This attribute enables the Vector Renderer to render reflections. If you select this option, all objects show up in Reflections. The attribute Reflection Depth controls how often a reflection is "traced". This attribute is comparable to the Reflection Depth attribute in the material.

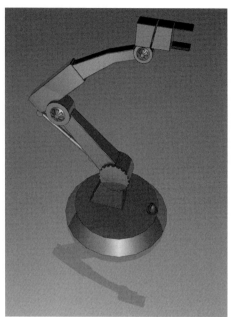

Illustration 13: The robot with a Mesh Gradient fill and reflections

Edge Options section

Enable this option to render your objects with an outline.

Edge Weight

This option lets you control the thickness of the outline. It is measured in points. If you render to a vector format, you can modify the line thickness later in software like Macromedia Flash or Adobe Illustrator. The option Edge Weight Presets provides you with some presets.

Edge Color

The overall color of the outline is controlled by the attribute Edge Color.

Edge Style

Edge Style controls the placement of the outline. If it's set to **Outline**, the object's contour is rendered as an outline. If it's set to **Entire Mesh**, the object's triangulation is vectorized.

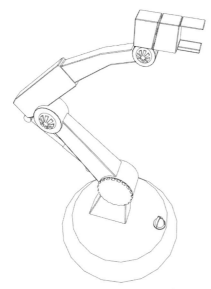

Illustration 14: The robot with Edge Style set to outlines

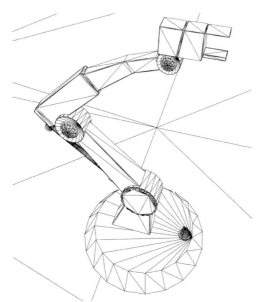

*Illustration 15: The robot with Edge Style set to Entire Mesh. This displays a
triangulated version of the polygon.*

Edge Detail

If this option is enabled, sharp edges between polygon edges are rendered as outline. The **Min Edge Angle** attribute acts as a threshold and gives you a global control where a line is drawn in the inside of the object. It decides at which angle an edge is drawn or not. The appearance of a line is also influenced by the smoothing angle. This means you can force the renderer to add and delete lines with the **Polygon → Normals → Soften/Harden** command. This workflow allows a local control and works for single parts of an object.

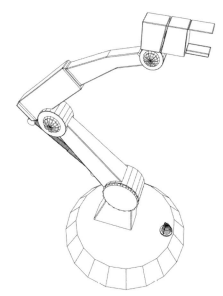

Illustration 16: The robot with Edge Style set to outlines and Edge Detail on. This shows the original polygonal faces. The distribution of the inner lines can be modified by setting soft/hard edges and the attribute Min Edge Angle.

Hidden Edge

If this option is enabled, the Vector Renderer displays all edges. This gives a wireframe-like look.

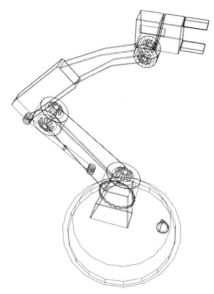

Illustration 17: The robot with Edge Style set to Hidden Edge

Render Layer

Objects on different Render Layers are rendered to different files. To compose them, these files can be imported in the Vector Graphics software. Shadows and reflections don't interact between objects on different render layers.

EXERCISE: CHARACTER OUTLINE

In the first exercise, you practice the use of the Vector Renderer. The goal is to get a nice distribution of outlines. Thanks to cybersign (*www.cybersign.de*) for the model of the peperoni character.

1   Open the file called start_peperoni.mb

This file contains a scene with a character. Select the Maya Vector Renderer. Go to the Maya Vector tab and make sure **Fill Object** is disabled and **Include Edge** is enabled. If you render the scene, you will see the peperoni character as an outline. The distribution of the outlines is odd; the face especially looks strange. The goal is to get the contour of the character and some specific lines "inside" the character.

Illustration 18: The default rendering of the peperoni character

2 Apply Soft/Hard edges to the model

You can easily change the distribution of the outline. Select the character and go to the **Edit Polygon** → **Normals** → **Soften/Harden**. If you use the default settings for the **Soften/Harden** command, the rendering looks like Illustration 19.

Illustration 19: The command Soften/Harden applies new values for the edge smoothing. If you render the scene with these values, the character looks similar to this.

3 Globally modify the look with the Min Edge Angle attribute

You can now enable the **Edge Detail** attribute. Play with the value for **Min Edge Angle** to get a feeling for what's going on. Decreasing the value will add more lines at the inner parts of the model. This gives you global control of the line distribution.

4 Get rid of the inner lines

For local control, do the following: Select the character and in the Channel Box under Inputs select *polySoftEdge1*. Enter a value of **180** for the attribute **Angle** in the polysmooth node of the character. This forces Maya to smooth all edges. If you go now to the Render Globals window and enter a value of **90** in the attribute **Min Edge Angle**, all the inner edges are gone. Now, only the outlines and hard edges of the polygon are displayed.

Illustration 20: If you apply a value of 180 for the Angle attribute in the polySmooth node and a value of 90 for the Min Edge Angle attribute, the rendering should look like this.

5 Modify locally the look by adding manually hard edges

Now you can use the **Soften/Harden** command for more local control.

Set the **Angle** attribute to **0**. Select a specific row of edges and apply the **Edit Polygon → Normals → Soften/Harden** command again. Make sure that the value for the **Angle** attribute is now **0**. In this example, a row of edges in the eye is selected to get more detail there.

Illustration 21: This row of edges is selected and modified to make it hard

Illustration 22: The resulting output should look like this

6 Fine-tune your scene

Now, you can proceed with the other edges until the look of the
rendering fits your needs. Keep in mind that you can delete the
construction history without losing the information of the hard edges. If
you like to smooth your low polygon model, make sure that the
attribute Keep Hard Edges in the option box of the Smooth and Smooth
Proxy command is enabled, to keep your work after smoothing.

EXERCISE: WORKING WITH FILLS

1 Open the scene start_robot.mb

In this scene, you find a simple poly model. Try out the different looks when using the Fill Objects attribute in the Vector Render Globals. You will see that Average Color gives you quite a good 3D impression of the object in vector format, combined with a moderate render time. Also, the file size is not too big.

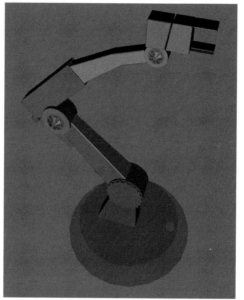

*Illustration 23: With Average Color chosen,
the resulting output should look like this*

2 Modify the bottom part

The upper parts of the robot give a good 3D impression. A problem appears at the bottom of the robot. The cylinder-like shape of the object looks too flat. To change this, you have to proceed similarly to step 5 of the previous example. Select two edges that are facing the camera and **Edit Polygons → Normals → Soften/Harden**. This is enough to indicate to the Vector Renderer that the bottom should be treated as a separate part of the object.

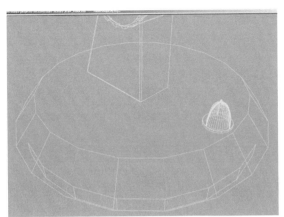

Illustration 24: Selecting these two edges and making them hard changes the look of the bottom part

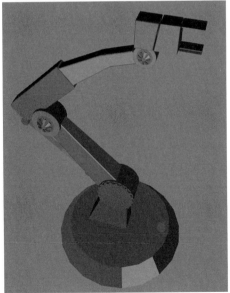

Illustration 25: The resulting image after modifying the bottom

3 Apply reflection and shadows

If you choose to render with reflections, highlight, and shadows, it can be useful to put each "pass" on a different layer for better control inside Flash MX. Using Maya's (SW) Render Layers doesn't give you this effect, because the Vector Renderer doesn't support different passes like color pass, specular pass, shadow pass, and reflection pass. There is another easy way to achieve this effect in Flash MX. Simply render the scene as one file and load it into Flash MX. You will see only one layer in the layer bar. Now select all objects and choose **Modify → Distribute to Layers**. After this, you will find new layers in the layer bar. Each single layer contains the fill, outline, shadows, and reflection pass.

Illustration 26: If you open the file robot_reflection_shadow.swf in Flash MX you see only one layer

EXAMPLE: WORKING WITH RENDER LAYERS

Open the file start_pepProps.mb

In this file you find the peperoni character and some props. In Maya's Layer Editor, switch to Render Layers and create two layers, one for the character and one for the props. Assign the objects to the Render Layer. If you like to work with shadows and reflections, keep in mind that these features are only calculated for objects on the same layer.

Then, open the Vector Render Render Globals window and turn **Enable Render Layer** on. You see a list of all layers where you can finally decide to render or not to render a single layer. Maya outputs each layer in a specific vector file. This happens only if you select **Render → Batch Render**. Hitting the **Render** button in the Render View window has no effect on the Render Layer output.

If you disable the *defaultRenderLayer* in the Render Globals, the **Render** button in the Render View window is disabled.

Using the command line vector render

If you finish your work and finally want to render your scene, you can do this without the Maya GUI. Open a DOS window and type:

```
mayaVectorRender -help
```

This shows you the options that are available with this command. To render a scene, move in the command prompt to the folder with your Maya scene, then type:

```
mayaVectorRender yourfilename
```

This starts the batch renderer in batch mode. In the command prompt, you can read information about the render time, output location, etc. The command takes the settings that are saved with your Maya scene.

11 Caustics & Global Illumination

Direct illumination occurs when a light source directly illuminates an object or objects in a scene. Indirect illumination occurs if light illuminates objects by reflection or transmission by other objects. Global Illumination is the technique used to describe Indirect illumination and Indirect illumination includes effects such as Caustics.

Caustics are light patterns formed by focused light. They are created when light from a source illuminates a diffuse surface via one or more specular reflections or transmissions. Examples of Caustic effects include the "hot spots" seen on surfaces when light is focused through a refractive glass or reflected off metal, or the patterns created on the bottom of a swimming pool from light shining through the water.

Global Illumination and Caustics cannot be simulated efficiently using standard raytracing methods. To overcome this problem, mental ray uses a mechanism based on Photon Maps. Light is emitted from the source in the form of energy (called Photons) and then followed as they bounce around a scene until they're absorbed or escape to infinity. These Photons are then stored in a Photon Map and used at render time to calculate illumination in a scene. Photons can be emitted from standard light sources as well as from user defined photon-emitting shaders.

In this chapter, you will learn the following:

- How to use Caustics
- How to fine-tune Caustics
- How to use Global Illumination
- How to fine-tune Global Illumination

Caustics

In this exercise, you will learn to enable Caustics and fine-tune its effects.

1 Open scene file cognacGlass_start.mb

Render the scene to see the initial results using Maya Software rendering. This is a simple scene consisting of a glass and a Spot Light. The glass and its contents have refractive materials, and the Spot Light casts raytraced shadows. You can see that the shadows cast by the glass are properly colored and transparent, but the image lacks the "hotspots" usually seen when light shines through glass.

Initial render using Maya Software renderer

2 Enable Caustics

- Open the **Render Globals** window and change your selected renderer to **mental ray**.

- In the **mental ray** tab of the **Render Globals**, scroll to the **Quality** setting and select the **PreviewCaustics** preset.

- Scroll to the **General** section and increase the Raytracing settings:

  Set **Max Refraction Rays** to **6**. This is the number of times the ray must go through a transparent surface before it stops.

  Set **Max Ray Depth** to **8** (Reflection rays + Refraction rays).

- Scroll to the **Caustics and Global Illumination** section and note that **Caustics** are now enabled.

  Increase **Max Refraction Photons** and **Max Photon Depth** to **6**. The photon goes through 6 transparent surfaces before hitting a diffuse surface (the wall) and stopping. Therefore, the default value of 5 would not produce proper results.

- Scroll to the **Translation** section of the **Render Globals**, and set **Export Verbosity** to **Progress Messages** so that you can check Maya's **Output Window** for progress messages when you render.

- See sections 1.30 and 2.7.1.8 of the mental ray reference documentation for more information.

3 Turn on photon emission

In order to use Caustics, at least one of the light sources in your scene must emit photons. Each photon emitted by the light source is traced through the scene until it either hits a diffuse surface or until it has been reflected or transmitted a maximum number of times as indicated by the photon trace depth. The Caustic Photon Map holds just those photons that have been specularly reflected or refracted, before hitting a diffuse surface where they are stored.

Note: It is also possible to use custom mental ray shaders as photon emitters.

- In the **Hypershade**'s **Lights** tab, select *spotLightShape1* and open the **Attribute Editor**.

- Scroll to the **mental ray** attribute section and turn on **Emit Photons** in the **Caustics and Global Illumination** subsection.

- **Energy** is the amount of light distributed by the light source. Each photon will carry a fraction of the light source energy and distribute it into the scene.

  Leave **Energy** at the default (**8000**) for now.

- The number of **Caustic Photons** emitted by the light source will determine the quality of the generated Caustics. More photons produce higher quality results, but also increase memory usage. A suggested workflow is to use the default number of photons or less while tuning your image, to produce quick, low-quality Caustics. You can increase the number of photons to produce higher-quality images.

  Leave **Caustic Photons** at the default number (**10000**) for now.

- **Exponent** acts like decay; the intensity increases as the value decreases. The default value of **2** simulates quadratic (realistic) decay. Leave this setting at the default value for now.

- The **Physical** option will not be used.

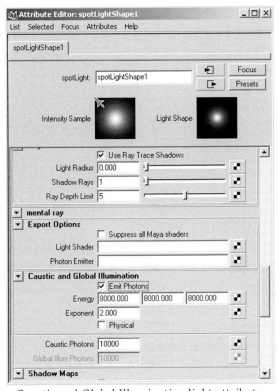

Caustic and Global Illumination light attributes

4 Test render the scene

You should now see Caustic effects around the glass, but the quality will not be very good; the Caustic effects will be spotty. Further tuning is needed to improve the appearance of Caustics.

Initial results of render with Caustics

5 Fine-tuning Caustics

- In the **mental ray** tab of the **Render Globals**, scroll to the **Caustics and Global Illumination** section.

  The appearance of Caustics can be fine-tuned using the Caustic Accuracy and Radius settings.

- **Radius** controls the maximum distance at which mental ray considers photons.

  For example, to specify that only photons within 1 scene unit away should be used, set **Radius** to **1**. When **Radius** is left at the default value of **0**, the renderer will itself calculate an appropriate radius based on your scene size. However, this default result is not always acceptable, as in this case. Increasing the **Radius** will generally decrease noise but give a more blurred result. To decrease noise without blurring details, it would be necessary to increase the number of Caustic photons emitted by your light source.

    Increase **Radius** in small increments and test render until you have acceptable results. Try a setting of **1.5** or **2**.

- **Accuracy** controls how many photons are considered during rendering. The default is 64; larger numbers make the Caustics smoother. For example, to specify that at most 100 photons should be used to compute the Caustic brightness, set **Accuracy** to **100**.

Increase **Accuracy** in small increments and test render until you have acceptable results. Try a setting of **100**.

- You may find that the Caustic effects are not bright enough. Raising or lowering the **Energy** of your light source will increase or decrease the brightness of your Caustics.

Open the **Attribute Editor** for the light and, in the **Caustics and Global Illumination** section, change the three **Energy** value fields equally until you have better results.

Try a setting of **12000 | 12000 | 12000**.

Caustic Radius 2.000, Accuracy 100, Energy 12000

- Changing the **Caustic Filter Type** to **Cone** can produce smoother results.

In the **mental ray** tab of the **Render Globals**, scroll to the **Caustics and Global Illumination** section and change **Caustic Filter** to **Cone**.

Results using Cone filter

- To further increase the quality of Caustic effects, you can increase the amount of emitted photons. This will slow down your rendering time, but improve image quality.

  In the **Caustics and Global Illumination** attributes for your light, increase **Caustic Photons**. Try a setting of **20000**.

20000 Caustic Photons, Accuracy 200, Radius 1.5

- Further improvements to Caustics generally require experimentation with the light's **Energy**, **Caustic Photons** and **Exponent** values, as well as the **Render Globals' Caustic Accuracy** and **Radius** values.

The scene file *cognacGlass_finished.mb* has the finished results of this exercise.

Global Illumination

In this exercise, you will enable Global Illumination and fine-tune the results.

1 Open scene file Global_start.mb

This scene consists of a bike in a garage. The garage door is animated open, allowing indirect light to spill into the scene and illuminate its contents. Go to the last frame of the animation where the illumination will be at it's fullest. We will tune from there.

2 Enable Global Illumination

- Open the **Render Globals** window and change your selected renderer to **mental ray**.

- In the **mental ray** tab of the **Render Globals**, scroll to the **Quality** setting and select the **PreviewGlobalIllum** preset.
- Scroll to the **Caustics and Global Illumination** section and note that **Global Illumination** is now enabled.

3 Turn on photon emission

As with Caustics, at least one of the light sources in your scene must emit photons.

- In the **Hypershade**'s **Lights** tab, select *spotLightShape1* and open the **Attribute Editor**.
- Under the **Spot Light** attribute section, turn **Intensity** to **0.** This means that all illumination in the scene will come solely from photons.
- Scroll to the **mental ray** attribute section and turn on **Emit Photons** in the **Caustics and Global Illumination** subsection.
- Leave **Energy** at the default (**8000**) for now.
- Leave **Caustic Photons** at the default number (**10000**) for now.
- Leave **Exponent** at its default value of 2 for now.

4 Test render the scene

There is very little illumination in the scene. Further tuning is needed.

5 Change the Exponent Value

As with Caustics, the Exponent attribute represents decay. To increase the chances of photons reaching the back of the garage, increase your energy values or turn **Exponent** to **1**.

6 Render the scene

Notice you can now see the bike at the back of the garage a little more clearly. There are more photons reaching this area, but we'll need to further tune to get rid of the hot areas where there is a greater concentration of photons.

Global Illumination Exponent 1, Energy 8000, 8000, 8000

7 Change the Energy Values

Lower values will produce less bright photons and lessen the chances of hot spots. Try a value of 4000 for each of the R,G,B channels and do a test render. If you find this too dark, try values of 5000.

Note: The message "no photons stored after emitting 10000 photons" means that photons emitted by the source don't hit any energy-storing object. One reason this can happen is the photon emitting source is emitting photons in the wrong direction.

8 Change the Radius

- In the **mental ray** tab of the **Render Globals**, open the **Caustics and Global Illumination** section.

- Scroll to the **Global Illumination Radius** section and increase this value from 0 to 1. The radius represents the size of the photons. Increasing this value will help smooth out the photons and get rid of that mottled look.

- Do a test render. If you still find that your photons are not smooth enough, increase the **Radius** to **2**.

- If you increase your **Radius** to **3**, you may find that there is little or no change in your render between this and when you used **2**. This is a good time to start increasing your **Global Illumination Accuracy** value.

Tip: Increase your **Radius** until you see no change in your render. Then start increasing the **Accuracy** value.

Exponent 1, energy 5000,5000,5000, radius 1

Exponent 1, energy 5000,5000, 5000, radius 2

9 Increase the Accuracy

- In the **mental ray** tab of the **Render Globals**, open the **Caustics and Global Illumination** section.

- Scroll to the **Global Illumination Accuracy** section and slowly increase this value. This will further refine your photons, helping to smooth them.

Radius 2, Global Illumination Accuracy 900

10 Change the Number of Photons

The brightness of the scene is good but there could still be a few areas to tune. The corners of the garage could be a little darker and the area behind the bike should be dark, since it's casting a shadow. Under the **mental ray** attribute section of the Spot Light, increase **Caustic Photons** value until you are satisfied with the results. Increasing this value will emit more photons into the scene, capturing more detail.

100000 photons emitted

200000 photons emitted

SUMMARY

Adding Caustics and Global Illumination to your scenes can help create more subtle and realistic light effects.

This chapter covered the following topics:

- Explaining Caustics and Global Illumination
- Enabling Caustics/Global Illumination in the Render Globals
- Emitting Photons from a light source
- Fine-tuning Caustic and Global Illumination effects

12 **Final Gather & HDRI**

mental ray for Maya's Final Gather process can be used with the Global Illumination solution to obtain a finer level of diffuse detail resolve, or it can also be used by itself as an independent rendering alternative.

Alias\Wavefront Lobby rendered using Final Gather, Global Illumination and HDR

In this chapter, you will learn the following topics:

- mental ray for Maya Final Gather theory
- How to setup a mental ray for Maya Final Gather render
- Combining Final Gather with Global Illumination
- HDRI theory
- Using HDRI images

Final Gather - Theory

With Final Gather, mental ray for Maya calculates the scene irradiance or total incoming illumination in the scene. Every object in your scene is, in effect, a light source. It is possible, therefore, to render a scene without any lights. This can be a very useful technique.

It is important to note that one ray generation is used in the Final Gather process. This differs from Global Illumination Photon Mapping where photons bounce around many times. Final Gather allows for one Final Gather ray emission and then contact with a surface to determine if there is a diffuse light contribution to the emitting surface points color value. Final Gather does not allow for multiple diffuse light bounces. Final Gather will calculate color bleeding and diffuse contributions from the first surface, but not from a secondary surface.

With Final Gather, a semi-hemispherical area above the point to be shaded is sampled to determine the indirect as well as direct illumination. This semi-hemispherical area is defined by the Min Radius and Max Radius values found in the Render Globals - Final Gather section.

Not all points are sampled with this approach. Rather, an averaging of nearby points is calculated, and this value is used for the sampled point. This technique is used, as Final Gather ray generation is too expensive to calculate for all sampled points.

The final result of the FG process is a value for how much light is incident upon each point in the scene.

Final Gather is useful in the following situations:

- In very diffuse scenes where Indirect illumination changes slowly.

- In the elimination of low-frequency noise when using Global Illumination, as well as low photon emission values.

- With finer detail resolution.

- When combined with Global Illumination, a more physically accurate solution is possible.

- For convincing soft shadow techniques.

- To help eliminate "dark corners".

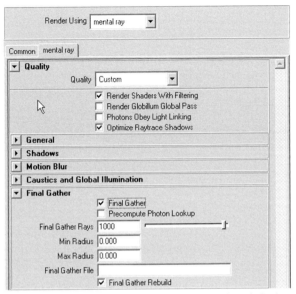

mental ray for Maya Render Globals - Final Gather default settings

Number of Final Gather Rays

This is the number of rays that are sent out from each sampled point. The default value is 1,000. However, for test render situations, 100 - 200 rays will often be sufficient. When rendering out for production, more Final Gather rays will be required.

Min Radius and Max Radius

The Min Radius and Max Radius attributes control the size of the sampling region within which the Final Gather rays search for irradiance information from other surfaces.

With the default 0 values, mental ray for Maya will calculate values that seem appropriate based on scene dimensions. This will speed things up. However, using the default values does not allow for a specific scene's individual geometry complexity. Ultimately, you will want to enter your own scene specific Min Radius and Max Radius values for optimal Final Gather results.

Typically, a good rule of thumb is to take 10% of your scene's overall dimension in Maya units for the Max Radius and then take 10% of that value for the Min Radius. Again, this is a starting point, as a particular scene may contain geometry that requires lesser or greater values for proper detail resolution.

Min Radius and Max Radius are functions of scene geometry detail level and how it is arranged in the scene. Every scene will be different and will require some initial adjusting for optimum results.

In the section on Combining Global Illumination and Final Gather, the interior architectural scene benefits from adjusting the default Min Radius and Max Radius values. This adjustment creates better diffuse detailing between the duct work and the ceiling and along the stairs.

In the Alias | Wavefront Lobby image depicted at the beginning of this chapter, Min Radius and Max Radius values were increased to 1.2 and 12, respectively. These values increased the diffuse detail precision at wall-to-wall and wall-to-ceiling intersections.

Irradiance

Irradiance can most easily be defined as total incoming illumination. It is an environmental lighting parameter that determines the amount of light that is incident upon a surface.

This irradiance attribute is found on each individual shader's Attribute Editor, under the mental ray section. It is used to map an incoming "illumination map", such as one created using convert to File texture, mental ray, or other texture map that may have been created. With this shader attribute mapped, the Final Gather solution takes the irradiance information from the texture map and not from surrounding surfaces.

Irradiance Color

This attribute controls the effects of Photon Mapping and Final Gather on a surface. For example, if a red ball is sitting on a white diffuse plane, the plane will acquire a red tinge from the ball. Irradiance Color allows for the control of this color bleeding effect.

Final Gather - Applying the Theory

With this series of workflows, you will discover that Final Gather can be affected and adjusted in several ways. The Final Gather solution can be affected by:

- The number of Final Gather rays
- The Min Radius and Max Radius
- The camera background color
- Colored Incandescence in the scene
- Ambient Color in the scene
- Irradiance contributions from shaders
- Irradiance Color mapping contributions from shaders
- Whether there are lights in the scene and their locations

Another technique for overall illumination, when doing a Final Gather render, includes the use of an HDR or High Dynamic Range Image, or using an out of camera view dummy surface (light card) with an incandescence value.

1 Open the file

The scene file consists of a space jet with assigned shaders. There is one Directional Light in the scene that has had its **Illuminates by Default** toggle disabled. The dome shader has a slight incandescence value. This is the "illumination" or irradiance contribution in the scene. The **Incandescence** could be supplanted with **Ambient Color** to get the same effect.

- Open the scene file *spaceJet_Start.mb*.

Note: It is important to note that color bleed will not occur in your scene if there are no lights, colored incandescence, or ambient color.

---

2 Turn off Maya's Default Lights

It is important to turn off Maya's **Default Lights**, otherwise a Directional Light will be created at render time.

- Go to the **Common Render Options** of **Render Globals** and turn the **Default Light** off.

3 Set up the FG render

- Go to **Render Globals** and change the **Render Using** field to indicate **mental ray**. Scroll down to the **Final Gather** section and turn **Final Gather ON**.

- Adjust the number of **Final Gather** rays to 100. This will speed the render time up considerably. This is a good starting point for test renders. Keep the **Min Radius** and **Max Radius** values at **0**.

- Render the scene.

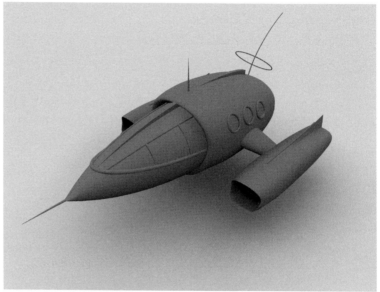

Space Jet Final Gather render - no lights - no color bleed

Notice the soft shadows on the underside of the space jet. The points being shaded under the space jet are hidden from the scene irradiance or illumination contribution from the incandescence on the dome shader. This results in a soft shadow effect.

Note: The scene will render out black if there are no lights or irradiance contribution from other surfaces in the scene. Try turning the dome shader's incandescence to 0. With no lights, the scene will render out black. The reason for this is there is no irradiance in the scene from any source.

---

4 Color bleed

Now, we will look at some techniques for introducing and adjusting color bleed when using the Final Gather process.

- Turn the **Illuminates by Default** toggle for the **Directional Light** on.
- Render out the scene. Notice the color bleed from the red space jet onto the white floor.
- Go to the **mental ray** section of the floor shader's **Attribute Editor**.
- Change the **Irradiance Color** to **50% grey**.
- Render out the scene. Notice the decrease in color bleed.

Note: Irradiance Color allows you to adjust the color bleed effect.

5 Map the Irradiance Color

Another technique that can be very useful is to map the Irradiance Color attribute.

- Select the *dome* shader and map the **Irradiance Color** with a **sky procedural**.
- Render out the scene.

6 Color bleed with no lights

With no lights in the scene, it is still possible to achieve the color bleed effect.

- Turn the **Illuminates by Default** toggle for the **Directional Light** off.
- Adjust the Ambient Color or add some "colored" Incandescence to the *space jet* shader.
- Render again. Notice the color bleed.

Note: With the space jet Final Gather scene, the default Final Gather Min Radius and Max Radius values of 0 are sufficient for good image quality. With the interior architecture scene, adjusting these values will give better image quality.

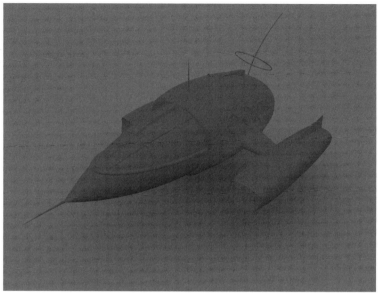

Space Jet Final Gather - lights off - color bleed

Note: Another technique for contributing lighting levels in a Final Gather rendered scene, include changing the camera's background color to a value other than black. Go to the Camera's Attribute Editor and change the Environment Background Color to 50% grey. Render the scene. This can also be a useful technique.

There are several ways to influence and adjust the Final Gather process.

Combining Final Gather and Global Illumination

Using Final Gather and Global Illumination together results in very fine diffuse detail resolution. The technique is particularly useful for interior architectural shots where lighting definition is a function of light contribution from interior and exterior sources.

We will start off by setting up the exterior lights and then move inside to setup the scene for Global Illumination. Once the scene is correctly illuminated using Photon Mapping, we will add Final Gather.

Interior Architectural Lighting using Final Gather and Global Illumination

Architectural Interior - Exercise Flow

We will setup the scene and then render out the file using mental ray for Maya. We will then render the scene out using Global Illumination and no Final Gather, just a Final Gather and then a combination of the two. Combining Global Illumination and Final Gather together results in the best image quality.

1 Open the scene file

- Open the scene file *interiorArchitectural_Start.mb.*

The scene contains an interior architectural shot with attendant lights and shaders. There are 6 pre-positioned lights in the scene: three linked Spot Lights for the translucent panels over the kitchen area, one linked Directional Light for exterior lighting, one Spot Light on the outside for interior direct illumination and shadows, and two Spot Lights for the lampshade over the dining area. The shaders in the scene are mostly File textures.

2 Setup the exterior light

- Select *spotLight5* and change the **Decay Rate** to **Quadratic** and the **Intensity** to **2500**.

- Turn **Raytrace Shadows ON**. Leave the shadow settings at their defaults.

Note: When setting up for Global Illumination and Final Gather, use the quadratic decay rate. This ensures that light levels in the scene decrease in intensity based on the inverse square law.

- Position *spotLight5* to generate shadows on the interior floor.

  This light is used for direct illumination and primary shadow generation.

3 The Translucent Panels

The three translucent panels in the kitchen generate warm light effects. The three Spot Lights overhead need to be linked to the translucent panels.

- Open the **Relationship Editor** and go to **Light Centric Mode**.

- **Link** the three Spot Lights to the translucent panels.

  The links are as follows:

      spotLight3 linked to pPlane3;

      spotLight2 linked to pPlane2;

      spotLight4 linked to pPlane1.

4 Exterior lighting

- Select *directionalLight1*.

- Using the **Relationship Editor**, link *directionalLight1* to the *terrace* geometry.

5 The Lamp Shade

The lamp hierarchy consists of three parts. The geometry, the shader, and the Spot Light setup. There are two spots lights in this lampshade arrangement. The first is linked to the lampshade geometry. The lampshade geometry gets its lighting information from this Spot Light exclusively. The second Spot Light that fits just inside the geometry is used for direct illumination, shadow generation, and photon emission.

- Using the **Relationship Editor** link *spotlight6* to the lampshade geometry.

  This Light Linking arrangement allows for controlled illumination of the warm light effect on the lampshade geometry.

- Select *spotLight1* and change the **Intensity** to **45** and **Decay Rate** to **Quadratic**.

    The intensity of *spotLight1* will be increased later, when Global Illumination and Final Gather are enabled.

6 Render Setup

- Go to **Render Globals** and set the **Resolution** to **320 x 240**.

- Using a **Render View** window, render the scene.

Because there is no Global Illumination occurring in the scene, the render is only using the direct illumination from the lights in the scene for illumination. If you render this scene out using the Maya renderer, the result will be the same.

mental ray for Maya render - no Global Illumination - no Final Gather

Global Illumination

Now we will introduce Global Illumination to the scene.

1 Turn on Global Illumination

- Go to **Render Globals** and turn **Global Illumination ON**. Set the following settings:

  Global Illumination Accuracy to **450**;

  Global Illumination Radius to **6.0**.

- Leave the other settings at their defaults.

2 Turn on Photon Emission

- select *spotLight1* and turn **Photon Emission** ON. Set the following settings:

  Energy to **4000, 4000, 4000**;

  Exponent to **2.0**;

  Physical to **OFF**;

  Global Illumination Photons to **25000**.

- The Attribute Editor for the *spotLight1* will look like this:

spotLight1 - Global Illumination - photon settings

3 Render

- Using a **Render View** window, render the scene.

Global Illumination - no Final Gather

Final Gather - no Global Illumination

1 Turn Global Illumination off

- Turn **Global Illumination OFF** in the **Render Globals** window.

- Turn **Photon Emission OFF** in the Attribute Editor of *spotLight1*.

2 Turn Final Gather on

- Go to the **Final Gather** section of **Render Globals** and enable Final Gather.

3 Adjust the number of Final Gather rays

- In the Final Gather section of Render Globals, change the number of rays to 125. This is a good value for test rendering. For a higher quality render, 400 - 600 rays will give very fine detailing.

4 Adjust the Min Radius and Max Radius

The Min Radius and Max Radius defines the search area, within which Final Gather rays will look for irradiance information from neighboring surfaces. The areas above the ducting, in the far corner, and along the wall on the left, are good examples of where the default 0 and 0 Min Radius and Max Radius values are not sufficient for optimum image quality. Adjusting the values to 8 and 20 respectively will remove these areas.

Final Gather - no Global Illumination - default Min Radius and Max Radius

Notice the poor diffuse solution behind the hand rail, the wall on the left, the ceiling, and above the ducting.

Final Gather - no Global Illumination - Min Radius 8 and Max Radius 20

Notice the splotchy areas have been reduced. Turning on jitter will sometimes help further assist with the removal of these areas.

5 Render the scene

- In a **Render View** window, render out the scene.

Final Gather and Global Illumination

We will now render the interior architectural scene out using Global Illumination and Final Gather.

1 Turn Global Illumination on

- In the **Global Illumination and Caustics** section of **Render Globals**, turn **Global Illumination** back **ON**. Use the same settings as previously described.

- In the **Quality** section of the **Render Globals** window, turn **Photons Obey Light Linking ON**.

2 Turn Final Gather on

- In the **Render Globals** window, turn **Final Gather ON**. Use the same settings as previously described.

3 Physical attribute

- In the **Attribute Editor** for the photon emitter, turn the **Physical** attribute **ON**.

- An adjustment to photon energy and light intensity may be required once this attribute is enabled.

- Try a *spotLight1* intensity of 350 and photon energy levels of 25000, 25000, 25000.

Note: When combining Global Illumination and Final Gather, turn the Physical flag on. This ensures that shading models in the scene behave in a physically correct manner, i.e. they do not amplify light by emitting more energy than was received.

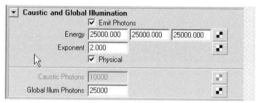

Photon emission settings showing the Physical attribute

- With the Physical attribute enabled, adjustments will be required to energy and intensity levels.

4 Precompute Photon Lookup

The Precompute photon Lookup toggle arranges irradiance to be stored with the Photon Map when Global Illumination is enabled. This toggle is only used if Global Illumination is turned on, i.e. photon emission is occurring in the scene. Fewer Final Gather points are required with this option as the Photon Map will carry a good approximation of the irradiance in the scene. This is because irradiance can be estimated with a single lookup instead of using a large number of photons. Enabling this feature will slow the Photon Mapping phase but will speed the Final Gather process. Ultimately, the render will be faster with this feature enabled.

- Go to the **Final Gather** section of **Render Globals** and turn **Precompute Photon Lookup ON**.

Global Illumination, Final Gather, and Physical attribute enabled

5 Render the scene

Notice the areas under the table are now correctly illuminated. With the Physical attribute enabled, light interacts with surfaces based on real world physics. The scene is now correctly illuminated.

- To increase the overall lighting levels, try increasing the photon energy to 30000, 30000, 30000.

Final Gather Filename

This allows Final Gather results to be stored in a file. This allows later frames to reuse Final Gather results from a frame rendered earlier. The file is saved into the current project's *mentalRay\finalgMap* directory.

To create a Final Gather map:

- Ensure that "Rebuild Final Gather" is turned ON
- Enter a file name in the Final Gather
- Render the scene out

Rebuild Final Gather

This is the default setting and will ignore any Final Gather map that has been generated previously. Turning this toggle off will force the Final Gather to use the results from a previous Final Gather render if a Final

Gather map was created. Use of this toggle will speed the Final Gather considerably.

It is important to note that if the number of rays is changed, the Final Gather map will be ignored and new Final Gather rays will be emitted. A glance into the Output window will reveal the following message in such an event:

```
RCFG 0.2  info : finalgMap/test1: final gather options
differ from ones currently used, content ignored
RCFG 0.2  info : overwriting final gather file
"finalgMap/test1"
```

If you are rendering out a still image and are not changing the Final Gather settings, turning the "Rebuild Final Gather" off can save considerable time.

When rendering out a camera animation sequence, it may be possible to get away with the Final Gather calculations of the previous frames. This will depend on how the irradiance changes during the course of the camera animation. In such an event, considerable time can be saved if the Rebuild Final Gather toggle is disabled. However, if there are objects in the scene that are moving, the irradiance values for the scene will have to be re-computed for each subsequent frame.

HIGH DYNAMIC RANGE IMAGING

The Final Gather process can also make use of a High Dynamic Range Image as the basis for illumination information in a scene. This is known as image-based lighting.

nappaValley.tif High Dynamic Range Image

What is an HDR Image?

An HDR Image has an extra floating point value that is used to describe the exponent or persistence of light at any given pixel. This overall illumination information is used in the Final Gather process. LDR (Low Dynamic Range) images, the kind that we are all familiar with, have limitations when it comes to describing the range of colors necessary to correctly describe light values precisely. Think of a dark cathedral with strong light spilling through a stain glass window - the range from dark to bright is too broad for a conventional LDR image. Such an LDR image will have "blown out" and very black areas.

Pixels that have a high floating point value (exponential value) are not affected very much by a darkening of the overall image. Pixels that have a lower persistence of light would be affected more by this same darkening operation.

Creating your own HDR Image involves taking several shots of the same subject matter with bracketed f-stops and then assembling the images into an HDR (floating point tiff) Image. There are applications available for this purpose.

Lesson 1 - Metal Ring

In this lesson, we will use the *nappaValley.tif* HDR Image as the source of illumination and reflection for a gold ring sitting on a table top.

Note:	When loading an HDR Image into Maya, a warning message will be generated (Maya cannot read the additional information included in HDR Images). Ignore this message while rendering with mental ray.

nappaValley.tif HDR file used as background and illumination source

1 Open the scene file

The scene contains a ring sitting on a table top. There is also a NURBS sphere surface that surrounds the scene. Assigned to this geometry is an HDR Image. The three surfaces are on separate layers.

- Open the scene file *ringHDR_Start.mb*.

2 Create and apply the HDR shading network

- In the **Hypershade**, create a Lambert shader.
- Map the **Ambient Color** attribute with a **File Texture.**
- Use the *nappaValley.tif* file in the sourceImages directory as the source file for the **File Texture** node.

- Apply the HDR shader to the background surface.

3 Create the gold metal shader

The gold shader makes use of a few techniques to achieve the polished metal effect. Setting the Diffuse, Eccentricity, and Specular Roll Off as indicated below, allows the color of the metal to be controlled by using the Specular Color attribute.

- Create a **Blinn** shader.

    Edit the shader attributes as follows:

    Color to dark yellow (H **47.68**, S **0.852**, V **0.875**);

    Diffuse to **0**;

    Eccentricity to **0**;

    Specular Roll Off to **1.0**;

    Reflected Color to **Black**;

    Specular Color to pale yellow (H **47.37**, S **0.98**, V **0.909**).

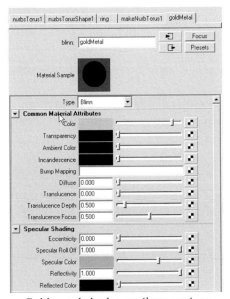

Gold metal shader attribute settings

4 Setup Render Globals

- In the **Render Globals** window, turn **Final Gather ON**.

- Set the number of **Final Gather** rays to **100**. This is sufficient for testing purposes. Leave the other **Render Globals** attributes at their default settings.

5 Render

- In a **Render View** window, render the scene.

6 Adjust the effect

To adjust the effect of the HDR Images irradiance contribution, go to the **Color Balance** section of the HDR shader's **File Texture** node. Change the Color Value to a value higher or lower than 1. Going higher will increase the amount of light contribution in the scene.

Try experimenting with other values.

Lesson 2 - Car Visualization

In this lesson, we will use the *nappaValley.tif* HDR Image as the illumination and reflection information for a car's body paint. We will also incorporate three Spot Lights into the scene for highlight control and added drama.

1 Open the scene

- Open the scene file *carHDR_Start.mb.*

Render using High Dynamic Range Image

2 Review the scene

- The scene consists of car geometry, a ground plane, background geometry, shaders, and Spot Lights.

3 Review the car paint shader

- In the Hypershade, graph the *layeredShader1* node.

The Layered Shader makes use of three individual layers. This allows specific control over the base layer's shading map, the clear coat layer, and the Reflectivity layer. A very similar shading network was introduced in the shading map section of Chapter Two. This shader has been further refined with a granite and clamp node on the specular channel of the shading map.

- Here is the *layeredShader* in the Hypershade:

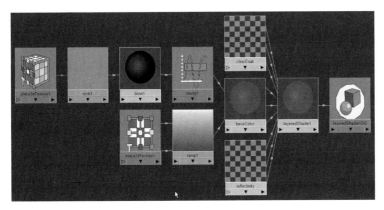

Shading network used for car paint

Recall from Chapter Two that a shading map allows for control over where the diffuse and specular information is placed on a surface. For automobile surfaces, this can be a very useful technique.

4 Create the HDR shader

- In the **Hypershade** create a **Blinn** shader.
- Map the **Ambient Color** attribute with a **File Texture.**
- Use the *nappaValley.tif* file as the source for the **File Texture.**

5 Review the Spot Light setup

There are three Spot Lights in the scene for increased highlight control.

6 **Review the other shaders in the scene**

There are other shaders in the scene that contribute to the image. Review the shaders for the wheels, tires, and glass.

Notice that the floor shader has had its Irradiance Color attribute adjusted to 20% grey. This value decreases the amount of color the floor acquires from the HDR Image.

7 **Setup Render Globals**

- In the **Render Globals** window turn, **Final Gather ON**.
- Use a value of 125 for the number of **Final Gather Rays.**
- Adjust **Min Radius** and **Max Radius** to values of **4** and **12**. This will give good results.
- Set the **Resolution** to **320x240**.

8 **Render the scene**

- In a **Render View** window, render the scene.

9 **Adjust the results**

- Adjust the results using methods you have learned in this chapter.

SUMMARY

The Final Gather and HDR render processes allow for precise diffuse light contributions in your scene.

In this chapter, we have reviewed:

- Final Gather and HDR theory
- Applied Final Gather theory
- Combining Global Illumination and Final Gather

13 mental ray Shaders

mental ray for Maya supports Maya-type shaders, textures, and lights, but it is also possible to use custom mental ray shaders.

This chapter will cover several examples of how to use custom mental ray for Maya shaders to create complex effects that may not be easily reproduced using another renderer.

In this chapter, you will learn the following:

- How to use Contour Shaders
- How to use mental ray Material Shaders
- How to use mental ray Photon Shaders
- How to use mental ray Shadow Shaders
- How to use mental ray Volume Shaders

- How to create a mental ray Double-Sided Shader

- How to use mental ray Light Shaders

INTRODUCTION

mental ray for Maya includes an extensive library of custom mental ray shaders. In addition to standard shaders, user defined shaders written in standard C or C++ can be precompiled and linked at runtime, or can be both compiled and linked at runtime.

You can create mental ray custom shaders the same way you create Maya shading nodes - with the **Hypershade**'s **Create** bar, **Hypershade**'s **Create** menu, or **Hypershade**'s **Create Render Node** window (**Create** → **Create Render Node**).

Showing mental ray nodes in the **Hypershade** is an advanced user feature. If you have no "**Create mental ray Nodes**" tab in your **Hypershade**, you have to add an environment variable to your *Maya.env* file.

- Create a plain text file named *Maya.env*.

  On Windows, save the file to "`drive:\Documents and Settings\username\My Documents\maya\version`" or "`drive:\Documents and Settings\username\My Documents\maya`".

  On Mac, save the file to "`/Users/username/Library/Preferences/AliasWavefront/maya/version`" or "`/Users/username/Library/Preferences/AliasWavefront/maya`".

  On UNIX, save the file to `~/maya/version` or `~/maya`. Make sure to capitalize the M in *Maya.env*.

  Make sure you only have one *Maya.env* file.

  On Windows and UNIX, you can change the location where Maya looks for *Maya.env* by setting the MAYA_APP_DIR environment variable. See the documentation for more information.

- Add this line to your text file:

  `MAYA_MRFM_SHOW_CUSTOM_SHADERS=1`

- Save the file in text format as *Maya.env* and restart Maya if it was open. Make sure you only have one *Maya.env* file.

For more information about environment variables and the *Maya.env* file, see the Basics guide in the Maya documentation. To read the documentation from within Maya, go to the **Help** → **Contents and Search** and do a search for "*Maya.env*".

Contour Shaders

Contour shader used with Maya Ramp Shader

mental ray for Maya's custom contour shaders can allow you to create cartoon-style images and other effects.

Contour shaders, along with other custom mental ray shaders, are found in the **Create mental ray Nodes** bar of your **Hypershade** window.

1 Open the file called contourShader_start.mb.

2 Apply a Contour Shader

- Open the **Hypershade**'s **Materials** tab and select *vaseRampShader*. In the **Hypershade**, select **Graph → Output Connections**. This will display the Shading Group used by the shader, *vaseRampShaderSG*.

- Select *vaseRampShaderSG* and open the **Attribute Editor**. Make sure to select the *vaseRampShaderSG* tab.

- Expand the **mental ray** attributes section.

- Open the **Create mental ray Nodes** bar in the Hypershade and expand the **Materials** section.

- MMB drag a *contour_shader_simple* node to the *vaseRampShaderSG*'s **Contour Shader** attribute.

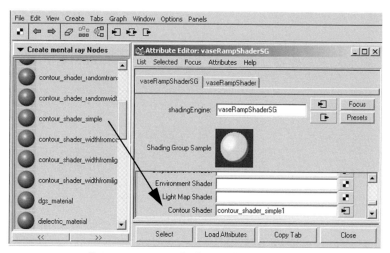

Connect contour shader to shading group

3 Adjust the contour shader settings

- Open the Attribute Editor for the *contour_shader_simple* node. There are two attributes you can set (Width and Color). This scene has the following settings:

    Width to **0.5**;

    Color to **Red**.

4 Set the mental ray for Maya Render Globals

- Change your selected renderer to **mental ray**.

- Open the **mental ray** tab in your Render Globals.

- In the **Quality** section, select a quality setting of your choice; this scene uses **Preview** quality.

- Turn off **Raytracing** in the **General** section to speed up render time.

5 Apply Contrast and Store Shaders

- In the Render Globals' **mental ray** tab, scroll down to the **Contours** section.

- MMB drag a contrast shader and store shader from the **Miscellaneous** section of the **Create mental ray nodes** bar of the Hypershade into the corresponding **Contour** attributes of the Render Globals. You have two options for each.

    This scene uses *contour_contrast_function_levels* for the **Contrast Shader** because it has many parameters that can be set; the simpler *contour_contrast_function_simple* shader can be used for fast computations if only the outlines of objects need to have contours.

This scene uses *contour_store_function* as a **Store Shader**. The simpler *contour_store_function_simple* shader does not store as much information and can be used if only the outlines of objects need contours.

Note: The Connection Editor may open when you try to connect your Store Shader. If this happens, toggle on "Show Hidden" in the Left Display and Right Display menus of the Connection Editor. Connect the Message attribute of the shader (on the left) to the Contour Store attribute of the mentalRayOptions (the Render Globals tab on the right).

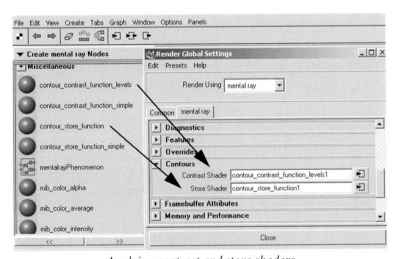

Applying contrast and store shaders

6 Apply an Output Shader to your camera

- In the Hypershade's **Cameras** tab, select the camera you are using to render: *perspShape*.

- Open the **Attribute Editor** for the *perspShape* camera and open up the **mental ray** section.

- MMB drag a *contour_composite* output shader from the **Output Shaders** section of the **Create mental ray nodes** bar of the **Hypershade** into the **Output Shader** attribute of the camera. No changes are made to the output shader's settings.

Note: You can use *contour_only* as an output shader if you want to render only the outlines. The *contour_ps* output shader creates PostScript code with black contours. Read more about output shaders in the mental ray shader reference documentation.

---

7 Tweak your settings

If you render the scene now, you will not see any contours; several changes must be made in order for them to render correctly.

- In the **Hypershade**, select the *contour_contrast_function_levels* node and open the **Attribute Editor**. These are the settings used in this scene:

  min_level is **0** and **max_level** is **1**. If your min and max level are both 0, you will not get any contours.

  zdelta is set to **0.4**; this number is the minimum depth difference required to cause a contour, measured in coordinate units.

  ndelta is set to **12**; this number is the minimum angle difference between normal vectors required to cause a contour, measured in degrees.

  diff_mat, **diff_label**, **diff_index** and **contrast** are all unchecked.

- Render the scene; you should now have thin red contours around your vase. Tweak your settings as desired. Try different values for the **zdelta** and **ndelta** attributes of your Contrast Shader. The *contourShader_finished.mb* file has the finished result of this exercise.

8 Contour shader types and settings

The images below illustrate only a few of the many effects possible using different contour shaders or contour contrast shader settings. For more information about the contour shaders included with mental ray for Maya, please consult the mental ray shader reference: open the documentation home page (**Help → Contents and Search**), click on **Reference**, then click on **mental ray shader reference**. Contour shaders are explained in Chapter Three: Contour Shaders.

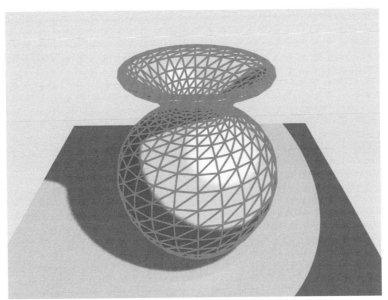

Contour_shader_simple with diff_index checked ON

- Turning **diff_index** on in the *contour_contrast_function_levels* node will create contours on the tessellation of your object. Open the scene file *contourShader_diffindex.mb* to examine this shader.

Contrast checked ON in contour_contrast_function_levels

- Turning **Contrast** on in the *contour_contrast_function_levels* node will create contours around different colors on the object. The Ramp Shader above uses a checker texture as its **Reflected Color**. **Diff_index** is not enabled in the above image. Open the scene file *contourShader_contrast.mb* to examine this shader.

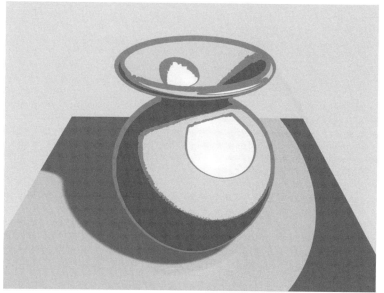

Contour_shader_widthfromlight

- The *contour_shader_widthfromlight* shader creates contours whose width depends on the angle between the surface normal and the distance to a light source. In the above image, **contrast** has also been checked **ON** in the contrast shader node. The scene file used for this image is *contourShader_widthfromlight.mb*.

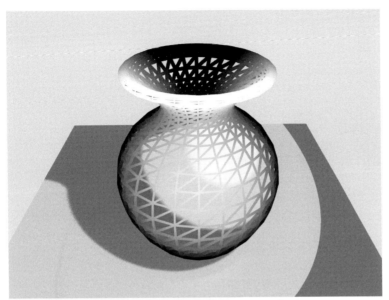

Contour_shader_depthfade contour shader

- Using a *contour_shader_depthfade* node as your shading group's **Contour Shader** allows you to have contours that change their width and color depending on the depth of the object. It is useful to turn on **Object Details** in your **Heads Up Display** (**Display** → **Heads Up Display**) to find out your object's distance from the camera; this can help you set the correct **Near_z** and **Far_z** values for this contour shader.

The above image also has **diff_index** checked ON in its *contour_contrast_function_levels* node.

Open the scene file *contourShader_depthfade* to examine this shading network.

Material Shaders

mental ray for Maya material shaders are similar to Maya's surface materials.

Two material shaders are included with mental ray for Maya: *dgs_material* and *dielectric_material*. These two shaders implement different physically based models of reflection and refraction.

The *dgs* in *dgs_material* stands for Diffuse-glossy-specular. The *dgs_material* shader can simulate mirrors, glossy paint or plastic, anisotropic glossy materials such as brushed metal, diffuse materials such as paper, translucent materials such as frosted glass, and any combination of these.

The *dielectric_material* shader is a physically based material shader which can be used to simulate dielectric media such as glass, water, and other liquids.

In this exercise, you will learn to use mental ray for Maya custom material shaders.

1 Open the file called crystalBall_start.mb

This scene has been set up for rendering with mental ray for Maya, using Caustics. There is one Point Light in the scene and it has been set to emit photons. The objects in the scene use regular Maya shaders. There should be no need to alter the light's settings or the Render Globals during this exercise.

You will use mental ray custom shaders to replace the regular Phong shader on the sphere and create a refractive crystal ball.

- Test render the scene if you wish.

2 Assign a mental ray custom material shader

- Open **Hypershade** and select the *phong1* material. In the **Hypershade**, select **Graph** → **Output Connections**. This will display the Shading Group used by the shader: *phong1SG*.

- Select *phong1SG* and open the **Attribute Editor**. Make sure to open the *phong1SG* tab.

- Expand the **mental ray** attributes section.

- Open the **Create mental ray Nodes** bar in the **Hypershade** and expand the **Materials** section.

- MMB drag a *dielectric_material* node to the *phong1SG*'s **Material Shader** attribute.

3 Assign a mental ray custom photon shader

Maya's regular shaders, such as Phong, Lambert, and Blinn, have Photon attributes by default. This is not the case with mental ray custom material shaders; in order to use photonic effects such as Caustics with a custom mental ray material shader, a photon shader must also be connected to the shading group.

- Open **Hypershade** and select the *phong1* material. Graph its output connections to display the Shading Group used by the shader: *phong1SG*.

- Select *phong1SG* and open the **Attribute Editor**. Make sure to select the *phong1SG* tab.

- Expand the **mental ray** attributes section.

- Open the **Create mental ray Nodes** bar in the Hypershade and expand the **Photonic Materials** section.

- MMB drag a *dielectric_material_photon* node to the *phong1SG*'s **Photon Shader** attribute.

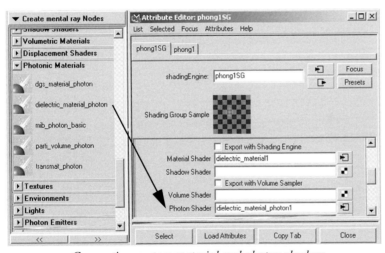

Connecting custom material and photon shaders

4 Change the settings for the custom shaders

The various settings for the custom mental ray shaders are at zero by default; they must be changed in order for the shaders to render properly. You can read more about the settings for these custom shaders in the mental ray shader reference section of the Maya documentation: open the documentation (**Help** → **Contents and Search**), click on **Reference**, then click on **mental ray shader reference**. Material shaders are explained in Chapter 2.3: Material Shaders.

- Select *dielectric_material1* in the **Hypershade**'s **Materials** tab, and open the **Attribute Editor**.

- Double-click the color swatch for the **Col** attribute to set the material's color. This scene used the following settings to create a pale blue color:

  H to **198;**

  S to **0.13;**

  V to **1.00.**

- Set the Index of Refraction (**Ior**) attribute to **2.00**. 2.00 is the refractive index of crystal.

- Set the **Phong_coef** attribute to **140**. This setting is used to compute normalized Phong highlights. It is similar to the **Cosine Power** attribute of a regular Maya Phong shader. Reducing this value will result in a larger highlight.

Tip: If Phong_coef is zero, only reflected rays will create highlight effects. Phong_coef could thus be left at zero if Final Gather or a mental ray physical light was being used to light the scene. This is not the case in this scene, therefore the Phong_coef attribute must be set in order for there to be highlights on the material. If the Col_out color is different from the color for Col and the Ior_out value is different than zero, the reflected color will be a combination of the two colors (Col_out and Col).

- Open the **Hypershade**'s **Utilities** tab and select the *dielectric_material_photon1* node, and open the **Attribute Editor**.

- The settings for the *dielectric_material_photon1* shader should match the *dielectric_material1* shader:

  Col to **pale blue;**

  Ior to **2.00;**

  Phong_coef to **140.**

Note: If the Col_out color is different from the color for Col and the Ior_out value is different than zero, the color of the Caustics will be taken from the Col_out swatch.

---

5 Render the scene

You may notice that it renders more quickly than it did originally, when no custom shaders were used.

Crystal ball with custom dielectric shader

Shadow shaders

It is possible to use mental ray shadow shaders to further customize the appearance of your object's shadows.

Note:	If photon effects (Caustics and/or Global Illumination) are used, using shadow shaders is generally not recommended, because light effects are properly determined by the photons. Shadow shaders used with Caustics/Global Illumination will not produce physically correct results, but can be used to "fake" certain shadow effects such as in this scene.

1 Open scene

You may either use the scene you created in the above exercise (Material Shaders), or open *crystalBall_finished.mb*.

2 Assign a shadow shader

- Open the **Hypershade** and select the *phong1* material. In the **Hypershade**, select **Graph → Output Connections**. This will display the Shading Group: *phong1SG*.

- Select *phong1SG* and open the **Attribute Editor**. Make sure to open the *phong1SG* tab.

- Expand the **mental ray** attributes section.

- Open the **Create mental ray Nodes** bar in the **Hypershade** and expand the **Shadows** section.

- MMB drag a *mib_shadow_transparency* node to the *phong1SG*'s **Shadow Shader** attribute.

3 Adjust the settings for the shadow shader

- In the **Hypershade**'s **Utilities** tab, select the *mib_shadow_transparency1* node and open the **Attribute Editor**.

- Set **Mode** to **3** in order to remove light dependency. You will not get any shadows if you leave this at 0.

- Double-click on the color swatch for the **Color** attribute to select your shadow color. You may wish to set it to a slightly darker color than that used by your crystal ball's material. This scene uses:

  H to **198;**

  S to **0.3;**

  V to **0.8.**

- Lighten **Transparency** to **grey** in order to produce transparent shadows.

Tip: You can soften your shadows by enabling **Area Light** in your light's mental ray attributes in order to convert it to a mental ray Area Light. This may slow down rendering time.

---

4 Render the scene

Custom shadow shader used for transparent shadows

Volume shaders

Volumetric materials scatter light to a certain degree, and can be used to realistically simulate effects such as fog, smoke, translucent glass, etc. Volume shaders can be assigned to particular objects by connecting to their Shading Group.

In this exercise, you will apply a volume shader to the crystal ball from the previous exercises.

1 Open scene file

You may use the scene file you created in the previous exercise (Shadow Shaders), or open *crystalBall_shadow_finished.mb*.

2 Assign a volume shader to the shading group

- Open the **Hypershade** and select the *phong1* material. In the **Hypershade**, select **Graph** → **Output Connections**. This will display the Shading Group: *phong1SG*.

- Select *phong1SG* and open the **Attribute Editor**. Make sure to open the *phong1SG* tab.

- Expand the **mental ray** attributes section.

- Open the **Create mental ray Nodes** bar in the **Hypershade** and expand the **Volumetric Materials** section.

- MMB drag a *parti_volume* node to the *phong1SG*'s mental ray **Volume Shader** attribute.

Note: Make sure you connect the volume shader to the shading group's Volume Shader attribute, found in the mental ray attribute section. Do not connect it to the Volume Material attribute, found in the Shading Group Attributes section.

---

3 Assign a photon volume shader

In order for the Caustic effects in this scene to work, the volume shader needs an equivalent photon volume shader as well.

- In the **Hypershade**, graph the input and output connections of the *phong1* material to display its Shading Group.

- Select *phong1SG* and open the **Attribute Editor**. Make sure to open the *phong1SG* tab.

- Expand the **mental ray** attributes section.

- Open the **Create mental ray Nodes** bar in the **Hypershade** and expand the **Photonic Materials** section.

- MMB drag a *parti_volume_photon* node to the *phong1SG*'s mental ray **Photon Volume Shader** attribute.

4 Adjust the volume shader settings

In order for the volume shaders to render properly, their settings must be adjusted. In this scene, the volume shader and the photon volume shader will use identical settings.

- In the **Hypershade**'s **Materials** tab, select the *parti_volume1* node and open the **Attribute Editor**.

- Try the following settings:

    Scatter is the color of the scattering medium - set this to a color of your choice. This scene uses a dull aqua color.

    Extinction determines how much light is absorbed or scattered in the medium. The higher the value, the denser the medium, and the more light is scattered. A value of **0** would indicate clean air or vacuum. Try setting this to **0.3**.

    Min_step_len and **Max_step_len** determine the step length for rays marching in a non-homogeneous medium - in other

words, they regulate accuracy. Try setting these to
Min_step_len = 0.03 and **Max_step_len = 0.1**.

- Select the *parti_volume_photon* node in the **Hypershade**'s **Utilities** tab and give it the same settings as the *parti_volume* node. You can also try experimenting with different settings.

5 Increase the light energy

The light source's energy values must be increased for the volume shaders to be properly lit.

- In the **Hypershade**'s **Lights** tab, select *pointLightShape1* and open the **Attribute Editor**.

- In the **Caustics and Global Illumination** subsection of the **mental ray** attributes section, increase **Energy** to **12000 I 12000 I 12000**.

6 Increase Caustic Photon Radius

If you render the scene now, you will see dots scattered throughout your image - these are the photons. Increasing the photon radius is one way to correct this effect.

- Open your **Render Globals** and click on the **mental ray** tab. Scroll to the **Caustics and Global Illumination section**.

- Set **Caustic Radius** to **2.000**.

7 Render the scene

Your crystal ball should now be uniformly translucent.

Volume shader creates translucent glass effect

Filling the crystal ball with "smoke"

You will now use some Maya textures and utility nodes to further enhance the volume shader's appearance.

8 Create a Volume Noise texture

A Volume Noise texture will be used to color the volume shader's Scatter attribute.

- In the **Create Textures** bar of the **Hypershade**, scroll to the **3D Textures** section and create a **Volume Noise** texture.

- Adjust the texture's attributes as desired. The settings used in the final scene are:

  Amplitude to **0.860**;

  Frequency Ratio to **1.370**;

  Frequency to **10.000**;

  Noise Type to **Wispy**;

  Color Gain to **dull yellow**;

  Color Offset to **dark blue-green**.

9 Connect the Volume Noise texture to the volume shaders

- Select the *parti_volume1* node in the **Hypershade's Materials** tab and open the **Attribute Editor**.

- MMB drag the Volume Noise texture to the *parti_volume1's* **Scatter** attribute.

- Repeat the above steps with the *parti_volume_photon1* node.

10 Adjust the volume shaders

If you render the scene now, you should see a wispy color effect inside your crystal ball. The "smoke" itself is, however, still uniformly distributed. You can increase the Non-uniform attribute of the volume shaders to randomize the distribution of the volumetric material. The Non-uniform attribute can be set to any number between 0 and 1.

- Select the *parti_volume1* node in the **Hypershade's Materials** tab and open the **Attribute Editor**.

- Increase the **Non-uniform** attribute to a value between 0 and 1. The final scene uses a value of **0.95**.

- Repeat the above steps with the *parti_volume_photon1* node.

11 Restrict the height of the smoke

Currently, the volumetric material fills the entire sphere. You can use the volume shader's **Height** attribute to limit the height of the material. When the volume shader's **Mode** value is set to **0**, the volumetric material fills the entire volume. When **Mode** is **1**, there will be clear air or vacuum anywhere above the **Height** setting.

- Select the *parti_volume1* node in the **Hypershade's Materials** tab and open the **Attribute Editor**.

- Set the **Mode** attribute to **1**.

- Set the **Height** attribute to **3**.

- Repeat the above steps with the *parti_volume_photon1* node.

12 Randomize the smoke height

A noise texture will be used to make the height more uneven.

- In the **Create Textures** bar of the **Hypershade**, scroll to the **2D Textures** section and create a **Noise** texture.

- Adjust the Noise texture's attributes as desired. The final scene uses the following settings:

  Amplitude to **0.790;**

  Ratio to **0.320;**

  Frequency Ratio to **1.970;**

  Noise Type to **Wispy.**

- Open the **Create Utilities** bar of the **Hypershade** and create a **Set Range** utility node.

  The Noise texture's output will return a value between 0 and 1, but the Height value for the smoke in the crystal ball should be higher than that. The Set Range utility will allow you to specify a new output range.

- MMB drag the *noise1* texture onto the *setRange1* node and choose "Other..." from the pop-up menu to open the **Connection Editor.**

- Connect *noise1*'s **Out Alpha** attribute to *setRange1*'s **Value X** attribute.

- Select *noise1* and open the **Attribute Editor.** Change the following settings:

  Min X to **2.000;**

  Max X to **4.000;**

  Old Min to **0.000;**

  Old Max to **1.000.**

- MMB drag *setRange1* onto the *parti_volume1* swatch. Choose "Other..." from the pop-up menu to open the **Connection Editor.**

- Connect *setRange1*'s **Out Value X** attribute to *parti_volume1*'s **Height** attribute.

- Repeat the previous two steps to connect *setRange1*'s **Out Value X** attribute with the *parti_volume_photon1* node's **Height** attribute.

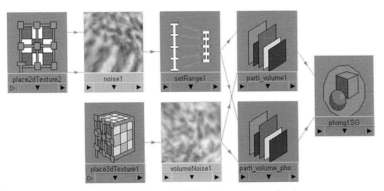

Final shading network for the volume shaders

13 Render the scene

The smoke inside the crystal ball now has uneven distribution and
height. The *crystalBall_smoke_finished.mb* file has the final results of this
exercise.

Smoky effect using volume shaders

Double-Sided mental ray Shaders

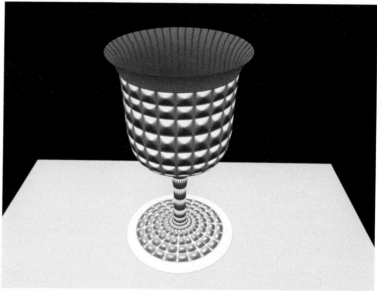

mib_twosided shader used to create a double-sided shader effect

mental ray for Maya's custom *mib_twosided* shader can be used to create a surface material with different properties (e.g. specular, diffuse, bump) for each face of the geometry to which it is assigned (a double-sided shader).

In order to achieve the double-sided shader effect with mental ray, you will have to use a different workflow than the one used for Maya's rendering engine. This workflow will be illustrated in the following exercise:

1 Open the file called Goblet_start.mb

2 Create the shaders and textures used for the two sides of the goblet

- In the **Create All Nodes** bar of the **Hypershade**, create a Blinn shader and a Lambert shader. Change the Blinn color to faded gold and the Lambert color to deep blue.

- Scroll down to the **2D Textures** section and **MMB** drag a Bulge texture on top of the Blinn shader and from the pop-up menu choose bump map.

- Open the **Attribute Editor** for the **2D placement** of the Bulge texture and set the following values:

   Coverage to **0.675 , 1.000**;

   Translate Frame to **0.060 , -0.065**;

   Repeat UV to **22.000 , 22.000**.

- From the **Create 2D Textures** section of the **Hypershade**, MMB drag a Grid texture on top of the Lambert shader and choose bump map from the pop-up menu.

- Open the **Attribute Editor** for the Grid texture and set the following values:

   U Width to **0.000**;

   V Width to **0.120**.

- Open the **Attribute Editor** for the Grid's 2D placement node and set the following values:

   Repeat UV to **0.00 , 50.000**.

3 Create a mib_twosided mental ray custom shader

- Open the **Hypershade**'s Materials tab and select *gobletLambert*.

   In the **Hypershade**, select **Graph** → **Output Connections**.

   This will display the Shading Group node used by the shader *GobletSG*.

- Select *GobletSG* and open the Attribute Editor. Make sure to select the *GobletSG* tab.

- Open the Create mental ray Nodes bar in the Hypershade and expand the Miscellaneous section.

- MMB drag a *mib_twosided* node onto the Surface Material port of *GobletSG*.

4 Assign materials to mib_twosided

- Open the **Attribute Editor** for the *mib_twosided* node.

- Open the **Hypershade**'s Materials tab and MMB drag the Lambert material onto the **Front** attribute of *mib_twosided*.

- MMB drag the Blinn material onto the **Back** attribute of *mib_twosided*.

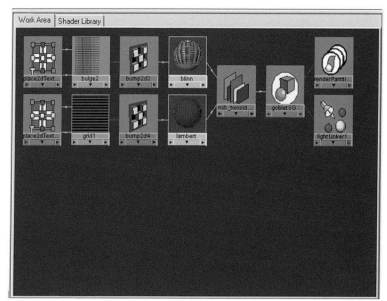

The shading network should look like the above image

5 Set your Render Globals

- In the **Render Globals** window, under **Render Using**, choose **mental ray**.

6 Render your scene

Light Shaders

mental ray Light Shaders can be used to replace the regular Maya lights at render time. This workflow will be illustrated in the following:

1 Open Light_Shader.mb

2 Create a mental ray Light Shader

- Open the **Create mental ray Nodes** bar in the **Hypershade** and expand the **Lights** section.

- Open the **Attribute Editor** window for the Spot Light and in the mental ray section scroll to the Export Options section.

- MMB drag a *mib_light_spot* node into the **Light Shader** port of the Spot Light.

■ In the **Hypershade** window, select the Spot Light node and display the output connections. Double-click the *coneShape* node and in the **Attribute Editor**, expand the **Render Stats** section. Turn on the **Volume Samples Override** and the **Depth Jitter** and set:

Volume Samples to **12.**

3 Adjust the attributes for the mib_light_spot node

■ Set the color to a pale yellow.

■ Turn **Shadow** to **ON**. This will result in volumetric shadows.

■ If **Atten** is **ON**, the light will start from the **start** value and will fade at the **stop** value.

■ Set the cone value to 4.

Note: If the Factor is different than 0, you will not get a volumetric shadow.

---

4 Render your scene

SUMMARY

Custom mental ray shaders can allow you to create complex shading and lighting effects. Custom shaders can be used with standard Maya texture and utility nodes, and integrated rendering is fully supported.

This chapter covered the following topics:

■ Using Contour Shaders to create outlines on and around objects

■ Using mental ray Material and Photon Shaders

■ Creating shadows with mental ray Shadow Shaders

■ Creating complex volumetric effects with mental ray Volume and Photon Volume shaders

■ Creating a double-sided shader with *mib_twosided* shader

■ Using mental ray Light Shaders

CHAPTER 13
Summary

Want to Learn More?

Alias|Wavefront publishes a variety of self-study learning materials that can help you improve your skills.

Visit

www.aliaswavefrontstore.com

and check out our books and training materials.